Th
of
Lancelot of the Laik.

Early English Text Society
Original Series, No. 6
1865
Second Edition 1870
Reprinted 1889, 1905, 1965
Price 42*s.*

Lancelot of the Laik:

A SCOTTISH METRICAL ROMANCE,

(ABOUT 1490–1500 A.D.)

RE-EDITED

FROM A MANUSCRIPT IN THE CAMBRIDGE UNIVERSITY LIBRARY,

WITH AN

INTRODUCTION, NOTES, AND GLOSSARIAL INDEX,

BY

W. W. SKEAT

Published for
THE EARLY ENGLISH TEXT SOCIETY
by the
OXFORD UNIVERSITY PRESS
LONDON · NEW YORK · TORONTO

Unaltered reprint 2006

ISBN 1 84384 100 2

Distributed for the Early English Text Society by
Boydell & Brewer Ltd,
PO Box 9, Woodbridge, Suffolk IP12 3DF
and Boydell & Brewer Inc,
688 Mount Hope Avenue, Rochester, NY 14620, USA
Website www.boydell.co.uk

Printed in Great Britain by
Antony Rowe Ltd, Eastbourne

PREFACE.

I.—DESCRIPTION OF THE MS., ETC.

A FORMER edition of the present poem was printed for the Maitland Club, in 1839, and edited by Joseph Stevenson, Esq. It has saved me all trouble of transcription, but by no means, I am sorry to say, that of correction. Those who possess the older edition will readily perceive that it differs from the present one very frequently indeed, and that the variations are often such as considerably to affect the sense. Many of the errors in it (such as *casualtyee* for *casualytee*, *grone*, for *gone*, *reprent* for *repent*) are clearly typographical, but there are others which would incline me to believe that the transcription was too hastily executed; several passages being quite meaningless. Near the conclusion of Mr Stevenson's preface we read : " The pieces which have been selected for the present volume[1] are printed with such errors of transcription as have crept into them by the carelessness of the scribe;" a statement which certainly implies that there was no intention on his part of departing from the original. Yet that he sometimes unconsciously did so to such an extent as considerably to alter (or destroy) the sense, the reader may readily judge from a few examples :—

[1] The volume contains other poems besides " Sir Lancelot."

PREFACE.

LINE.	EDITION OF 1839.	TRUE READING OF THE MS.
26.	fatil (*fatal*),	fatit (*fated*).
285.	unarmyt (*unarmed*),	enarmyt (*fully armed*).
682.	can here,	cam nere.
700.	rendit (*rent*),	vondit (*wounded*).
764.	refuse (*refusal?*),	reprefe (*defeat*).
861.	felith (*feeleth*),	fetith (*setteth*).
1054.	vyt,	rycht.
1084.	speiris,	spuris.
1455.	cumyng (*coming*),	cunyng (*skill*).
1621.	he war,	be war (*beware*).
1641.	promyſ,	punyſ (*punish*).
2010.	ane desyne,	medysyne.
2092.	born,	lorn (*lost*).
2114.	havin,	harm.
2142.	Hymene (!),	hyme (*him*).
2219.	such,	furth (*forth*).
2245.	al so y-vroght,	al foly vroght.
2279.	chichingis (!),	thithingis (*tidings*).
2446.	love,	lore (*teaching*). Etc.

Several omissions also occur, as, *e. g.*, of the word " off" in l. 7, of the word " tressore " in l. 1715, and of four whole lines at a time in two instances ; viz., lines 1191-4, and 2877-80. It will be found, in fact, that the former text can seldom be safely quoted for the purposes of philology ; and I cannot but think Mr Stevenson's claim of being accurate to be especially unfortunate ; and the more so, because the genuine text is much simpler and more intelligible than the one which he has given.

The original MS. is to be found in the Cambridge University Library, marked Kk. 1. 5. It formerly formed part of a thick volume, labelled " Tracts ;" but these are now being separated, for greater convenience, into several volumes. The MS. of " Lancelot " has little to do with any of the rest as regards its subject, but several other pieces are in the same hand-writing ; and, at the end of one of them, an abstract of Solomon's proverbs, occur the words, "Expliciunt Dicta Salamonis, per manum V. de F."[1] This hand-writing, though close, is very regular, and my own impression certainly is that the scribe has almost always succeeded in preserving the sense of the poem, though there is much confusion in the dialectal forms, as will be shewn presently.

The present text is as close a fac-simile of the MS. as can be represented by printed letters, every peculiarity being preserved as far as practicable, even including the use of *y* for *þ* (or *th*); so that the reader must remember that *yow* in l. 94 stands for *thow*, and *yis* in l. 160 for *this*, and so on; but this ought not to cause much difficulty. The sole points of difference are the following:

1. In the MS. the headings "Prologue," "Book I." etc., do not occur.

2. The lines do not always begin (in the MS.) with a capital letter.

3. The letters *italicized* are (in the MS.) represented by signs of contraction. One source of difficulty is the flourish over a word, used *sometimes* as a contraction for *m* or *n*. I have expanded this flourish as an *m* or *n* wherever such letter is manifestly required; but it also occurs where it is best to attach to it no value. In such instances, the flourish occurs most frequently over the last word in a line, and (except very rarely) only over words which have an *m* or *n* in them. It would thus seem that their presence is due to the fact of the scribe wanting employment for his pen after the line had been written, and that the flourish therefore appears over certain words, not so much because the *n* is *wanting* in them, as because it is *there already*. Such words have a special attraction for the wandering pen. Still, in order that the reader

---

[1] See Mr Lumby's editions of "Early Scottish Verse" and "Ratis Raving," both edited for the E. E. T. S. from this MS. Only the latter of these is in the hand-writing of V. de F.

may know wherever such flourishes occur, they have all been noted down ; thus, in l. 46, the stroke over the *n* in " greñ " means that a long flourish occurs drawn over the whole word, and the reader who wishes to expand this word into " gren*e* " or " gren*n* " may easily do it for himself, though he should observe that the most usual form of the word is simply "gren," as in lines 1000, 1305.

In a few nouns ending in -*l*, the plural is indicated by a stroke drawn through the doubled letter ; as in *perillis*, *sadillis*, etc. ; and even the word *ellis* (else) is thus abbreviated.

4. I am responsible for all hyphens, and letters and words between square brackets; thus, " with-outen " is in the MS. " with outen ; " and " knych[t]ly " is written " knychly." Whenever a line begins with a capital letter included between two brackets, the original has a blank space left, evidently intended for an illuminated letter. Wherever illuminated letters actually occur in the MS., they are denoted in this edition by large capitals.

5. We find, in the MS., both the long and the twisted *s* (ſ and s). These have been noted down as they occur, though I do not observe any law for their use. The letter "ß" has been adopted as closely resembling a symbol in the MS., which apparently has the force of double *s*, and is not unlike the " *sz* " used in modern German hand-writing. It may be conveniently denoted by *ss* when the type "ß" is not to be had, and is sometimes so represented in the " Notes."

6. The MS. is, of course, not punctuated. The punctuation in the present edition is mostly new ; and many passages, which in the former edition were meaningless, have thus been rendered easily intelligible. I am also responsible for the headings of the pages, the abstract at the sides of them, the numbering of the folios in the margin, the notes, and the glossary ; which I hope may be found useful. The greatest

care has been taken to make the text accurate, the proof-sheets having been compared with the MS. *three times* throughout.[1]

II.—DESCRIPTION OF THE POEM.

The poem itself is a loose paraphrase of not quite fourteen folios of the first of the three volumes of the French Romance of Lancelot du Lac, if we refer to it as reprinted at Paris in 1513, in three volumes, thin folio, double-columned.[2] The English poet has set aside the French Prologue, and written a new one of his own, and has afterwards translated and amplified that portion of the Romance which narrates the invasion of Arthur's territory by " le roy de oultre les marches, nomme galehault" (in the English *Galiot*), and the defeat of the said king by Arthur and his allies.

The Prologue (lines 1-334) tells how the author undertook to write a romance to please his lady-love ; and how, after deciding to take as his subject the story of Lancelot as told in the French Romance, yet finding himself unequal to a close translation of the whole of it, he determined to give a para-

---

[1] This refers to the edition printed in 1865. In executing the present reprint, the proof-sheets have been once more compared with the MS., and a very few insignificant errors have been thus detected and rectified.

[2] "As to the Romance of Sir Lancelot, our author [Gower], among others on the subject, refers to a volume of which he was the hero ; perhaps that of Robert de Borron, altered soon afterwards by Godefroy de Leigny, under the title of *Le Roman de la Charrette*, and printed, with additions, at Paris by Antony Verard, in the year 1494.

> For if thou wilt the bokes rede
> Of Launcelot and other mo,
> Then might thou seen how it was tho
> Of armes," etc. (GOWER : *Confessio Amantis*, Book iv.)

Quoted from Warton's English Poetry, vol. ii., p. 234, *ed.* 1840. I quote this as bearing somewhat on the subject, though it should be observed that *Le Roman de la Charrette* is not the same with *Lancelot du Lac*, but only a romance of the same class. Chaucer also refers to Lancelot in his Nonnes Prestes Tale, l. 392 ; and it is mentioned in the famous lines of Dante (*Inf.* v. 127)—
" Noi leggevamo un giorno per diletto
Di Lancilotto, come amor lo strinse," &c.

phrase of a portion of it only. After giving us a brief summary of the earlier part by the simple process of telling us what he will *not* relate, he proposes to begin the story at the point where Lancelot has been made prisoner by the lady of Melyhalt, and to take as his subject the wars between Arthur and Galiot, and the distinction which Lancelot won in them; and afterwards to tell how Lancelot made peace between these two kings, and was consequently rewarded by Venus, who

"makith hyme his ladice grace to have" (l. 311).

The latter part of the poem, it may be observed, has not come down to us. The author then concludes his Prologue by beseeching to have the support of a very celebrated poet, whose name he will not mention, but will only say that

" Ye fresch enditing of his laiting toung
Out throuch yis world so wid is yroung," etc.[1] (l. 328.)

The first Book introduces us to King Arthur at Carlisle.[2] The king is visited by dreams, which he imagines to forebode misfortune; he therefore convokes all his clerks, and inquires of them the meaning of the dreams, proposing to hang them in the event of their refusal. Thus strongly urged, they tell him that those on whom he most relies will fail him at his need; and when he further inquires if this evil fate can be averted, they answer him very obscurely that it can only be remedied by help of the water-lion, the leech, and the flower; a reply which the king evidently regards as unsatisfactory. Soon after an aged knight, fully armed, enters the palace, with a message from King Galiot, requiring him to give "tribute and rent." Arthur at once refuses, somewhat to the astonishment of the knight, who is amazed at his hardihood. Next arrives a message from the lady of Melyhalt, informing Arthur of the

[1] He does not necessarily imply that the poet invoked was still alive; and we might almost suppose Petrarch to be meant, who was more proud of his Latin poem called "Africa" than of his odes and sonnets. See Hallam's Literary History (4 vols.), vol. i., p. 85. But this is pure conjecture.
[2] But the French has "Cardueil." See l. 2153.

actual presence of Galiot's army. We are then momentarily introduced to Lancelot, who is pining miserably in the lady's custody. Next follows a description of Galiot's army, at sight of the approach of which King Arthur and his "niece," Sir Gawain, confer as to the best means of resistance. In the ensuing battle Sir Gawain greatly distinguishes himself, but is at last severely wounded. Sir Lancelot, coming to hear of Sir Gawain's deeds, craves leave of the lady to be allowed to take part in the next conflict, who grants him his boon on condition that he promise to return to his prison. She then provides for him a red courser, and a complete suit of red armour, in which guise he appears at the second battle, and is the "head and comfort of the field;" the queen and Sir Gawain beholding his exploits from a tower. The result of the battle convinces Galiot that Arthur is not strong enough at present to resist him sufficiently, and that he thus runs the risk of a too easy, and therefore dishonourable, conquest; for which excellent reason he grants Arthur a twelvemonth's truce, with a promise to return again in increased force at the expiration of that period. Sir Lancelot returns to Melyhalt according to promise, and the lady is well pleased at hearing the reports of his famous deeds, and visits him when asleep, out of curiosity to observe his appearance after the fight.

In the Second Book the story makes but little progress, nearly the whole of it being occupied by a long lecture or sermon delivered to Arthur by a "master," named Amytans, on the duties of a king; the chief one being that a king should give presents to everybody—a duty which is insisted on with laborious tediousness. Lines 1320-2130 are almost entirely occupied with this subject, and will be found to be the driest part of the whole narrative. In the course of his lecture, Amytans explains at great length the obscure prophecy mentioned above, shewing that by the water-lion is meant God the Father, by the leech God the Son, and by the flower the Virgin

Mary. Though the outline of a similar lecture exists in the old French text, there would seem to be a special reason for the length to which it is here expanded. Some lines certainly seem to hint at events passing in Scotland at the time when the poem was composed. Thus, "kings may be excused when of tender age" (l. 1658); but when they come to years of discretion should punish those that have wrested the law. Again we find (l. 1920) strong warnings against flatterers, concluding (l. 1940) with the expression,

"Wo to the realme that havith sich o chans!"

Such hints may remind us of the long minorities of James II. and James III.; and, whilst speaking on this subject, I may note a somewhat remarkable coincidence. When King Arthur, as related in Book I., asks the meaning of his dream, he is told that it signifies that "they in whom he most trusts will fail him" (l. 499); and he afterwards laments (l. 1151) how his "men fail him at need." Now when we read that a story is current of a prophetess having told James III. that he was destined to "fall by the hands of his own kindred,"[1] and that that monarch was in the habit of consulting *astrologers*[2] (compare l. 432) as to the dangers that threatened him, it seems quite possible that the poem was really composed about the year 1478; and this supposition is consistent with the fact that the hand-writing of the present MS. copy belongs to the very end of the fifteenth century.

Towards the end of the Second Book, we learn that the twelvemonth's truce draws near its end, and that Sir Lancelot again obtains permission from the lady to be present in the approaching combat, choosing this time to be arrayed in "armys al of blak" (l. 2426).

[1] Tytler's History of Scotland (Edinburgh, 1841), vol. iv., p. 216.
[2] The French text does not say anything about "astronomy." We may especially note the following lines, as *not* being in the French, viz., lines 1473-1496, 1523-1542, 1599-1644, 1658-1680, and the long passage 1752-1998.

In the Third Book Galiot returns to the fight with a host thrice as large as his former one. As before, Gawain distinguishes himself in the first encounter, but is at length so "evil wounded" that he was "the worse thereof evermore" (l. 2706). In the second combat, the black knight utterly eclipses the red knight, and the last thousand (extant) lines of the poem are almost wholly occupied with a description of his wonderful prowess. At the point where the extant portion of the poem ceases, the author would appear to be just warming with his subject, and to be preparing for greater efforts.

In continuance of the outline of the story, I may add that the French text[1] informs us how, after being several times remounted by Galiot, and finding himself with every fresh horse quite as fresh as he was at the beginning of the battle, the black knight attempted, as evening fell, to make his way back to Melyhalt secretly. Galiot, however, having determined not to lose sight of him, follows and confronts him, and earnestly requests his company to supper, and that he will lodge in his tent that night. After a little hesitation, Lancelot accepts the invitation, and Galiot entertains him with the utmost respect and flattery, providing for him a most excellent supper and a bed larger than any of the rest. Lancelot, though naturally somewhat wearied, passes a rather restless night, and talks a good deal in his sleep. Next day Galiot prays him to stay longer, and he consents on condition that a boon may be granted him, which is immediately acceded to without further question. He then requests Galiot to submit himself to Arthur, and to confess himself vanquished, a demand which so amazes that chieftain that he at first refuses, yet succeeds in persuading Lancelot to remain with him a little longer. The day after, preparations are made for another battle, on which occasion Lancelot wears Galiot's armour, and is at first mistaken for him, till Sir Gawain's acute vision detects that the armour

[1] See Appendix.

really encases the black knight. As Lancelot now fights on Galiot's side, it may easily be imagined how utter and complete is the defeat of Arthur's army, which was before victorious owing to his aid only; and we are told that Arthur is ready to kill himself out of pure grief and chagrin, whilst Sir Gawain swoons so repeatedly, for the same reason, as to cause the most serious fears to be entertained for his life. At this sorrowful juncture Lancelot again claims his boon of Galiot, who, in the very moment of victory, determines at last to grant it, and most humbly sues for mercy at the hands of Arthur, to that king's most intense astonishment. By this very unexpected turn of affairs, the scene of dolour is changed to one of unalloyed joy, and peace is immediately agreed upon, to the satisfaction of all but some true-bred warriors, who preferred a battle to a peace under all circumstances. Not long after, Galiot discovers Lancelot with eyes red and swollen with much weeping, and endeavours to ascertain the reason of his grief, but with small success. After endeavouring to comfort Lancelot as much as possible, Galiot goes to visit King Arthur, and a rather long conference takes place between them as they stand at Sir Gawain's bedside, the queen being also present. In the course of it, Galiot asks Arthur what price he would pay to have the black knight's perpetual friendship; to which Arthur replies, he would gladly share with him half of everything that he possessed, saving only Queen Guinevere. The question is then put to Gawain, who replies that, if only his health might be restored, he would wish to be the most beautiful woman in the world, so as to be always beloved by the knight. Next it is put to Guinevere, who remarks that Sir Gawain has anticipated all that a lady could possibly wish, an answer which is received with much laughter. Lastly, Arthur puts the question to Galiot himself, who declares that he would willingly, for the black knight's sake, suffer that all his honour should be turned into shame, whereat Sir Gawain allows himself to be outbidden. The queen then obtains a brief private conference with Galiot, and prays him to obtain for her an interview with the black knight, who promises to do what he can to that end. He accordingly sounds the black knight upon the subject, and, finding him entirely of the same mind, does all he can to promote their acquaintance, and is at last only too successful; and at this point we may suppose the Scottish Romance to have stopped, if indeed it was ever completed. For some account of the Romance of Lancelot, I may refer the reader to Professor Morley's English Writers, vol. i., pp. 568—570, and 573; to "Les Romans de la Table Ronde," par M. Paulin Paris; and to the Prefaces to the "Seynt Graal," edited by Mr Furnivall for the Roxburghe Club, 1861, and "La Queste del Saint Graal," also edited by the same for the same club in 1864. In the last-named volume short specimens are given from thirteen MSS. at Paris, ten of which contain the Romance of Lancelot. There are also manuscript copies of it in the British Museum, viz., MSS. Harl. 6341 and 6342, Lansdowne 757, and MS. Addit. 10293.

III.—THE DIALECT OF THE POEM.

In coming to discuss the dialect, we find everywhere traces of considerable confusion; but it is not at all easy to assign a satisfactory reason for this.[1] Certain errors of transcription soon shew that the scribe had before his eyes an older copy, which he mis-read. Thus, in l. 433, we find "set," where the older copy must have had "fet," and which he must have misread as "fet;" and again, in lines 2865, 2883, he has, by a similar confusion between "f" and "ſ," written "firſt" instead of "fift." It is most probable that the older copy was

[1] For many valuable remarks upon the dialect of the poem I am indebted to Mr R. Morris.

written in the Lowland Scottish dialect (the whole tone of the poem going to prove this), as shewn by the use of *ch* for *gh*, as in *bricht* for *bright*, (unless this be wholly due to the scribe); by the occurrence of plurals in *-is*, of verbal preterites and passive participles in *-it*, and of words peculiarly Scottish, such as *syne* (afterwards), *anerly* (only), *laif* (remainder), *oftsyss* (oft-times), etc. Moreover, the Northern *r* is clearly indicated by the occurrence of such dissyllables as *gar-t*, 2777, *lar-g*, 2845, *fir-st*, 2958, 3075; with which compare the significant spellings *harrmful*, 1945, and *furrde*, 2583. But, on the other hand, it would appear as if either the author or the copyist had no great regard for pure dialect, and continually introduces Southern and Midland forms, mixing them together in an indiscriminate and very unusual manner. We find, for example, in line 1765,

"B*eith* larg and iff*is* frely of thi thing,"

the Scottish form *iffis* (give) and the Southern *beith* in close conjunction; and we find no less than six or seven forms of the plural of the past tense of the verb "to be;" as, for example, *war* (3136), *reir* (818), *ware* (825), *waren* (3301), *veryng* (2971), *waryng* (443), etc. If we could suppose that the scribe was not himself a Scotchman, we might in some measure account for such a result; but the supposition is altogether untenable, as the peculiar character of the handwriting (resembling that found, not in English, but in *French* MSS.) decides it to be certainly Scottish; as is also evident from the occurrence, in the same hand-writing, of a Scotticised version of Chaucer's " Flee from the press."

The best that can be done is to collect a few instances of peculiarities.

1. The broad Northumbrian forms *a, ane, baith, fra, ga, haill, hame, knaw, law, sa, wat*, although occasionally retained, are also at times changed into *o, one, boith, fro, go, holl, hom, know,*

low, so, and *wot.* Thus, at the end of l. 3246, we find *haill,* which could not have been altered without destroying the rime; but in l. 3078, we find it changed, in the middle of the line, into *holl.* In l. 3406, we find *sa,* but only three lines further on we find *so* twice.

So, too, we not only find *tane* (taken), *gais* (goes), but also the forms *tone* and *goſ.* See lines 1071, 1073.

2. The true plural form of the verb is shewn by lines 203, 204, "Of quhois fame and worschipful dedis
Clerkis into diuerſ bukis *redis*,"

where alteration would have ruined the rime utterly; and the same termination (*-is*) is correctly used in the imperative mood, as, ——" ſo *giffis* ws delay" (l. 463);
"And of thi wordis *beis* trew and stable" (l. 1671);

but the termination *-ith* is continually finding its way into the poem, even as early as in the fourth line,

"*Uprisith* arly in his fyre chare;"

and in the imperative mood also, as,

"*Remembrith* now it stondith one the poynt" (l. 797).

The most singular point of all, however, is this—that, not content with changing *-is* into *-ith* in the 3rd person singular, the scribe has done the same even in the 2nd person, thus producing words which belong to no pure example of any distinct dialect. Observe the following lines:—

"O woful wrech, that *levis* in to were!
To schew the thus the god of loue me sent,
That of thi seruice no thing is content,
For in his court yhoue [= thou] *lewith* in disspar,
And vilfully *sustenis* al thi care,
And *schapith* no thinge of thine awn remede,
Bot *clepith* ay and *cryith* apone dede," etc. (ll. 84-90).

Here *levis* is altered into *lewith*, not only unnecessarily, but quite wrongly. For similar mistakes, see ll. 1019, 1369, 1384,

2203. For examples of correct usage, see ll. 1024, 1337, 1796, 2200, 2201.

3. But the terminations which are used in the most confused manner of all are *-en*, *-yne*, and *-ing* or *-yng*. Thus we find the non-Scottish infinitives, *telen* (494), *makine* (191); the constant substitution of *-ing* for *-and* in the present participle;[1] a confusion between the past participial ending *-ine* (more correctly *-yn*), and the present ending *-and*, thus producing such forms as *thinkine* (34), and *besichyne* (418); and also a confusion between *-ing* and the past participial ending *-en*, as *fundyng* for *funden* (465), *fallyng* for *fallen* (1217, 1322, 3267), *swellyng* for *swollen* (1222), and *halding* for *halden* (2259). We even find *-ing* in the infinitive mood, as in *awysing* (424), *viting* (to know, 410), *smyting* (1326), *warnnyng* (1035), *passing* (2148), *fchewing* (2736), etc.; and, lastly, it occurs in the plural of the indicative present, instead of the Midland *-en*; as in *passing* (1166), *biding* (2670), and *levyng* (3304).[2]

It may safely be concluded, however, that the frequent occurrence of non-Scottish infinitives must not be attributed to the copyist, since they are probably due rather to the author; for in such a line as

"Of his desir to viting the sentens" (l. 410),

the termination *-ing* is required to complete the rhythm of the line.

In the same way we must account for the presence of the prefix *i-*, as in the line

"Quharwith that al the gardinge was I-clede" (l. 50).

[1] We find the true forms occasionally, as *obeisand* (641), *plesand* (1731), *thinkand* (2173), *prekand* (3089), and *fechtand* (3127). Compare the form *seruand* (122).

[2] "The Scottish pronunciation of *-ing* was already, as it still is, *-een*; and the writer, knowing that the correct spelling of *dwellin*, for example, was *dwelling*, fancied also that *fallen*, *halden* (Sc. *fallyn*, *haldyn*) were *fallyng*, *haldyng*. Lyndesay and Gawain Douglas often do the same. Compare *gardinge* (l. 50), *laiting* (l. 327)."—J. A. H. Murray.

This prefix never occurs in vernacular Scottish; but we may readily suppose that this and other numerous Southern forms of words are due (as in Gawain Douglas and Lyndesay) to the author's familiarity with Chaucer's poems, as evinced by the similarity of the rhythm to Chaucer's, and by the close resemblance of several passages. Compare, for instance, the first seventy lines of the Prologue with the opening passages of "The Flower and the Leaf," and "The Complaint of the Black Knight;" and see notes to ll. 432, 1608. Indeed, this seems to be the only satisfactory way of accounting for the various peculiarities with which the poem abounds.

Mr J. A. H. Murray, in his remarks printed in the preface to Mr Lumby's edition of "Early Scottish Verse," comes to a similar conclusion, and I here quote his words for the reader's convenience and information. "There is no reason, however, to suspect the scribe of *wilfully* altering his original; indeed, the reverse appears manifest, from the fact that the 'Craft of Deyng' has not been assimilated in orthography to 'Ratis Raving,' but distinctly retains its more archaic character; while in 'Sir Lancelot,' edited by Mr Skeat for the Early English Text Society, from the handwriting of the same scribe, we have a language in its continual Anglicisms quite distinct from that of the pieces contained in this volume, of which the Scotch is as pure and unmixed as that of the contemporary Acts of Parliament. With regard to the remarkable transformation which the dialect has undergone in Sir Lancelot, there seems reason, therefore, to suppose that it was not due to the copyist of the present MS., but to a previous writer, if not to the author himself, who perhaps affected *southernism*, as was done a century later by Lyndesay and Knox, and other adherents of the English party in the Reformation movement. The Southern forms are certainly often shown by the rhyme to be original, and such a form as *tone* for *tane* = taken, is more likely to have been that of a Northerner trying to write

Southern, than of a Southern scribe, who knew that no such word existed in his dialect. The same may be said of the *th* in the second person singular. A Scotch writer, who observed that Chaucer said *he liveth*, where he himself said *he lyves*, might be excused for supposing that he would also have said *thou liveth* for the Northern *thow lyves;* but we can hardly fancy a Southern copyist making the blunder.'

4. We find not only the Northumbrian forms *sall* and *suld*, but also *shall*, *shalt*, and *shuld*.

5. As regards pronouns, we find the Scottish *scho* (she) in l. 1169; but the usual form is *sche*. We find, too, not only the broad forms *thai*, *thair*, *thaim*, but also *thei* (sometimes *the*), *ther*, and *them*. As examples of forms of the relative pronoun, we may quote *who*, *quho*, *whois*, *quhois* (whose), *quhom*, *qwhome* (whom), *quhat*, *qwhat* (what), and *whilk*, *quhilk*, *quhich*, *quich*, *wich* (which). *Wich* is used instead of *who* (l. 387), and we also find *the wich*, or *the wich that*, similarly employed. The nominative *who* does not perhaps occur as a *simple* relative, but has the force of *whoso*, or *he who*, as e. g., in l. 1102 ; or else it is used interrogatively, as in l. 1172.

6. Many other peculiarities occur, which it were tedious to discuss fully. It may suffice, perhaps, to note briefly these following. We find both the soft sound *ch*, as in *wich*, *sich*, and the hard sound *k*, as in *whilk*, *reke* (reach), *streke* (stretch), etc.; which are the true Northern forms.

Mo is used as well as *more*.

Tho occurs for *then* in l. 3184 ; and for *the* in l. 247.

At occurs as well as *that ; atte* as well as *at the*, 627, 1055.

The short forms *ma* (make), *ta* (take), *sent* (sendeth), *stant* (standeth), are sometimes found ; the two former being Northumbrian.

Has is used twice as a *plural* verb (ll. 481, 496).[1]

---

[1] "The plural in Scottish always ends in *-s* after a noun or when the verb is separated from its pronoun ; we still say *the men hes, the bairns sings, them*

ȝha (yes) occurs in l. 2843; but we also meet with ȝhis, or yis; with reference to which Mr Morris writes:—"The latter term was not much in favour with the people of the North. Even now yes sounds offensive to a Lancashire man. 'Hoo cou'd naw opp'n hur meawth t' sey eigh (yea) or now (no); boh simpurt on sed iss; th' dickons iss hur on him too.—*Tim Bobbin.*'" In fact, the distinction between ȝha and ȝhis, which I have pointed out in *William of Palerne* (Glossary, s. v. ȝis), viz., that ȝha merely assents, whilst ȝhis shews that the speaker has an opinion of his own, is in this poem observed. Thus, in l. 2843, ȝha = "yes, I admit that I do;" but in l. 514, yis = "yes, but you had better do so;" in l. 1397, ȝhis = "yes, indeed I will;" and in l. 3406, ȝis = "yes, but I cannot accept your answer."[1] The true distinction between *thou* and *ye* (William of Palerne, Pref. p. xli) is also generally observed. Thus the Green Bird, in the Prologue, considers the poet to be a fool, and calls him *thou*; but the clerks, in addressing Arthur (l. 498) politely say *ye*. And again, Amytans, when rebuking Arthur, frequently calls him *thou*, without any ceremony. Cf. ll. 659, 908, 921, 2839, &c.

As regards the vocabulary, we find that some Northumbrian terms have been employed, but others thrown aside. Thus, while we find the Northumbrian words *thir* (these), *traist* (trust), *newis* (neives, fists), *radour* (fear), etc., we do not, on the other hand, meet with the usual Scottish word *mirk*, but observe it to be supplanted by *dirk* (l. 2471). So, again, *eke* is used in the sense of *also*, instead of being a verb, as more usual in Northern works. We may note, too, the occurrence of *frome* as well as *fra*, and the Scottish form *thyne-furth* (thenceforth) in l. 2196.

'*at cums*, not *have*, *sing*, *come*. Notice the frequent use of *th* for *t*, as in l. 497, *Presumyth* = *presumit*, presumed, it being presumed."—J. A. H. Murray. [Or, *presumyth* may be the pl. imperative, as in *Remembrith* (l. 797), already noticed.—ED.]

[1] "This ȝis is the common form in the Scottish writers, though *ay* is largely the modern vernacular."—J. A. H. Murray.

The spelling is very various. We find even four forms of one word, as *cusynace, cusynece, cusynes, cwsynes;* and, as examples of eccentric spelling, may be quoted *qsquyaris* (squires, l. 3204), whilst in l. 3221 we find *sqwar*.

Both in the marginal abstract and in the notes I have chiefly aimed at removing minor difficulties by explaining sentences of which the construction is peculiar, and words which are disguised by the spelling. For the explanation of more uncommon words, recourse should be had to the Glossarial Index.

APPENDIX.

EXTRACTS FROM THE FRENCH ROMANCE OF "LANCELOT DU LAC."

As it seems impossible to do justice to the story of Lancelot without giving due attention to the famous French Romance, and since a portion of the French text is really necessary to complete even that fragment of it which the Scottish author proposed to write, the following extracts have been made with the view of shewing (1) the general outline of the earlier part of the story, (2) the method in which the Scottish author has expanded or altered his original, and (3) the completion of the story of the wars between Arthur and Galiot.[1]

I. Headings of the chapters of the French Romance, from its commencement to the end of the wars with Galiot.

[The commas are inserted by the present editor, and the expansions marked by italics.]

¶ Cy commence la table du premier volume de la table ronde lancelot du lac.

¶ Comment apres la mort de vterpandragon roy du royaulme de logres, & apres la mort aramon, roy de la petite bretaigne, le roy claudas de la terre Descosse mena guerre contre le roy ban de benoic et le roy boort de gauues tant quil les desherita[2] de leurs terres. Fueillet. i. *Claudas, king of Scotland, deprives king Ban and king Boort of their lands.*

---

[1] The extracts are from the Paris edition of 1513, 3 vols. folio, a copy of which is in the King's Library in the British Museum. There are also two other editions in the Museum, one in the Grenville Library, 3 vols. Paris, 1494, folio; the other in one folio volume, Paris, 1520.   [2] See ll. 1447-1449.

xxiv HEADS OF THE EARLY CHAPTERS OF THE FRENCH ROMANCE.

Claudas besieges Ban in the Castle of Trible.

¶ Comment le roy claudas assiegea le chasteau de trible auquel estoit le roy ban de benoic, et comment ilz parlementerent ensemble. f.   i.

King Ban, his wife, and his son Lancelot repair to the court of Arthur.

¶ Comment le roy ban de benoic, accompaigne de sa femme et de son filz lancelot, auecques vng seul escuyer, se partirent du chasteau de trible pour aller querir secours deuers le roy Artus a la grant bretaigne. Fueillet   ii.

The Castle of Trible is treacherously given up to Claudas.

¶ Comment apres ce que le roy ban fut party de son chasteau de trible, le seneschal a qui il auoit baille la garde trahit ledit chasteau, et le liura es mains du roy claudas. Fueillet.   ii.

King Ban dies of grief, and Lancelot is taken away by the lady of the lake.

¶ Comment le roy ban mourut de dueil quant il veit son chasteau ardoir et brouyr. Et comment la dame du lac emporta son filz lancelot.[1] Fueillet.   iiii.

¶ Comment la royne helaine, apres que le roy fut mort et elle eut perdu son filz, se rendit nonnain en labbaye du monstier royal. Fueillet.   v.

¶ Comment le roy de gauues mourut | & comment la Royne sa femme, pour paour de claudas, sen partit de son chasteau pour aller au monstier royal, ou sa seur estait rendue. et comment ses enfans Lyonnel et Boort luy furent ostez. Fueillet   vi.

The two sisters, widows of kings Ban and Boort, retreat to a monastery.

¶ Comment la royne de Gauues, apres que son seigneur fut mort et que elle eut perdu ses deux enfans, se vint rendre au monastere ou estoit sa seur la royne de benoic. Fueillet   vi.

Merlin's love for the lady of the lake.

¶ Comment merlin fut engendre du dyable : Et comment il fut amoureux de la dame du lac. Fueillet vii.

Sir Farien secretly nourishes the two sons of king Boort, and is made seneschal to king Claudas.

¶ Comment le cheualier farien, qui auoit tollu a la royne de Gauues ses deux enfans, les emporta en sa maison | et les feist nourrir vne espace de temps. Et comment le roy claudas fut amoureux de la femme du dict Farien | et pource le fist son seneschal. Fueillet viii.

Claudas accuses Sir Farien of treason.

¶ Comment le roy claudas fist appeller son cheualier farien de trahison par ladmonnestement de sa femme, disant quil gardoit les deux enfans du roy boort de gauues   Fueillet.   viii.

Claudas, in disguise, visits Arthur's court.

¶ comment le roy claudas en maniere de cheualier estrange, se partit du royaulme de gauues pour aller en la grant bretaigne a la court du roy artus pour veoir sa puissance & son gouuernement. Fueillet   x.

The lady of the lake informs Lancelot that he is a king's son.

¶ Comment la dame du lac bailla a lancelot vng maistre pour linstruyre comme il appartenoit a filz de roy. Fueillet   xii.

¶ Comment la royne helaine alloit faire chascun iour

[1] Lines 215, 220.

son dueil au lieu ou son seigneur mourut | et de la alloit au lac ou elle perdit son filz. Fueillet xv.

¶ Comment le bon Religieux qui auoit dit nouuelles a la royne helaine de son filz lancelot, print conge de elle, et sen vint au roy artus en la grant bretaigne. Fueillet xvi.

¶ Comment la dame du lac enuoya sa damoyselle a la court du roy claudas, pour delyurer les deux enfans au roy boort que claudas tenoit en prison. Fueillet xvii. *The lady of the lake seeks to deliver the sons of king Boort.*

¶ Comment farien, seneschal du roy claudas par le commandement de son seigneur, alla querir en prison les deux filz au roy de Gauues. Fueillet xviii.

¶ Comment les deux enfans au roy de gauues blecerent le roy claudas, & occirent dorin son filz | et comment la damoyselle du lac les emmena en semblance de deux leuriers. fueil. xix. *Lyonnel and Boort wound king Claudas, and slay his son Dorin.*

¶ De la grant ioye et du grant honneur que la dame du lac fist aux deux enfans quant elle les veit en sa maison. Fueillet xx.

¶ Comment le roy claudas mena tres grant dueil pour la mort de dorin son filz que boort auoit occis. Fueillet xx. *Claudas bewails his son's death.*

¶ Comment farien et le peuple de la cyte de gauues sesmeurent contre le roy claudas a cause que il vouloit faire mourir les deux filz au roy boort de gauues. Fueillet. xxi.

¶ Comment le roy claudas se partit de gauues | et comment ceulx dudit lieu le vouloient occire, se neust este farien le bon cheualier. f. xxiii. *Farien saves Claudas' life.*

¶ Comment le roy claudas se deffendit vaillamment contre ceulx de Gauues qui le vouloyent occire. Fueillet. xxv.

¶ Comment lyonnel et boort perdirent le boire et le manger pource quilz ne scauoyent nouuelles de leur maistres | lesquelz estoyent demourez auec le roy claudas | & comment la dame du lac enuoya vne sienne damoyselle a gauues pour les amener. Fueillet. xxvii.

¶ Comment, par le conseil des barons de gauues : leonce & lambegues sen allerent auecques la damoyselle pour veoir leurs seigneurs lyonnel et boort. Fueillet xxviii. *Leonce and Lambegues go to seek Lyonnel and Boort.*

¶ Comment la dame du lac sen retourna apres ce quelle eut monstre a leonce et a lambegues les enfans du roy de gauues leurs seigneurs, et comment lesditz cheualiers sen retournerent a gauues. Fueillet xxx.

¶ Comment le roy claudas retourna a gauues, pour soy venger de la honte quon luy auoit faicte, et pour la mort de son filz. Fueil. xxxi. *Claudas meditates revenge.*

¶ Comment lappointement fut fait entre le roy claudas et les barons, par le moyen de farien et lambegues son nepueu. fueillet. xxxiii.

Death of Farien.

¶ Comment farien | sa femme, et son nepueu lambegues sen partirent pour aller veoir lyonnel et boort, qui estoyent au lac | & comment farien mourut. Fueillet. xxxv.

The widow of king Boort sees her children and Lancelot in a vision, and dies.

¶ Comment les deux roynes menerent saincte vie au monstier royal | et comment celle de gauues veit ces deux enfans & lancelot en aduision | et comment elle trespassa de ce siecle. Fueillet. xxxv.

Arthur holds a tournament, and Banin, son of king Ban, is the victor.

¶ Comment le roy artus assembla le iour de pasques tous ses barons, & tint grant court a karahes, et comment banin le filleul au Roy ban emporta le pris du behourdys celluy iour. Fueillet. xxxvi.

The lady of the lake sends Lancelot to Arthur to be knighted, and provides for him white armour.

¶ Comment la dame du lac se pourpensa de mener lancelot au roy artus pour le faire cheualier,[1] et elle luy bailla armes blanches, et partit du lac a tout quarante cheualliers pour le conuoyer. Fueillet xxxvii.

Of the wounded knight who came to Arthur's court.

¶ Comment vng cheuallier naure, lequel auoit vne espee fichee en la teste et deux troncons de lance parmy le corps,[2] vint a la court du roy artus | et comment la dame du lac le mena deuant le roy artus, et luy prya quil le fist cheualier. Fueillet xxxix.

Lancelot is knighted.

¶ Comment messire yuain, a qui le roy Artus auoit recommande lancelot, alla faire sa requeste audit roy artus, que le lendemain il fist ledit lancelot cheualier, et comment ledit lancelot defferra le cheualier naure.[3] Fueillet. xli.

How the white knight defended the lady of Nohalt,

¶ Comment la dame de noehault[4] enuoya deuers le roy artus, luy supplier quil luy enuoyast secours contre le Roy de norhombellande qui luy menoit guerre. Et comment Lancelot requist au roy artus quil luy donnast congie dy aller | & il luy octroya. Fueillet xlii.

and won the battle for her.

¶ Comment le nouueau cheualier aux armes blanches vainquit la bataille pour la dame de noehault. Fueillet xliii.

¶ Comment lancelot apres ce quil se fut party de la dame de noehault, se combatit auec vng cheualier qui lauoit mouille. Fueillet xlv.

How Lancelot conquered the "Sorrowful Castle."

¶ Comment lancelot conquist vaillamment par sa force et proesse le chasteau de la douloureuse garde que nul aultre ne pouoit conquerre.[5] Fueillet xlv.

How Arthur hears of it, and sends Gawain to see if it is true.

¶ Comment les nouuelles vindrent au roy artus que la douloureuse garde estoit conquise par la cheualier

---

[1] Line 223. [2] Lines 237-245. [3] Lines 249-252.
[4] Line 255. [5] Lines 257-259.

aux armes blanches | Et le roy y enuoya messire gauuain pour en scauoir la verite. Fueillet xlviii.

¶ Comment messire Gauuain fut mys en prison | et comment le roy et la royne entrerent en la premiere porte de la | et la veirent des tumbes ou il y auoit escript que monseigneur gauuain estoit mort, et plusieures aultres cheualiers. Fueillet. xlix. *Gawain is imprisoned, and supposed to be dead.*

¶ Comment vne damoyselle de lhostel de la dame du lac feist assauoir au cheuallier blanc que monseigneur gauuain & ses compaignons estoyent emprisonnez par celluy qui auoit este seigneur de la douloureuse garde. Fueillet l. *Lancelot hears of Gawain's imprisonment,*

¶ Comment le blanc cheualier se combatit encontre celluy qui auoit este seigneur de la douloureuse garde, qui tenoit en prison messire gauuain et ses compaignons.[1] Fueillet. l. *and delivers him and his companions.*

¶ Comment le cheuallier blanc emmena le cheualier conquis en vng hermitaige. et comment ledit cheualier conquis luy rendit audit hermitage gauuain & ses compaignons. f. lii.

¶ Comment messire gauuain et ses compaignons sen vindrent par deuers le roy artus qui estoit a la douloureuse garde. Et comment le roy et la royne furent ioyeulx quant ilz les virent. Fueillet. liii. *Gawain returns to Arthur and his Queen at Douloureuse Garde.*

¶ Comment le cheuallier blanc retourna a labbaye ou il auoit laisse ses escuyers | et comment il sceut lassemblee qui deuoit estre entre le roy artus et le roy doultre les marches, & comment il conquist le cheualier qui disoit mieulx aymer le cheualier qui auoit naure que celluy qui lauoit este.[2] Fueillet. liiii. *Lancelot hears of the war to come between Arthur and Galiot.*

¶ Comment messire gauuain se mist en queste pour trouuer le blanc cheuallier.[3] Et comment la meslee dentre les gens au roy des cent cheualiers et les gens de la dame de noehault fut appaisee. Fueillet lv. *Gawain goes to seek the white knight,*

¶ Comment le blanc cheualier vainquit lassemble dentre les deux roys | et comment il fut naure du roy des cent cheualiers. Fueillet. lvi. *who is wounded in the battle against Galiot by the king-of-a-hundred-knights.*

¶ Comment apres que le cheualier qui auoit gangne le tournoyement dentre le roy doultre les marches sen fut alle, le roy artus & la royne genieure se partirent pour aller en leurs pays. Fueillet lvii. *Arthur and Queen Genure return home.*

¶ Comment messire gauuain se combatit a brehainsans-pitie, et le rua par terre. et comment apres ilz sen allerent a la douloureuse garde : & comment les deux pucelles que messire Gauuain menoit luy furent tollues. Fueillet. lviii.

[1] Lines 263, -4.   [2] See ll. 244, -5.   [3] Line 267.

Lancelot ends the adventures of the "Sorrowful Castle."	¶ Comment lancelot print congie de son mire ∣ et comment il mist a fin les aduentures de la douloureuse garde. Fueillet lx.
Lancelot is again victorious in the combat between Arthur and Galiot.	¶ Comment messire gauuain recouura les deux pucelles qui luy auoyent este tollues, Et comment lancelot vainquit la seconde assemblee dentre le roy artus & le roy doultre les marches. Fueillet lxi.
Gawain returns to Arthur's court.	¶ Comment messire gauuain retourna a la court du roy artus apres la seconde assemblee dentre le roy artus & le roy doultre les marches, et comment lancelot vainquit le cheualier qui gardoit le gue. Fueillet lxiii.

[*Here begins the Scotch Translation.*]

Arthur's evil dreams.	¶ Comment le roy Artus songea plusieurs songes ∣ et apres manda tous les saiges clercs de son royaulme pour en scauoir la signifiance.[1] Fueillet lxiiii.
Galiot defies Arthur.	¶ Comment le roy doultre les marches, nomme gallehault, enuoya deffier le roy artus[2] ∣ et comment Lancelot occist deux geans empres kamalot.[3] Fueillet lxv.
Lancelot is assailed by forty knights, and imprisoned by the lady of Melyhalt.	¶ Comment lancelot occist vng cheualier qui disoit moins aymer le cheualier naure que celluy qui lauoit naure.[4] ∣ et comment il fut assailly de .xl. cheualliers, et mys en prison de la dame de mallehault.[5] Fueillet lxviii.
Lancelot, released from prison, is again victorious against Galiot.	¶ Comment gallehault assembla au roy artus vng iour durant que lancelot estoit en prison[6] ∣ et comment le lendemain lancelot fut deliure de prison[7] ∣ et vainquit lassemblee dentre les deux roys.[8] Fueillet lxvii.
Arthur is reproved by Amytans, and Galiot proposes a truce for a year.	¶ Comment le roy artus fut reprins de ses vices, et moult bien conseille par vng cheualier qui suruint en son ost[9] ∣ Et comment gallehault donna tresues au roy Artus iusques a vng an.[10] Fueillet lxix.
Lancelot returns to the lady of Melyhalt.	¶ Comment lancelot, apres ce quil eut vaincu lassemblee, retourna en la prison de la dame de mallehault[11] ∣ et comment elle le congneut, a son cheual et par les playes quil auoit, que cestoit celluy qui auoit vaincu lassemblee.[12] Fueillet lxxii.
Gawain, with 39 comrades, departs to seek the red knight.	¶ Comment messire gauuain, soy quarantiesme de compaignons, se mist en queste pour trouuer le cheuallier qui auoit porte lescu vermeil a lassemblee dentre le roy artus et Gallehault.[13] Fueillet lxxii.
The lady of Melyhalt accepts Lancelot's ransom.	¶ Comment la dame de mallehault mist a rancon le cheuallier quelle tenoit en prison, et le laissa aller quant elle veit quelle ne peult scauoir son nom.[14] fu. lxxiii.

[1] Lines 363-527. [2] Lines 540-592. [3] Line 280.
[4] Lines 233-252. [5] Lines 281-292. [6] Lines 634-894.
[7] Lines 895-974. [8] Lines 975-1138. [9] Lines 1275-2130.
[10] Lines 1543-1584. [11] Lines 1139-1152. [12] Lines 1181-1274.
[13] Lines 2161-2256. [14] Lines 2347-2442.

¶ Comment messire gauuain et ses compaignons re-   The truce ended,
tournerent de leur queste¹ | et comment apres les treues   Galiot again attacks Arthur.
faillies galehault vint assembler contre le roy artus, &
tous ses gens en furent moult troublez.² fu.   lxxiiii.

¶ Comment gallehault suyuit le cheuallier aux noires   Galiot gains over the black knight.
armes,³ & fist tant par belles parolles quil lemmena en
son ost, dont le roy artus et tous ses gens en furent
moult troublez.   Fueillet   lxxviii.

¶ Comment lancelot par sa prouesse conquist tout,   Lancelot induces Galiot to submit to Arthur.
et fist tant que gallehault crya mercy au roy artus.
fu.   lxxix.

¶ Comment gallehault fist tant que la royne vit lance-   The Queen and Lancelot meet.
lot | & comment ilz se arraisonnerent ensemble. fu. lxxxi.

¶ Comment la royne congneut lancelot apres ce   The Queen knows Lancelot from his adventures that he tells her.
quil eut longuement parle a elle, & quil luy eut compte
de ses aduentures. & comment la premiere acointance
fut faicte entre la royne & lancelot par le moyen de
galehault. fu.   lxxxii.

¶ Comment la premiere acointance fut faicte de   Galiot becomes acquainted with the lady of Melyhalt.
galehault & de la dame de malehault par le moyen
de la royne de logres, & comme[nt] lancelot & galehault sen alloyent esbatre & deuiser auecques leurs
dames. fu.   lxxxiiii.

II. The Chapter of the French romance from which the
translator has taken the beginning of his First Book is here
given, in order to shew in what manner he has treated his
original. It begins at Fol. lxiii. *a*, col. 1.

Comment le roy artus songea plusieurs songes, et   Arthur's evil dreams.
  apres manda tous les sages clercz de son
  royaulme pour en scauoir la signifiance.

OR dit le compte que le roy artus auoit longue-   King Arthur being at Cardueil,
ment seiourne a cardueil. Et pource ny auenoit
mie grandement de aduentures, il ennuya moult aux   his knights are annoyed at meeting with no adventures.
compaignons du Roy de ce quilz auoient si longuement
seiourne, & ne veoient riens de ce quilz souloyent veoir.
Principallement keu le seneschal en fut trop ennuye Et
en parloit moult souuent, et disoyt deuant le roy que
trop estoit ce seiour ennuyeulx, & trop auoit dure. Le
roy luy demande "Keu | que vouldriez vous que nous   Sir Kay counsels that they should go to Camelot.
feissons?" "Certes," fait keu, "ie conseilleroye que
nous allissions a kamalot | car la cite est plus aduan-

¹ Lines 2504-2530.   ² Lines 2531-3268.
³ Lines 3343-3487.

tureuse que vous ayez | et la nous verrions souuent et
orrions choses de merueilles que nous ne voyons pas icy.
Nous auons seiourne ia icy plus de deux moys, et
oncques ne y veismes gueres de choses aduenir." "Or
alons donc," fait le roy, "a Kamalot, puis que vous le
conseillez." Lendemain deust partir le roy | mais la
nuyct luy aduint vne merueilleuse aduenture. Il songa
que tous les cheueulx de sa teste cheoient, et tous les
poilz de sa barbe, dont il fut moult espouente. Et par
ce demoura encores en la ville. La tierce nuyt apres il
songa que il luy estoit aduis que tous les dois luy
cheoient fors les poulces, & lors fut plus esbahy que
deuant.

A Lautre nuyct songea il que tous les ortelz des
piedz luy cheoient fors les poulces. de ce fut si
trouble que plus ne peult. "Sire," fait son chappelain
a qui il lauoit dit, "ne vous chaille | car songes ne sont
pas a croire ;" le roy le dit a la royne, et elle respond
tout ainsi que luy auoit fait son chappelain. "En
verite," dist il, "ie ne laisseray pas la chose ainsi" | il
fait mander ses euesques et archeuesques quilz soient a
luy au .ix iour ensuyuant a kamalot, & quilz amainent
auec eulx tous les plus sages clercz quils pourroient
auoir et trouuer. A tant se part de cardueil & sen va
par les chasteaulx et par les citez | tant que au neuf-
niesme iour est venu a kamalot, et aussi sont venus les
clercz du pays. Il leur demande conseil de son songe,
et ilz elisent dix des plus sages : le roy les fist bien
enserrer, et dist que iamais nen sortiroient de prison
deuant quilz luy auroient dit la significance de son songe.
Ilz esprouuerent la force de leur science par neuf iours,
et puis vindrent au roy, & dirent quilz nauoient riens
trouue. "Ainsi maist dieu," dit le roy, "ia ainsi
neschapperez." Et ils demandent respit iusques au
troisiesme iour ensuyuant, et il leur donne. Les .iii
iours passez, ilz reuiennent deuant le roy, et dient que
ilz ne peuent riens trouuer | et demandent encores autre
delay | et ilz ont. Et de rechief vindrent pour de-
mander aultres troys iours de dilacion, ainsi que le roy
auoit songe de tierce nuyt en tierce nuyt. "Or sachez,"
fait le roy, "que iamais plus nen aurez." Quant vint
au tiers iour ilz dirent quilz nauoient rien trouue ; "ce
ne vault rien," fait le roy, "ie vous feray tous destruire
se vous ne me dictes la verite ;" et ils dirent. "Sire
nous ne vous en scairions que dire" Lors se pense le
roy quil leur fera paour de mort. Il fait fair vng grant
feu, & commanda en leurs presences que les .v. y fus-

sent mis, et que les autres cinq soyent penduz | mais *The five who are to be hung, having the cords round their necks, offer to speak out.*
priueement deffent a ses baillifz quilz ne les menassent
que iusques a la paour de mourir. Quant les cinq qui
furent menez aux fourches euerent les cordes entour
leurs colz, ils eurent paour de mourir, et dirent, que se
les aultres cinq le vouloyent dire, ilz le diroyent. La
nouuelle vint au .v. que len menoit ardre | et ilz dirent
que, se les autres le vouloyent dire, ils le diroyent | ils
furent amenez ensemble deuant le roy, et les plus sages
dirent | "sire, nous vous dirons ce que nous auons *They stipulate not to be held as liars if their interpretations fail.*
trouue | mais nous ne vouldrions mie que vous nous
tenissiez a menteurs se il ne aduenoit | car nous vouldrions bien quil nen fust rien, et voulons, comment quil
en aduiengne, que vous nous asseurez que ia mal ne
nous en aduiendra;" et il leur promet. Lors dist lung
de eulx qui pour tous parla. "Sire, sachez que ceste *The dreams mean that he will lose his land and his honour.*
terre et tout honneur vous conuiendra perdre et ceulx
en qui plus vous fiez vous fauldront; telle est la substance et signifiance de voz songes." De ceste chose fut
le roy moult effraye, "Or me dictes," fait il, "sil est *Arthur asks if anything can avert such fate.*
chose qui men peult garantir." "Certes," fait le
maistre, nous auons veu une chose | Mais cest si grande
merueille que on ne le pourroyt penser, et ne la vous
osons dire." "Dictes," fait il, "seurement | car pis ne
me pouez vous dire que vous mauez dit." "Sire, riens *He is told, "nothing, except the savage lion and the leech without medicine, by help of the counsel of the flower."*
ne vous peult garder de perdre tout honneur terrien fors
le lyon sauluaige, et le mire sans medecine, par le conseil de la fleur, & se nous semble estre si grande folie
que nous ne losions dire | Car lyon sauluaige ne y peult
estre, ne mire sans medecine | ne fleur qui parlast |" le
roy est moult entreprins de ceste chose: mais plus en
fait belle chiere que le cueur ne luy apporte. Ung iour *Arthur goes to the chase.*
alla le roy chasser au boys bien matin | et mena auec
luy messire gauuain, keu le seneschal, et ceulx qui lui
pleust. Si laisse icy le compte a parler de luy, et
retourne a parler du cheualier dont messire Gauuain
aporta le nom en court.

Q̇vant[1] le cheuallier qui lassemblee auoyt vaincu *Lancelot on his wanderings.*
se partast de la ou il se combatist a son hoste,
il erra toute iour sans autre aduanture trouuer. Il se
logea la nuyt chiez une veufue dame a lyssue dune
forest a cinq lieues angleches pres de kamelot. Le
cheualier se leua matin, et erra, luy et ses escuyers et sa *He meets an esquire,*
damoyselle, tant quil encontra vng escuyer. "Varlet,"
fait il, "scez tu nulles nouuelles?" "Ouy," fait il, *and asks him, "what news?"*

[1] There is no trace of the rest of this chapter in the Scottish poem.

xxxii   THE FRENCH CONTINUATION OF THE SCOTCH POEM.

<small>"The queen," he says, "is at Camelot."</small>
"ma dame la royne est icy pres a kamalot." "quelle royne" fait il "Le fe*m*me au roy artus," fait lescuyer.
<small>Lancelot goes on till he sees a large house, a lady, and her damsel.</small>
Le cheuallier sen part, et cheuauche tant quil treuue vne maison forte, et voit vne dame en son surcot, qui regardoit les prez et la forest | & auoit auec elle vne damoiselle.
<small>He regards her fixedly.</small>
Le cheuallier se arreste, et regarde la dame moult longuement tant quil oublie tout autre chose. Et maintenant passa vng cheuallier arme de toutes
<small>An armed knight, passing, asks him what he is regarding so closely.</small>
armes, qui luy dist. "Sire cheualier, que attendez vous?" et celluy ne respo*n*d mot | car il ne la pas ouy. Et le cheualier le boutte, et luy demande quil regarde.
<small>He replies, that he looks at what pleases him.</small>
"Je regarde," fait il, "ce q*u*e me plaist: Et vous nestes mie courtois, qui de mo*n* penser me auez iecte." "Par
<small>The knight asks if he knows who the lady is,</small>
la foy que vous deuez o dieu," fait le cheuallier estrange, scauez vous bien qui la dame est que vous regardez?" "Je le cuyde bien scauoir," fait le bon cheuallier. "Et
<small>and he replies that he knows it is the queen.</small>
q*u*i este elle," fait lautre. "Cest ma dame la royne." "Si maist dieu, estrangement la congnoissez, deables vous font bien regarder dames." "Pourquoy," faict il. "Pource que vous ne me oseriez suyuir par deuant la Royne la ou ie yroye." "Certes," faict le bon cheuallier, "se vous osiez aller la ou ie vous oseray suyuir, vous aurez passez de couraige tous les plus gra*n*s oseurs qui oncques furent." A tant sen part le cheualier. Et
<small>The stranger takes Lancelot home to lodge with him,</small>
le bon cheuallier va apres. Et quant ilz ont vne piece alle, lautre luy dist, "vous he[r]bergerez ennuyt auec moy, et le matin ie vous meneray la ou ie vous diz;" et le bon cheuallier luy demande sil conuient ainsi faire.
<small>and he is well entertained.</small>
"Oy" | fait il. Et il dist que donc lottroyera il. Il geut la nuyt chez le cheuallier sur la riuiere de kamalot, et fut moult bien herberge, et sa pucelle | et ses escuyers.

III. Our last extract will shew exactly where the Scottish poem suddenly ceases, and how the story was probably continued. For the latter purpose, four chapters of the French Romance are added beyond the point where the Scotch ends; and it is possible (judging from lines 306-312 of the Prologue) that the author did not intend to go very much further. The passage begins, in the French copy, at Fol. lxxvii. *b*, col. 1; and, in the Scotch poem, at l. 3427.

<small>Galiot gives Lancelot his own horse.</small>
Lors descent de son cheual, et la baille au cheualier. Et celluy si y monte sans arrest. Et gallehault monta sur vng autre, et vient a son conroy | Si prent auec

soy les dix mille, et dit quilz voisent assembler deuant ; "et vous," fait il au roy vend, "viendres apres, si ne assemblerez mie si tost comme ceulx cy seront assemblez | mais quant les derrains de ceulx de dela seront venus, vous assemblerez, & moy mesmes vous iray querir." A tant amaine les dix mille pour assembler,[1] Et quant il fut entre en la bataille il fist sonner ses busines tant que tout en retentissoit.[2] Quant le noir cheuallier les ouyt venir, si luy sembla que grant effort de gens eut la, si se retrait vng pou vers les siens, et les appella entour luy, & leur dist. "Seigneurs, vous estes tous amys du roy. Or y perra comment vous le ferez."[3] Et messire yuain, qui les vit venir, dist a ses gens, "Or soyes tous asseurs que nous ne perdrons au iourdhuy par force de gens."[4] Et ce disoit il pource quil cuidoit que les gens gallehault fussent tous venus.[5] *said gives orders to his own men.* *He commands the trumpets to be sounded.* *Lancelot harangues his men.* *Sir Yvain comforts Arthur's soldiers.*

Quant les .x.m. de gallehault sassemblerent, si fut grande la noise, et moult en abbatent a leur venir | mais quant messire yuain vint, si reconforta moult les gens du roy artus | et tous les fuyans retournent auec luy. Et gallehault sen va arriere a son conroy, et commande quilz cheuauchent fermement | et quilz se frappent es gens du roy artus[6] de telle maniere[7] que nul dentreulx ne demeure a cheual "Vous estes tous frays. Or y perra comment vous le ferez." A tant cheuauchent les conroys deuers leurs gens, Car ilz auoyent ia du pire. Et quant le conroy de Gallehault fut venu, si changa moult laffaire | Car moult y auoyt grant effort de gens. Et fut a leur venue le cheualier noir mis a terre.[8] Et aussi les six compaignons qui toute iour auoyent este pres de luy.[9] Lors vint gallehault, qui le remonta sur le cheual mesmes ou son corps seoit.[10] Et si tost comme il fut monte, il sen reuint a la meslee aussi frays comme il auoit le iour este. Et quant il vint aux coups donner, tous ceulx qui le veoyent sen esmerueilloyent, Ainsi dura la bataille iusques a la nuyt. Et quant il vint au soir ilz se departirent | et toutesfoys les gens du roy Artus en eurent du meilleur. Le bon cheualier se departit de lost le plus coyement quil peut,[11] et sen alla par vng chemin entre les prestz et vng tertre, et cuyda que nul ne le veist | mais Galle- *Galiot orders charge.* *Galiot's reserve arriving, his men awhile prevail.* *Galiot again remounts Lancelot.* *Night arriving, the hosts retreat.* *Lancelot tries to depart unobserved,*

---

[1] Line 3432. [2] Lines 3435-3440.
[3] Lines 3441-3476. [4] Lines 3477-3480.
[5] Lines 3481-3484. [6] Lines 3485, 6.
[7] Line 3487 *and last*. [8] Compare lines 3365-3368.
[9] Lines 3369, 70. [10] Compare lines 3391-3426.
[11] Compare line 1140.

but is followed by Galiot,	hault sen print tres bien garde, et picqua tant son cheual qui luy fut au deuant par vne adresse, et le vint rencontrer au pied du tertre. Si le salue, et dit 'que dieu le conduit.' Et celuy le regarde en trauers, et luy a a moult grant peine rendu son salut. "Bel amy," fait galehault, "qui estes vous?" "Sire," fait il, "ie suis vng cheualier, ce pouez vous veoir." "Certes," fait galehault, "cheualier estes vous meilleur qui soit	& vous estes lhomme du monde que plus ie vouldroye
who prays him to lodge with him for that night.	honnourer,[1] et si vous suis venu prier que vous herbergez ceste nuyt auec moy." Et il luy dist ainsi comme sil ne lauoit huy veu, "Qui estes vous, sire, qui me auez prie de me he[r]berger?" "Je suis gallehault, le sire de ces gens icy, vers qui vous auez au iourdhuy garanty le royaulme de logres, lequel ie eusse ia conquis se ne fust vostre corps." "Comment" (fait il) "vous estes ennemy de monseigneur le roy artus, et me priez de
Lancelot at first refuses, till Galiot agrees to do whatever Lancelot may require of him,	herberger?	Auec vous ne herbergeray ie mie en ce point." "Haa sire," faict gallehault, "plus feray ie pour vous, et si nay mye a commencer. Et ie vous prie que vous y herbergiez par tel conuenant que ie feray tout ce que me scaurez requerre." A tant se arresta le cheuallier, et dist a gallehault; "Sire, vous promettez assez	mais ie ne scay comment il est du rendre"	et gallehault luy dist. "Sire, se vous he[r]-
and promises to entertain him sumptuously; whereupon they return together to Galiot's camp.	bergez ennuyt auec moy, ie vous donneray tout ce que vous oserez diuiser de bouche, et bien vous en feray seur," Et lors luy fiance, & apres luy promet bailler bons plaiges; Adonc sen vont tous deux en lost.

¶ Comment gallehault suyuit le cheuallier aux noires armes, et fist tant par belles parolles quil lemmena en son ost, donc le roy artus & tous ses gens en furent moult troublez.

Gawain, seeing Lancelot with Galiot,	Messire gauuain auoyt veu aller le cheuallier au noir escu, & le eust voulentiers suiuy sil eust peu monter a cheual. Lors regarde contre val la riuiere,
tells the Queen that now they are all lost;	et voit gallehault et le cheuallier noir qui retournoyent pour venir a lost, et dist a la royne, "Haa dame, or pouons nous bien dire que nous sommes gens perdus	regardez que gallehault a conquis par scauoir," Et elle regarde, & voyt que cest le cheuallier noir que gallehault emmaine; si en est tant iree quelle ne peut dire mot. Et messire gauuain se pasme en pou dheure plus de
and swoons away more than three times.	trois fois. Le roi artus vint leans	et ouyt le cry que chascun disoit, "il est mort, il est mort." Si vint a luy, et lembrassa, et commenca a plorer moult tendre-

[1] Compare lines 2845-8.

ment. Et reuient monseigneur Gauuain de pasmoison; Et quant il veit le roy artus, il commence a le blasmer, et dit. "Ores est venu le terme que les clercz vous disrent. Regardez le tresor que vous auez huy perdu. celluy vous toldra terre qui toute iour la vous a garantie par son corps, et se vo*us* fussiez preudhomme vous leussiez retenu, ainsi comme a fait le plus preudhomme qui viue, qui par cy deuant lemmaine." Lors voit le roy gallehault, qui emmenoit le cheuallier, dont il a tel dueil que a pou quil ne est cheut | mais de plorer ne se peut tenir, et toutesfois faict il la plus belle chere q*ui*l peut pour son nepueu reconforter. Et si tost q*ue* il vit en la salle, il fist gra*n*t dueil | aussi fist chascun preudhomme.

He tells Arthur that his time of misfortune is come;

for their protector is lost.

Arthur also sees Galiot, and is deeply grieved, but tries to comfort his nephew.

TAnt sont allez gallehault et le cheualier quilz sont venus empres lost, Adonc luy dist le cheualier, "Sire, ains que ie entre dedans vostre ost, faictes moi p*ar*ler aux deux pl*us* preudhommes que vous ayez et esquelz vous fiez le plus." Et gallehault lottroye. Lors sen va en son tref, et prent deux des hommes du mo*n*de ou plus il se fie, et leur dist, "Venez auec moy et vous verrez le plus riche homme du monde." "Comme*n*t," font ilz, "nestes vous mie le plus riche qui soit au monde?" "Nenny," dist il | "mais ie le seray ains que ie dorme." Ces deux estoyent le roy premier conquis | et le roi des cent cheuallliers. Qua*n*t ilz virent le cheuallier, si lui firent moult grant ioye | Car ilz le congneurent bien par ses armes. Et le cheuallier leur demanda qui ilz estoient | et ilz se nommerent sicomme vous auez ouy | et il leur dist. "Seigneurs, vostre sire vous faict moult grant honneur | Car il dit que vous estes les deux hommes du monde que plus il ayme, et entre luy et moy a vne conuenance que ie vueil que vous oyez | Car il ma fiance que pour en nuyt herberger auec luy me donnera ce que ie luy vouldray demander." Et gallehault dist | "vous dictes verite." "Sire," faict le cheuallier, "ie vueil encores auoir la seurte de ses hommes." Et gallehault dist, "Dictes moy comme*n*t." "Ilz me fianceront," fait le cheuallier, "q*ue* se vous me faillez de co*n*uenant, ilz vous guerpiront et sen viendront auec moy la ou ie diray," Et gallehault dit que ainsi le veult | et il le fait fia*n*cer. Lors appella gallehault le roy premier co*n*quis a vne part, et luy dist. "Allez auant & dictes a mes barons quilz assemblent maintenant a monstre si honnorablement comme ilz pourront, et gardez que en mon tref soient to*us* les deduys que le*n* pourra trouuer en

Galiot and Lancelot arrive at Galiot's camp,

and Lancelot asks to speak with the two men whom Galiot most trusts.

Galiot takes him to the "first-conquest" king and the king of a hundred knights, and

Lancelot repeats to them his compact with Galiot,

and takes their pledge that they will forsake Galiot if he breaks his agreement, and will go with himself (Lancelot).

tout lost." Lors sen va celluy au ferir des esperons, &
fist le commandement de son seigneur. Et gallehault
tient le cheualier aux parolles, luy & son seneschal,
tant que le commandement fust fait. Si ne demoura
gueres que encontre eulx vindrent deux cens barons qui
tous estoient hommes de gallehault, .xxviii. roys, et les
autres estoient ducz et contes ; la fut le cheuallier telle-
ment honnoure que oncques si grant feste ne fut pour
vng homme mescongneu comme len fit pour luy a celle
fois | et disoient grans & petis, " Bien viengnez, la fleur
de la cheualerie du monde " | et il en auoit grant honte.
Ainsi vindrent iusques au tref de gallehault, si ne pour-
roient estre comtez les deduys et les instrumens qui leans
estoient. A telle ioye fut receu, et quant il fut desarme,
gallehault luy fit apporter vne robe moult riche, et il la
vestit. quant le manger fut prest, ilz se assirent a table,
et furent noblement seruis, et le cheualier fut moult
honnoure.

Apres manger commanda gallehault a faire quatre
litz desquelz lung estoit plus grant que les
aultres. Quant les litz furent si richement atournez,
gallehault maine le cheuallier coucher. Et dist. " Sire,
vous gerrez icy ; " " Et qui gerra de la ? " fait le cheua-
lier. " Quattre sergens," faict gallehault, " qui vous
seruiront | Et ie iray en vne chambre par dela, affin que
vous soyez icy plus en paix." " Haa, Sire, pour dieu,"
faict il, " ne me faictes gesir plus ayse que ces aultres
cheualiers | car tant ne me deuez a vilennir." " Nayez
garde," faict galehault, " Car ia pour chose que vous
faciez pour moi vous ne serez tenu a villain." A tant
sen part gallehault. Et le cheuallier commence a penser
au grant honneur que gallehault luy faisoit. Si lenprise
moult | puis se coucha, et tantost il sendormit | car
moult estoit las ; Et quant gallehault sceut quil fut
endormy, le plus coyement quil peut se coucha en vng
autre lit empres luy | et es deux aultres litz se coucher-
ent deux cheualiers, et nestoyent en la chambre que
eulx quatre, sans plus. La nuyt se plaint moult le
cheualier en son dormant, et gallehault loit bien, car il
ne dormoit gueres. Ains pensa toute la nuyt a le retenir.
Lendemain le cheualier se leua et alla ouyr messe ; et ia
estoit gallehault leue | car il ne voulut mie que le
cheualier laperceust. Quant ilz vindrent du monstier,
le cheualier demanda ses armes, & gallehault demande
pourquoy. Et il dist quil sen vouloit aller. Et galle-
hault luy dist. " Beau doulx amy, demourez | et ne
cuydez mye que ie vous vueille deceuoir. Car vous

noserez ia riens demander que vous nayez. Et sachez
que vous pourriez bien auoir compagnie de plus riche
homme que ie suis | mais vous ne laurez iamais a
homme qui plus vous ayme." "Sire," faict le cheual-
lier, "ie demoureray donc puis quil vous plaist. Car *Galiot induces*
meilleure compaignie que la vostre ne pourroye ie mye *him to stay,*
auoir | Mais ie vous diray presentement le don pour-
quoy ie demoureray auec vous | et se ie ne lay, ie ny
demoureray ia." "Sire," fait gallehault, "dictes seure- *but again pro-*
ment et vous laurez, se cest chose que ie puisse acom- *mises to do for*
plir;" Et le cheuallier appella ses deux plaiges et dist *asks.*
deuant eulx, "Je vous demande," fait il, "que si tost *Lancelot then de-*
que vous serez au dessus du roy artus, que vous luy *mands that Galiot*
alliez crier mercy si tost comme ie vous en semondray." *self to Arthur.*
Quant gallehault lentent, si en est tout esbahy, et com-
mence a penser. Et les deux roys luy dirent. "A
quoy pensez vous icy endroit, de penser nauez mestier |
car vous auez tant couru que vous ne pouez retourner."
"Comment," faict Gallehault, "cuydez vous que ie me *Galiot is con-*
vueille repentir | se tout le monde estoit mien si luy *founded, and*
oseroye ie bien donner. mais ie pensoye a vng seul mot *grants Lancelot's*
quil a dit | mais ia dieu ne maist," dist il, "se vous *request.*
nauez le don | car ie ne pourroye riens faire pour vous
ou ie peusse auoir honte. Mais ie vous prye que ne me
tollez vostre compagnie pour la donner a aultruy;" et
le cheualier luy creanca. Ainsi demoura | et ilz se
asseirent au manger qui estoit appreste. Si font moult
grant ioye par tout lost du cheualier qui est demoure.
Ainsi passerent celle nuyt. Lendemain gallehault et *Lancelot remains*
son compaignon allerent ouyr messe, et gallehault luy *with him another*
deist | "Sire, il est huy iour dassembler; voullez vous *night.*
armes porter?" "Ouy," dist il. "donc porterez vous
les miennes," fait gallehault, "pour le commencement."
Et il dist quil les porteroit voulentiers | "mais vous ne
porterez armes," feist il a gallehault, "si non comme
mon sergent?" "Non," dist il. Lors firent apporter
les armes, & armerent le cheuallier du fort haulbert, &
des chausses qui trop estoyent longues & lees; Lors se
armerent les gens de gallehault. et pareillement les gens *Next day, the*
du roy Artus, & passerent les lices de telz y eut. Toute- *hosts are again*
ffoys le roy auoyt deffendu que nul ne les passast. Si *armed for battle.*
y eut de bonnes ioustes en pou dheure | si se assembler-
ent tous les ostz deuant la lice, & commencerent a faire
armes. Le roy artus estoit a son estandart, et auoit
commande que ilz menassent la royne a sauluete se la
descomfiture tournoit sur eulx | quant tous les ostz
furent assemblez et le bon cheualier fust arme, si cuida

chascun que ce fust gallehault, & disoyent tous. "Voicy gallehault, voicy gallehault" | messire gauuain le congneust bien & dist. "Ce nest mye gallehault | ains est le cheualier aux armes noires, le meilleur cheualier du monde" | & si tost comme ilz furent assemblez, oncques ne se tint le roy Artus ne ses gens depuis que le cheualier y fut arriue | et trop se desconfortoyent du bon cheualier qui contre eulx estoit, si furent menez iusques a la lice. car trop estoient grans gens auec gallehault. au partir des lices ce tindrent vne piece et souffrirent longuement | mais le souffrit ny peut riens valoir. Grant fut le meschief des gens au roy artus. et dit le compte que le cheualier neust mie moins de peine de tenir les gens de gallehault que ilz ne passassent oultre la lice quil auoit de chasser les gens au roy Artus. Et nompourtant moult les auoit supportez | & il les eut mis oultre a force sil eust voulu | mais il demoura emmy le pas pour les aultres detenir. Lors regarda tout entour de luy, et commenca a hucher | "gallehault, gallehault." et gallehault vient grant alleure, et dist. "bel amy, que voulez vous?" "quoy," faict il, "ie vueil que mon conuenant me tenez;" "Par ma foy," fait gallehault, "ie suis tout prest de lacomplir puis quil vous plaist." Lors picque le cheual des esperons & vient iusques a lestandart ou le roy artus estoit, qui faisoit si tresgrant dueil que a peu quil ne se occioit pource quil estoit desconfit. Si estoit ia la royne montee, et lemmenoyent quarante cheualliers. Et monseigneur gauuain, que on vouloit emporter en lictiere | mais il dit quil aymeroit mieulx mourir en ce point que veoir toute cheualerie morte et honnye : si se pasma tellement que len cuydoit bien que il mourust incontinent.

¶ Comment lancelot par la prouesse conquis tout, et fist tant que galehault cria mercy au roy artus.

Vant le cheualier veit gallehault prest dacomplir son conuenant, il iura bien que oncques si loyal compaignon ne fut trouue. Il en a telle pytie quil en souspire moult fort, & dit entre ses dens. "Haa dieu, qui pourra ce desseruir?" & gallehault cheuauche iusques a lestandart et demande le roy artus. Il vient auant moult dolent & esmaye comme celluy qui tout honneur et toute ioye terrienne cuyde auoir perdue; Et quant gallehault le voit, si luy dit. "sire, roy artus, venez auant, & nayez paour | car ie vueil a vous parler." et quant le roy louyt, il sesmerueille moult que ce peult estre; Et de si loing comme galehault le voit venir, il descend de son cheual et se agenouille, et dit. "Sire,

ie vous viens faire droit de ce que ie vous ay meffait; *and submits himself to him humbly.*
si men repens, et me metz en vostre mercy."

QVant le roy lentend, il a merueilleusement grant *Arthur, overjoyed, praises God.*
ioye, et lieue les mains vers le ciel, louant Dieu
de ceste aduanture | et se le roy fait bonne chere, en-
cores la faict meilleure Gallehault. et il se lieue de
genoulx, & sentrebaisent, en font moult grande chere
lung a lautre. lors dist Gallehault | "sire, faictes vostre
plaisir de moy | car ie metz en vostre saisine mon corps
pour en faire ce que il vous plaira. Et sil vous plaist, *Galiot, first asking Arthur's leave, dismisses his troops to their tents.*
ie yray retraire mes gens arriere, & puis reuiendray a
vous incontinent." "Allez doncques," fait le roy | "car
ie vueil parler a vous." A tant sen part gallehault &
reuient a ses gens | & les en faict aller. Et le roy
enuoya apres la royne, qui sen alloit faisant grand dueil.
et les messages cheuauchent tant que ilz lattaingnent |
et sont venus a elle, & luy comptent la ioye que aduenue
leur est. Et elle ne le peult croire tant quelle voy les
enseignes que le roy luy enuoye. tant coururent les
nouuelles que monseigneur gauuain le sceut, lequel en
eut grant ioye sur tous les aultres, et dist au roy. *The Queen and Sir Gawain rejoice greatly.*
"Sire, comment a ce este?" "Certes, ie ne scay," fait
il: "mais ie croy que telle a este le plaisir de nostre
seigneur." moult est grande la ioye, & moult se esmer-
ueille chascun comment ce peult estre aduenu. Galle-
hault dist a son compaignon. "que voulez vous que ie
face? iay fait vostre commandement; & le roy ma dit
que ie retourne | mais ie vous conuoyeray auant iusques
a voz tentes." "Haa sire," fait le cheualier, "aincoys
vous irez au roy & luy porterez le plus grant honneur
que vous pourrez. Et tant auez fait pour moy que ie
ne le pourroye desseruir | mais tant vous prye, pour *Lancelot prays Galiot not to reveal where he is, and they return to their tents.*
dieu | et pour lamour que vous auez a moy, que nul ne
sache ou ie suis" | ainsi sen vont parlant iusques a leurs
tentes. chascun scait que la paix est faicte | mais
plusieurs en sont dolens | car mieulx aymassent la
guerre que la paix. lors sont descenduz les deux
compaignons, et si tost quilz furent desarmez, Galle-
hault print vne de ses meilleures robbes pour aller a la
court. et feist cryer par tout son ost que chascun sen
allast, fors tant seullement ceulx de son hostel. Apres *Galiot commits his guest to the care of the two kings, and departs to speak with Arthur.*
appella les deux roys, et leur baille son compaignon, &
leur commande quilz facent autant de luy comme de
son corps mesmes. A tant monte Gallehault, et sen
va a la court du roy artus. Et le roy luy vint alen-
contre, et la royne qui ia estoit retournee, & la dame de
malehault auec plusieurs dames & damoyselles. A tant

Arthur and Galiot go together to the tower where Gawain lies ill.	vont en la bretesche ou monseigneur gauuain gisoit malade. et quant il sceut que gallehault venoit, il sefforce de belle chere faire, comme celluy qui oncques mes ne lauoit veu de si pres. lors luy dist	"bien soyez vous venu comme de celluy dont ie desiroye moult lacointance	car vous estes lhomme du monde qui plus
Gawain welcomes Galiot.	doibt estre prise & ayme a droit de toutes gens. Et ie cuyde que nul ne scait si bien congnoistre preudhomme comme vous & bien y a paru." Ainsi parle messire gauuain a gallehault, & il luy demande comment il luy est	et Gauuain dist. "Jay este pres de mort. mais la grant amour qui est entre vous & le roy ma guery."
The Queen, the King, and Gawain rejoice at Galiot's coming,	Moult font grant ioye le roy artus & la royne & monseigneur gauuain de la venue de gallehault	et tout le iour ont parle de amour et daccointance. Mais du noir cheualier ne tiennent ilz nulles parolles	ains passent le iour a resiouyr lung lautre tant quil vint au vespre. Lors demande gallehault congie de ses gens aller veoir.
but he, soon after, departs to see Lancelot for a short time, promising to return.	Et le roy le luy donne	"mais vous reuiendrez," fait il, "incontinent;" et gallehault le luy octroye	si senreuient a son compaignon & luy demande comment il a lepuis fait	et il luy respondit que bien; "Sire," fait gallehault, "comment feray ie	: le roy ma moult prie que ie retourne a luy, & il me feroit mal de vous laisser
Lancelot tells Galiot to do whatever Arthur wishes.	en ce point." "Haa, sire cheualier, pour dieu mercy, vous ferez ce que monseigneur le roy vouldra. car iamais a plus preudhomme que il est ne eustes accointance. Mais ie vueil que vous me donnez vng don." Et galle-
He charges Galiot again not to ask his name, but to tell him about Arthur.	hault luy dist. "Demandez ce quil vous plaira	car ie ne vous escondiroye iamais;" "Sire," fait il, "ie vous remercye. Vous me auez donne que vous ne me demanderez mon nom deuant que ie le vous diray." "Et ie men tiendray a tant puis que vous le voulez," dit gallehault. "Et ne doubtez pas que ce eust este la premiere chose que ie vous eusse demande, si men tairay a tant." Lors luy demanda de laccointance du roy artus	mais il ne nomme mie la royne	et gallehault dit que "le roy est moult preudhomme, & moult me poyse que ie ne lay congneu pieca	Car moult en
Galiot praises the Queen,	feusse amende	mais ma dame la royne est sy vaillante que oncques plus honneste dame ne vey." et quant le cheualier ouyt parler de la royne, si se embronche et
and Lancelot sheds tears.	commence a souspirer durement. et gallehault le regarde et se esmerueille moult pource que les larmes luy cheoyent des yeulx, si commence a parler daultre chose.

Quant ilz ont longuement parle ensemble, le cheualier noir luy dist. "Allez, si ferez a monsei-

THE FRENCH CONTINUATION OF THE SCOTCH POEM. xli

gneur le roy compaignie, et si escoutez sy vouz orrez de moy nulles parolles, & vous me compterez demain ce que vous aurez ouy." "Voulentiers, sire," faict gallehault | lors le accolle, et dit aux roys. "Je vous baille en garde cest homme comme le cueur de mon ventre." Ainsi sen va gallehault & le cheuallier demeure en la garde de deux preu[d]hommes du pays de Gallehault | mais il ne fault mye demander sil fust honnore | car len faisoit assez plus pour luy quil neust voulu. celle nuyt geurent les deux roys au tref gallehault pour lamour du cheualier & luy firent entendant quilz ny coucheroyent mye | & ilz le firent coucher ainsi que Gallehault auoit fait lautre nuyt. Au commencement dormit le cheualier moult fort, et quant vint a mynuit si commenca a soy tourner, et commenca a faire vng dueil si grant que tous ceulz qui entour luy estoyent sen esueillerent. Et en son refrain disoit souuent. "Haa chetif, que pourray ie faire?" Et toute nuyt demena tel deuil. Au matin se leuerent les deux roys le plus coyement quilz peurent | & moult se merueillent quil pouoit auoir. daultre part fut gallehault leue, & vint a son tref veoir son compaignon. Il demande aux deux roys que son compaignon fait. Et ilz luy dient quil auoit toute nuyt mene grant dueil. Lors entre en la chambre ou il estoit, et si tost comme il le ouyt venir il essuye ses yeulx; Adonc gallehault, cuidant que il dormist, saillist dehors de la chambre incontinent; apres le cheualier se leua. Et gallehault vit que il auoit les yeulx rouges et enflez. Adonc le prent par la main, et le tyre a part, et luy dist. "Beau doulx compaignon, pourquoy vous occiez vous ainsi? dont vous vient ce dueil que vous auez toute nuyt demene, & le desplaisir que vous auez? Je vous prye pour dieu que vous me diez la cause, et ie vous ayderay se nul homme mortel y peult conseil mettre;" & commence a plourer si durement comme sil veist mort la chose du monde que mieulx aymast. Lors est gallehault moult a malayse et luy dit, "Beau doulx compaignon, dictes moy vostre mescheance | car il nest nul homme au monde, sil vous auoit riens forfait, que ie nen pourchassasse vostre droit." Et il dist que nul ne luy a riens meffait. "beau doulx amy, pourquoy menez vous doncques si grant dueil? Vous poise il que ie vous ay fait mon maistre & mon compaignon?" "Haa," fait il, "vous auez assez plus fait pour moy que ie ne pourroye desseruir, ne riens du monde ne me met a malaise que mon cueur, qui a toute paour que cueur mortel pourrait

Lancelot asks Galiot to return to Arthur, and to report to him all the conversation.

Lancelot sleeps with the two kings in Galiot's tent;

but awakes at midnight, and makes a great moaning.

Galiot comes to see after Lancelot,

finds him with his eyes red and swoln,

and conjures him to tell him what the matter is.

Lancelot cries bitterly,

and says that it is his heart, which has all the dread that it is possible for mortal heart to have.

auoir. Si doubte moult que vostre grant debonnairete ne me occie." De ceste chose est gallehault moult a malayse, si reconforte son compaignon. Apres allerent ouyr masse. Quant vint que le prestre eut fait trois parties du corps de nostre seigneur, gallehault se trait auant, et tient son compaignon par la main, & luy monstre le corps de nostre seigneur que le prestre tenoit entre ses mains; Puis luy dist. "doncques ne croyez vous pas bien que cest le corps de nostre saulueur?" "Voirement le croy ie bien," fait le cheualier. Et gallehault luy dist. "beau doulx amy, or ne me mescreez mye que ces trois parties de chair que ie vois en semblance de pain, ia ne feray en ma vie chose que ie cuyde qui vous ennuye: mais toutes les choses que ie scauray qui vous plairont, pourchasseray a mon pouoir." "sire," fait il, "grant mercys." A tant se taisent iusques apres la messe | et lors demanda gallehault a son compaignon quil fera; "Sire," fait il, "vous ne laisserez mie le roy en ce point | ains yrez luy faire compaignie." "Sire," faict il, "grant mercys;" A tant sen part de luy, si le rebaille aux preudhommes de la court du roy artus. si font de luy grant signeurie sicomme ilz peuent.

ET quant vint apres disner, sy furent le roy & la royne & gallehault appuyez au lict de messire gauuain, tant que messire gauuain dist a gallehault. "Sire, or ne vous poise dune chose que ie vous demanderay." "Certes," fait galehault, "non fera il." "sire, celle paix qui fut entre vous & mon oncle, par qui fut elle, par la chose au monde qui plus vous aymez?" "Sire," fait il, "vous me auez tant coniure que ie le vous diray. Vng cheualier la fist." "Et qui est le cheualier?" fait messire gauuain. "Si maist dieu," fait gallehault, "ie ne scay." "Qui fut celluy aux noires armes?" deist messire gauuain. "Ce fut," fait il, "vng cheualier;" "Tant," fait il, "en pouez vous bien dire | mais acquitter vous conuient." "Je me suis acquite de ce que me coniurastes. Ne plus ne vous en diray ores | ne rien ne vous en eusse ores dit, se vous ne me eussiez coniure." "Par dieu," faict la royne, "ce fut le cheuallier noir | mais faictes le nous monstrer." "Qui | moy, dame?" faict gallehault, "ie le vous puys bien monstrer sicomme celluy qui riens nen scait!" "Taisez vous," fait la royne, "il est demoure auec vous, & hier porta voz armes." "Dame," fait il | "il est vray | mais ie ne le vys oncques puis que ie party du roy a la premiere fois." "comment," fait le roy, "ne le cognoissiez vous mye | ie cuydoye que il fust de vostre terre." "Si maist dieu, non est," fait gallehault. "certes," fait le roy, "ne de la myenne non est il mye" | Moult tindrent longuement gallehault a parolle le roy et la royne pour auoir le nom du cheualier | mais plus nen peurent traire. et messire gauuain craint quil ne ennuye a gallehault, si dist au roy. "Or en laissez a tant le parler. certes le cheualier est preudhomme, & pleust a dieu que ie luy ressemblasse." Moult loe messire gauuain le cheualier. Si en ont la parolle laissee | et gallehault la recommence et dit. "Sire, veistes vous oncques meilleur cheuallier que celluy au noir escu?" "certes," fait le roy, "ie ne vy oncques cheualier de qui ie aymasse mieulx laccointance pour cheualerie;" "Non" | fait gallehault. "Or me dictes," faict gallehault, "par la foy que vous deuez a ma dame qui cy est, combien vous vouldriez auoir donne pour auoir son accointance a tousioursmais?" "Si maist dieu," faict il, "ie luy partiroye la moytie de tout ce que ie pourroye auoir, fors seullement de ceste dame." "Certes," fait gallehault, "assez y mettriez. Et vous, messire gauuain, se dieu vous doint sante que tant desirez, quel meschief en feriez vous pour auoir compaignie a si preudhomme?" Et quant messire gauuain lot, si pense vng petit comme celluy qui ne cuyde iamais auoir sante. "Se dieu me donnoit la sante que ie desire | ie vouldroye orendroit estre vne des plus belles dames du monde, par conuenant quil me aymast tous les iours de sa vie." "par ma foy," fait gallehault, "assez y auez mis." "Et vous, madame, quel meschef feriez vous par conuenant que vng tel cheualier fust tousiours en vostre seruice?" "par dieu," fait elle, "messire gauuain y a mis toutes les offres que dame y peult mettre." Et monseigneur gauuain & tous aultres se commencerent a rire. "Gallehault," fait messire gauuain, "qui tous nous auez adiurez par le serment que ie vous coniuray, ores qui vouldriez vous y auoir mys?" "Si maist dieu," faict gallehault, "ie y vouldroye auoir tourne mon honneur a honte, par tel si que ieusse a tousioursmais vng si bon cheualier en ma compaignie." "Sy maist dieu," faict messire gauuain, "plus y auez mys que nous." et lors se pensa messire gauuain que cestoit le noir cheualier qui le paix auoit faicte | car pour luy auoit tourne son honneur a honte, quant il veit quil estoyt au dessus. Et le dist gauuain a la royne, & se fut la cause dont gallehault fut plus prise; Moult tindrent longuement parolles du cheualier.

and Galiot will not disclose the knight's name,

but asks Arthur if he ever saw a better knight, and what he would give to know him henceforth.

"Half of all I have, except my wife," says Arthur.

"And what would you give, Gawain?"

"I should like to turn woman if he would love me all his life."

"I can offer no more than Gawain," says the Queen.

"Well," says Galiot, "I would turn all my honour into shame, for his sake."

So Gawain concludes that it was the Black Knight who brought about the peace.

xliv   THE FRENCH CONTINUATION OF THE SCOTCH POEM.

The Queen walks away with Galiot, tells him she loves him much, and prays him to let her see the Black Knight.

et la royne sadressa, et dist quelle sen voulloit aller vers la bretesche pour veoir les prez, et gallehault la conuoye : si le print la royne par la main & luy dist. "Gallehault, ie vous ayme moult, & il est vray que vous auez le cheualier en vostre baillie, & par aduenture il est tel que ie le congnois bien ; si vous prie si cher que vous auez mamour, que vous faciez tant que ie le voye." "Dame," fait gallehault, "ie nen ay encores nulle saisine | & ne le vy puis que la paix fut faicte de moy & du roy.   Et se il estoit or en mon tref, si y conuien-

He promises to do all he can for her;

droit il aultre voulente que le vostre & que la mienne. Et bien saichez que tant me auez coniure que ie mettray tout le pouoir que ie pourray. comment vous pourrez

and the Queen says, "I shall be sure to see him if you try,

parler a luy ?" "se vous en faictes vostre pouoir," fait elle, "ie le verray bien, & ie men attens a vous, et faictes tant que ie soye vostre a tousiours : car cest vng des hommes du monde que ie verroye plus voulentiers." "Dame," fait il, "ie en feray mon pouoir." "Grant

for he is in your custody. Send and get him."

mercys," fait elle. "Or gardez que ie le voye au plus tost que vous pourrez | car il est en vostre baillie, ie le scay bien | et se il est en vostre terre, enuoyez le querre." Atant sen part gallehault & sen vient au roy.

Arthur wishes Galiot's people and his own to be brought nearer to one another.

Et monseigneur gauuain & le roy lui dient. "gallehault, ie suis deliure de mes gens, ores faictes approcher voz gens des nostres, ou ie feray approcher les nostres des vostres | Car nous sommes a priuee mesgnie." "Sire," faict gallehault, "ie feray approcher les miens daultre part de cest riuiere si que mon tref sera endroit le vostre, et sera vne nef appareillee en quoy nous passerons dicy la et de la icy." "Certes," fait le roy, "moult auez bien dit."

Galiot returns to Lancelot,

LOrs sen va Gaillehault en sa tente, et trouue son compaignon moult pensif. Il luy demande comment il a puis faict ; Et il dist, "bien, se paour ne me mestriast." et gallehault dist, "de quoy auez vous telle paour?" "que ie ne soye congneu," dist il. "or nen ayez mie paour, car vous ny serez ia congneu, se

tells him what the King, Gawain, and the Queen have said of him,

vostre voulente ne y est ;" Lors luy compte les offres que le roy et messire gauuain ont faict pour luy, et ce que la royne dit | et comment la royne la tenu a grant parlement de le veoir | et comme il luy respondit. "et saichez que elle na de nully si tres grant desir de veoir comme de vous. Et monseigneur la Roy ma prye que ie face mes gens approcher | car nous sommes trop loing

and asks him what answer he shall give the Queen.

lung de lautre. Or me dictes que vous voulez que je face | car il est en vostre plaisir." "Je loue que vous facez ce que monseigneur le roy vous prye ;" "Et a ma dame que respondray ie, beau doulx amy?" "Certes," fait il, "ie ne scay." Lors commence a souspirer. Et gallehault luy deist. "Beau doulx amy, ne vous esmayez point | mais dictes moy comment vous voulez quil soit | car bien saichez quil sera ainsi comme vous vouldrez | et ie aymeroye mieulx estre courrouce a la moytie du monde que a vous tout seul. ores me dictes quil vous en plaist." "Sire," faict ledit cheualier, " ce que vous me louerez | car ie suis en vostre garde desormais." "Certes," fait gallehault, "il me semble que pour veoir ma dame la royne il ne vous peult empyrer." Lors apperceut galehault assez de son penser, & le tient si court quil luy octroye ce quil demande | "mais il conuiendra," faict il, "que il soyt faict celeement, que nul ne le saiche | fors moy et vous." Et gallehault dit que il ne se soulcye point. "Or dictes," (fait le cheualier a gallehault,) "a ma dame que vous me auez enuoye querre." "Sur moy en laissez le surplus," dit Gallehault. Lors sen part a tant, et commanda ses trefz a tendre la ou il auoit en conuenant au roy | et son seneschal fist son commandement.

Lancelot sighs,

and says, "Whatever you advise."

"There will be no harm in seeing her," answers Galiot.

Lancelot says the matter must be managed secretly; and they agree that Galiot shall tell the Queen he has sent to seek for Lancelot.

¶ Comment gallehault fist tant que la royne veit Lancelot, Et comment ilz se araisonnerent ensemble, et parlerent de plusieurs choses.

How Guinevere and Lancelot meet and talk.

A Tant sen partit gallehault & sen vient au tref du roy, & si tost comme la royne le voit, si luy courut a lencontre, & luy demande comment il auoit exploycte la besongne. "dame," faict il, "ie en ay fait tant que ie craing que lamour de vostre pryere ne me tolle la chose du monde que ie ayme plus." "Sy maist dieu," faict elle, "vous ne perderez riens par moy que ie ne vous rende ou double | mais que y pouez vous," fait elle, "perdre?" "Celluy mesmes que vous demandez," fait gallehault | "Car ie doubte quil ne se courrouce, et que ie ne le perde a tousiours." "Certes," faict elle, "ce ne pourray ie pas rendre | mais ia par moy ne le perderez, se dieu plaist. Et touteffoys dictes moy quant il viendra" | "dame," fait il, "quant il pourra | car ie lay enuoye querre, et croy que il ne demourra mye longuement." De leur conseil entendit ung peu la dame de mallehault qui sen prenoit garde et nen faisoit mye semblant. Lors sen partit gallehault et vient a ses gens qui estoyent logez la ou il auoit commande.

The Queen asks Galiot what he has done for her.

"Sent to seek for your knight," says he.

Galiot returns to his men,

Q Vant il fut descendu, il parla a son Seneschal et luy deist | "quant ie vous enuoyeray querir, venez a moy, vous & mon compaignon en ce lieu la."

and tells his Seneschal to bring Lancelot when he sends for him.

xlvi THE FRENCH CONTINUATION OF THE SCOTCH POEM

Et le roy des cent cheualiers, qui son seneschal estoit, dist que moult voulentiers feroit son commandement & son plaisir. Lors salua Gallehault son compaignon, et sen retourna a la court. Et quant la royne veit gallehault qui estoit venu, elle luy dist que il gardast bien et loyaulment ce quil luy auoit promis. Et il luy dist | "dame, ie cuyde que vous verrez ennuyt ce que vous auez tant desire." Quant elle ouyt ce, si en fut moult ioyeuse, et moult luy ennuya ce iour pour sa voulente acomplir du desir que elle auoit de parler a celuy ou toutes ses pensees estoyent. Lors luy deist Gallehault, "nous yrons apres souper en ce vergier la aual" | et elle luy octroye. Quant ce vint apres souper, si appelle la royne | la dame de mallehault | et dame Lore de cardueil, une sienne pucelle, et sen vont tout droit la ou gallehault auoyt dit | et gallehault prent ung escuyer et luy dist. "Va et dy a mon seneschal que il viengne la ou ie luy commanday." Et celuy y va. Apres ne demoura guaires que le seneschal y vint, luy et le cheualier. Ilz estoyent tous deux de grant beaulte; Quant ilz approcherent, si congneut la dame de mallehault le cheualier comme celluy que elle auoyt eu maint iour en sa baillie. Et pource quelle ne vouloit mye que il la congneut, se embroncha, et ilz passent oultre. le seneschal les salue. Et gallehault dit a la royne. "Dame, lequel vous semble il que se soit?" | et elle dit. "Certes, ilz sont tous deux beaulx cheualliers | mais ie ne voy corps ou il puisse auoir tant de prouesse que le noir cheualier auoit." "or saichez, dame, que cest lung de ces deux" | a tant sont venuz auant, et le cheuallier tremble si que a peine peult saluer la royne, & la royne sen esmerueille. lors se agenouillent eulx deux, et le cheualier la salue | mais cest moult pourement | car moult estoit honteux. Lors se pense la royne que cest il. Et gallehault dit au seneschal. "allez, si faictes a ces dames compaignie." Et celuy fait ce que son sire luy commande. A doncques la royne prent le cheualier par la main & le assiet iouxte elle. Sy luy fait moult beau semblant & dit en riant. "Sire, moult vous auons desire, tant que, dieu mercy et gallehault, vous voyons. et nonpourtant encores ne croy ie mye que ce soit celluy que ie demande | & gallehault ma dit que cestes vous | & encores vouldroye scauoir qui vous estes par vostre bouche mesmes, se vostre plaisir y estoit." Et celuy dit que il ne scait | et oncques ne la regarda au visaige. Et la royne ce esmerueille que il peult auoir, tant quelle souspeconne une partie de ce quil a. Et gallehault, qui

Marginalia:
- Galiot then goes back to the Queen, says he thinks she will see her knight that evening, and appoints to meet her in an Orchard below.
- After supper the Queen goes to the Orchard,
- and Galiot sends for his Seneschal and the Knight,
- who come.
- The Queen at first cannot think that either is the black knight,
- but one is so bashful that she fixes on him,
- seats him by her, smiles on him, says she has so longed to see him,
- and now he must tell her who he is. "I don't know," he answers.

THE FRENCH CONTINUATION OF THE SCOTCH POEM. xlvii

le voigt si honteux, pense quil veult dire a la royne son
penser seul a seul. lors sen vient messire gauuain celle
part, et fait rasseoir les damoyselles pour ce que leuees ses-
toient encontre luy. Puis commencent a parler de maintes
choses. Et la Royne dit au cheuallier, "Beau sire,
pourquoy vous celez vous de moy? Certes il ne y a
cause pourquoy; nestes vous mie celluy qui porta les
noires armes, et qui vainquist lassemblee?" "Dame,
nenny" | "et nestes vous pas celluy qui porta lende-
main les armes a gallehault?" "Dame, ouy;" "Donc
estes vous celluy qui vainquistes lassemblee qui fut
faicte le premier iour par deuers nous et par[1] deuers
Gallehault?" "Dame, non suis." Quant la royne ot
ainsi parler le cheualier, a donc appercoit elle bien quil
ne veult mie congnoistre quil eust vaincue lassemblee,
si len prise mieulx la royne | car quant vng homme se
loe luy mesmes, il tourne son honneur a honte | et
quant aultruy le loe, adonc il est mieulx prise. "Or
me dictes," fait la royne a lancelot | "qui vous fist
cheuallier?" "Dame," fait il, "vous;" "Moy?" fait
elle, "Et quant?" "Dame," fait il, "vous remembrez
vous point quant vng cheuallier vint a Kamalot, lequel
estoyt naure de deux troncons de lance au corps, et
dune espee parmy la teste, et que vng varlet vint a
court en vng vendredy, et fut cheualier le dymenche, et
deffera le cheuallier?" "De ce," fait elle, "me souient
il bien | et se dieu vous aist, feustes vous ce que la
dame du lac amena en court vestu dune robe blanche?"
"Dame, ouy." "Et pourquoy dictes vous donc que ie
vous fis cheuallier?" "Dame," fait il, "ie dys vray |
Car la coustume est telle que nul ne peut estre cheual-
lier sans ceindre espee. Et celluy de qui il tient lespee,
le faict cheuallier; de vous la tiens ie. Car le roy ne
la me donna onques. Pour ce dis ie que vous me feistes
cheualier." De ce est la royne moult ioyeuse | "ou vous
en allastes vous au partir de court?" "Dame, ie men
allay pour secourir la dame de noehault;" "Et durant ce
temps me mandastes vous riens?" "Dame, ouy | ie vous
ennoyay peux pucelles." "Il est vray," dist la royne.
"Et quant vous partistes de noehault, trouuastes vous nul
cheuallier qui se reclamast de moy?" "Dame, ouy; vng
qui gardoit vng gue, et me dist que descendisse de dessus
mon cheual et le vouloit auoir, et ie luy demanday a qui il
estoit | et il dist a vous. Puis luy demanday apres, qui le
commandoyt. Et il me dist quil nauoyt nul commande-
ment que le sien. Et adoncques remys le pied en lestrief et

[1] The original has *pat*.

Galiot leaves the two to them-selves,

and the Queen asks the knight, "Are not you he who wore the black armour, and overcame everyone?"

"No, I am not," saith he,

refusing to praise himself.

"Then who made you a knight, and when?"

"You, at Kama-lot, when the pieces of a spear were drawn out of the wounded knight,

and you girded on my sword, thus knighting me,

and I went away to help the Lady of Noehault, and sent you two damsels.

Then I met a man, who said he was your knight,

and I fought him (for which I crave your pardon).	remontay	Car ie estoye ia descendu	et luy dis que il ne lauoyt point, et me combatis a luy. Et ie scay bien que ie vous fis oultraige, si vous en crie mercy"	"Certes a moy ne en feistes vous point	Car il nestoyt mye a moy	et luy sceuz mauluais gre de ce quil ce reclama de
After that I took the Sorrowful Castle, and there I saw you thrice,	moy. Mais or me dictes on vous en allastes la?" "Dame, ie men allay a la douloureuse garde"	"& qui la conquist?" "Dame, ie y entray"	"et ne vous y viz ie oncques." "Ouy, plus de troys foys." "Et en quel temps?" fist elle. "Dame," fist il, "vng iour que ie vous demanday se vous vouliez leans entrer ; Et vous deistes ouy	et estiez moult esbahye par semblant." "Et quel escu portiez vous?" "Dame, ie portay a la premiere foys vng escu blanc a vne bande de belif vermeille. Et
last when you thought you had lost Gawain and his companions,	lautre foys vng ou il y auoyt deux bendes"	"Et vous vys ie plus?" "Ouy, la nuyt que vous cuidiez auoir perdu messire Gauuain et ses compaignons, et que les gens cryoyent que len me prenist ; Je vins hors a tout mon escu a troys bendes." "Certes," faict elle, "ce poise moy	car se on vous eust detenu, tous les enchantements feussent demourez	Mais or me dictes, fustes
and I helped to deliver him from prison."	vous ce qui iettastes messire Gauain de prison?" "Dame, ie y ayday a mon pouoir." "Certes," faict elle, "en toutes les choses que vous me dictes ie nay trouue si non verite. Mais or me dictes qui estoit en vne tour-
The Queen asks the knight who was in the turret above his room there.	nelle dessus la chambre monseigneur." "Dame, cestoyt vne pucelle que ie ne villennay oncques	Car ma dame du lac la me auoyt enuoyee	si me trouua en ceste tournelle	il fut assez qui la honnora pour moy. Quant ie
"A damsel whom I never dishonoured, but I asked her not to leave till she saw my messenger or me, which I then forgot, and kept her there a very long time."	ouy nouuelles de monseigneur Gauuain, si en fut moult angoisseux, et men party de la Damoyselle qui auecques moy debuoit venir, et luy priay que elle ne se remuast tant que elle eust mon messaige ou moy. Si fus si surprins de tresgrant affaire que ie loubliay	et elle fut plus loyalle uers moy que ie ne fus courtois vers elle	car oncques ne se remua iusques a ce quelle eut mes enseignes, et ce fut grant piece apres."
How the Queen knew Lancelot.	Comment la royne congneut Lancelot apres quil eut longuement parle a elle, et quil luy eut compte de ses aduentures. Et comment la premiere acointance fut faicte entre lancelot et la royne genieure par le moyen de gallehault.
When she heard of this damsel the Queen knew it must be Lancelot,	Quant la royne eut parle de la damoiselle, si scait bien que cest Lancelot. Si luy enquist de toutes les choses quelle auoit ouy de luy, et de toutes le trouua vray disant ; "Or me dictes," fait elle, "vous vy ie puis?" "Ouy, dame, telle heure que vous me eustes

THE FRENCH CONTINUATION OF THE SCOTCH POEM. xlix

bie*n* mestier | car ieusse este noye a kamalot se ne eussiez vous este." "Comment! feustes vous celluy que daguenet le fol print?" "Dame, prins fus ie sans faulte." "Et ou alliez vous?" "Dame, ie alloye apres v*n*g cheuallier." "Et vous combatistes vous a luy" | "dame, ouy." "Et dillec ou allastes vous?" "Dame, ie trouuay deux gra*n*s villains que me occirent mo*n* cheual | mais messire yuain, qui bonne aduenture ayt, men donna v*n*g." "Ha, ha," fait elle, "ie scay bien qui vous estes; Vous auez nom lancelot du lac." Il se taist. "Par dieu," faict elle, "pourneant le celez | long temps a que messire Gauuain apporta nouuelles de vostre nom a cou*r*t;" Lors luy compta comment messire yuain auoit compte que la damoyselle auoit dit | cest la tierce. "Et anten quelles armes portastes vous?" "Vnes vermeilles." "Par mo*n* chef cest verite. Et auant hier pourquoy feistes vo*u*s tant darmes comme vous feistes?" Et il commenca a souspirer. "Dictes moy seurement | Car ie scay bien que pour aulcune dame ou damoyselle le feistes vous, et me dictes qui elle est, par la foy que vous me deuez." "Haa, dame, ie voy bien quil le me conuient dire, cestes vo*us*." "Moy?" faict elle. "Voire, dame." "Pour moy ne ro*m*pistes vous pas les troys lances que ma pucelle vous porta?" "Car ie me mis bien hors du mandement, dame; ie fis pour elle ce q*ue* ie deu*z*, et pour vous ce que ie peux." "Et combien a il que vous me aymez tant?" "Des le iour que ie fus tenu pour cheuallier, et ie ne lestoye mye" | "Par la foy que vous me deuez, dont vindrent ces amours que vous auez en moy mises?" "dame," fait il, "vous le me feistes faire qui de moy feistes vostre amy, se vostre bouche ne me a me*n*ty." "Mon amy!" faict elle, "comment?" "Dame," fait il, "ie vins deuant vous quant ie eu prins congie monseigneur le roy | si vous commanday a dieu, et dis que ie estoye vostre cheuallier en tous lieux. Et vous me dictes que vostre amy et vostre cheuallier voulliez vous que ie feusse. Et ie dys, "a dieu! dame." Et vous distes "a dieu! mon beau doulx amy!" Ce fut le mot qui preudhomme me fera, se ie le suis, ne oncques puis ne fus a si grant meschef que il ne men remembrast. Ce mot ma conforte en to*us* mes ennuys. Cest mot ma de tous maulx guary. Cest mot ma fait riche en mes pouretez;" "Par ma foy," fait la royne, "ce mot fut en bo*n*ne heure dict | et dieu en soyt aoure | ne ie ne le prenoye pas acertes comme vous feistes, et a maint preudhomme ay ie ce dict ou ie ne pensay oncques riens que le dire. Mais la coustume est

and asks him if he was the knight whom Daguenet took. He answers "Yes;" and that two rascals killed his horse, and Ywain gave him another.

"Ah, then your name is Lancelot," says she,

"and for what lady or damsel did you do such feats of arms the day before yesterday?"

"For you, Lady; and for you I broke the three lances that your maiden brought me

for you had made me your friend, and said I was your knight in all lands, and bid me adieu as your own sweet friend.

That word has never left me, but always been my strength and wealth."

telle des cheualliers que font a mainte dame semblant de telles choses dont a gueres ne leur est au cueur." Et ce disoit elle pour veoir de combien elle le pourroit mettre en malaise ; Car elle veoit bien quil ne pretendoit a autre amour que a la sienne | mais elle se delectoyt a sa malaisete veoir, et il eut si grant angoisse que par vng pou quil ne se pasma | & la royne eut paour quil ne cheist, si appella gallehault, et il y vint acourant. Quant il voyt que son compaignon est si courrouce, si en a si grant angoisse que plus ne peut. "Haa, dame," fait gallehault, "vous le nous pourrez bien tollir, et ce seroit trop grand dommaige." "Certes, sire, se seroit mon ;" "Et ne scauez vous pour qui il a tant fait darmes ?" faict gallehault. "Certes, nenny," faict elle | "mais, se il est veoir ce qui ma este dict, cest pour moy ;" "Dame, se maist dieu, bien len pouez croire | car aussi comme il est le plus preudhomme de tous les hommes | aussi est son cueur plus vray que tous aultres." "Voirement," fait elle, "diriez vous quil seroit preudhomme se vous scauiez quil a fait darmes puis quil fut cheuallier." Lors luy compte tout ainsi comment vous auez ouy | "et saichez quil a ce faict seullement pour · moy," fait elle. Lors luy prie gallehault, & dist. "Pour dieu, dame, ayez de luy mercy, et faictes pour moy ainsi comme ie fis pour vous quant vous men priastes." "Quelle mercy voulez vous que ien aye ?" "Dame, vous scauez que ie vous ayme sur toutes, et il a fait pour vous plus que oncques cheualier ne fist pour dame, et sachez que la paix de moy et de monseigneur neust ia este faicte se neust il este." "Certes," faict elle, "il a plus faict pour moy que ne pourroye desseruir, ne il ne me pourroyt chose requerre dont ie le peuisse esconduyre | mais il ne me requiert de riens | ains est tant melencolieux que merueilles." "Dame," fait gallehault, "auez en mercy ; il est celluy qui vous ayme plus que soy mesmes. Si maist dieu, ie ne scauoye riens de sa voulente quant il vint, fors quil doubtoit de estre congneu, ne oncques plus ne men descouurit." "Je en auray," fait elle, "telle mercy comme vous vouldrez." "Dame, vous auez fait ce que ie vous ay requis ; aussi doy ie bien faire ce que vous me requerez." Se dit la royne, "il ne me requiert de riens." "Certes, dame," fait gallehault, "il ne ose | car len ne aymera ia riens par amours que len ne craigne | mais ie vous en prie pour luy, & se ie ne vous en priasse, si le deussiez vous pourchasser. Car plus riche tresor ne pourriez vous conquester." "Certes," fait elle, "ie le scay bien et ie en feray tout ce que vous commanderez." "Dame," fait Gallehault, "grant mercy. Je vous prie que vous luy donnez vostre amour, et le retenez pour vostre cheuallier a tousiours, et deuenez sa loyalle dame toute vostre vie | et vous le aurez fait plus riche que se vous luy auiez donne tout le monde." "Certes," faict elle, "ie luy ottroye que il soyt mien | et moy toute sienne, et que par vous soyent amendez tous les meffaitz." "Dame," faict Gallehault, "grant mercy. Or conuient il commencement de seruice;" "Vous ne deuiserez riens," fait la royne, "que ie ne face." "Dame," faict il, "grant mercy | donc baisez le deuant moy pour commencement de vrayes amours." "Du baiser," faict elle, "ie ne voy ne lieu ne temps | et ne doubtez pas," faict elle, "que ie ne le voulsisse faire aussi voullentiers quil feroit | mais ces dames sont cy qui moult se merueillent que nous auons tant fait, si ne pourroyt estre que ilz ne le vissent. Nompourtant, se il veult, ie le baiseray voullentiers." Et il en est si ioyeulx que il ne peult respondre si non tant quil dict. "Dame," faict il, "grant mercy" | "dame," faict Gallehault, "de son vouloir nen doubtez ia | Car il est tout vostre, bien le saichez, ne ia nul ne sen apperceuera ; Nous troys serons ensemble ainsi comme se nous conseillions" | "Dequoy me feroye ie pryer" | faict elle | "plus le vueil ie que vous." Lors se trayent a part, et font semblant de conseiller. La Royne voyt que le cheuallier nen ose plus faire, si le prent par le menton, et baise deuant Gallehault assez longuement. Et la dame de Mallehauli (*sic*) sceut de vray que elle le baisoyt. Lors parla la Royne qui moult estoyt sage & vaillant dame. "Beau doulx amy," faict elle, "tant auez faict que ie suys vostre ; Et moult en ay grant ioye. Or gardez que la chose soyt celee. Car mestier en est. Je suys une des Dames du monde dont len a greigneur bien dict, Et se ma renommee empiroyt par vous, il y auroyt layde amour et villaine | et vous, Gallehault, ie vous prye que mon honneur gardez | Car vous estes le plus saige | Et se mal men venoyt, ce ne seroyt si non par vous ; Et se ien ay bien et ioye, vous me lauez donnee." "Dame," faict Gallehault, "il ne pourroyt vers vous mesprendre, et ien ay bien faict ce que vous me commandastes. Or vous prye que faciez ma voulente ainsi comme iay fait la vostre ;" "Dictes," fait elle, "tout ce quil vous plaira hardyment | car vous ne me scauriez chose commander que ie ne face." "Dame," faict il, "donc mauez vous ottroye que ie seray son compaignon a tousiours." "Certes," fait elle, "se de ce vous failloit, vous auriez mal employe la peine que vous auez prinse pour luy et pour moy." Lors prent le cheuallier par la main, et dict. "Gallehault, ie vous donne ce cheualier a tousiours sans ce que iay auant eu, et vous le me creancez ainsi" | et aussi le cheualier luy creance | "scauez vous," fait elle, "Gallehault, que ie vous ay donne lancelot du lac, le filz au roy ban de benoic ;" Ainsi luy a fait le cheualier congnoistre, qui moult en a grant honte. Lors a gallehault greigneure ioye quil neust oncques | car il auoit maintesfois ouy dire, comme parolles vont, que cestoyt le meilleur cheualier et le plus preux du monde, et bien scauoit que le roy ban auoit este moult gentil homme, et moult puissant de amys et de terre.

Ainsi fut faicte la premiere acointance de la royne et de lancelot par gallehault | et Gallehault ne lauoit oncques congneu que de veue, et pource luy fait creancer quil ne luy demanderoit son nom tant quil luy dist, ou autre pour luy. Lors se leuerent tous troys, et il anuytoit durement. Mais la lune estoyt leuee, si faisoit cler | Si que elle luysoyt par toute la praerie | Lors sen retournerent a vne part contrement les prez droit vers le tref le cheualier, & le seneschal et gallehault vint apres luy & les dames tant quilz vindrent endroit les tentes de gallehault. Lors enuoya Gallehault son compaignon a son tref, et prent conge de la royne, et gallehault la conuoye iusques au tref du Roy. Et quant le roy les veyt, si demanda dont ilz venoyent. "Sire," fait Gallehault, "nous uenons de veoir ces pres a si peu de compaignie comment vous veez." Lors se assient, et parlent de plusieurs choses ; si sont la Royne et Gallehault moult ayses.

AV chef de piece se leua la royne, et sen alla en la bretesche ; gallehault la conuoya iusques la. Puis la commande a dieu, et dist quil sen yroit gesir auec son compaignon. "Bien auez fait," dit la royne, "il en sera plus ayse" | A tant sen part gallehault, et vient au roy prendre congie, et dist quil ne luy desplaise, et que il yra gesir auec les gens pource quil ny auoyt geu de grant piece, et dist. "Sire, ie me doibz pener de faire leur voulente | car ilz me ayment moult." "Sire," fait messire gauuain, "vous dictes bien, et len doit bien honnorer telz preudhommes qui les a." Lors sen part gallehault et vient a son compaignon ; Ilz se coucherent tous deux en vng lict, et deviserent la une piece. Si nous laisserons ores a parler de gallehault &

THE FRENCH CONTINUATION OF THE SCOTCH POEM.   liii

de son compaignon, et dirons de la royne qui est venu en la bretesche.

Qvant gallehault fut party, la royne sen alla en vne fenestre, et commence a penser a ce que plus luy plaisoyt. La dame de mallehault saprocha delle quant elle la vit seulle, et luy dist le plus priueement que elle peut. "Haa, dame! pourquoy ne est bonne la compaignie de quatre?" La royne le ouyst bien, si ne dit mot, et fait semblant que riens nen ouyt. Et ne demoura gueres que la dame dist celle parolle mesmes; la royne lapella et dist. "Dame, pourquoy auez ce dit?" "Dame," fait elle, "pardonnez moi, ie nen diray ores plus | car par aduenture en ay plus dit que a moy napartient | & len ne se doit mi faire plus priuee de sa dame que len est | car tost en acquiert on hayne." "Si maist dieu," fait la royne, "vous ne me pourriez riens dire dont vous eussiez ma haine | ie vous tiens tant a saige et a courtoyse, que vous ne diriez riens qui fust encontre ma voulente | Mais dictes hardyment | Car ie le vueil, et si vous en prie." "Dame," fait elle, "donc le vous diray ie | Je dy que moult est bonne la compaignie de quatre; Jay huy veu nouueau accointement que vous auez faict au cheuallier qui parla a vous la bas en ce vergier. Et scay bien que cest la personne du monde qui plus vous ayme, et vous ne auez pas tort se vous laymez | car vous ne pourriez vostre amour mieulx employer;" "Comment," fait la royne, "le congnoissez vous?" "Dame," fait elle, "telle heure a este ouen que ie vous en eusse bien peu faire refus comme vous en pouez ores faire a moy | car ie lay tenu vng an et demy en prison. Cest celluy qui vaincquit lassemblee aux armes vermeilles | & celle de deuant hier aux armes noires, les vnes & les autres luy baillay ie; Et quant il fut auant hier sur la riuiere pensif, et ie luy voulu mander que il fist vaillamment armes, ie ne le faisoye sinon pour ce que ie esperoye quil vous aymast; si cuydoye telle heure fust que il me aymast | Mais il me mist tost hors de cuyder, tant me descouurit de son penser." Lors luy compta comment elle lauoyt tenu en prison an et demy | et pourquoy elle lauoit prins. "Or me dictes," fait la royne, "quelle compaignie vault mieulx de quatre que de troys | car mieulx est vne chose celee par trois que par quatre." "Certes non est cy endroit, et si vous diray. Vray est que le cheualier vous ayme, et aussi fait il gallehault, et desormais se conforteront lung lautre en quelque terre quilz soient. Car icy ne seront ilz pas longuement: et vous

Queen Guinevere goes to the window to think,

and the Lady of Mallehault asks her why four are bad company.

At first Guinevere will not hear this, but the Lady repeats it; the Queen asks why she says it, and the Lady asks pardon, as perhaps she has said too much.

"No," says Guinevere,

"speak boldly out; I wish it."

"Then I must say that I think four very good company. I saw the new acquaintance you made to-day, and know he is the man who loves you most in the world.

I kept him a year and a half in prison, and gave him both the red and the black arms in which he won the tourneys;

and I thought then that he loved me, but he soon undeceived me."

The Queen answers, "But tell me why four are better company than three."

"Because, though your knight loves you, he loves Galiot too, and they will not stay here

THE FRENCH CONTINUATION OF THE SCOTCH POEM.

long, but you will; and if you have no one else to tell your thought to, you will be forced to keep your faith to yourself; but if you will let me be a fourth, we can comfort one another."

demourerez cy toute seule, et ne le scaura nul fors vous | ne si ne aurez a qui descouurir vostre pensee, si porterez ainsi vostre faix toute seulle | mais sil vo*us* pleust que ie fusse la quarte en la comp*ai*gnie entre nous deux dames, nous solacierons ainsi co*m*me entre eulx deux cheualiers feront, si en seriez plus aise." "Scauez vous," fait la royne, "qui est le cheuallier?" "Se maist dieu," fait la dame, "nen*n*y." "Vous auez bien ouy co*m*ment il se couurit vers moy." "Certes," faict la royne, "moult estes apparceuante, et moult conuien-

Queen Guinevere agrees to this with great joy,

droit estre sage qui vous vouldroit rien embler, & puis que ainsi est que vous lauez aperceu, et que vous me requerez la compagnie, vous laurez | mais ie vueil que vous portez vostre faix ainsi co*m*me ie feray le mie*n*." "Dame," faict elle, "ie feray ce que il vous plaira, pour ci haulte compaignie auoir." "En verite," faict la royne, "vous laurez | car meilleure compaignie que vous ne pourroye ie mye auoir." "Dame," fait elle, "nous serons ensemble toutes les heures quil vous plaira."

and tells the Lady that the knight is Lancelot of the Lake.

"Jen suys ioyeuse," faict la Royne. "Et no*us* affer-merons demain la compaignie de nous quattre." Lors luy compte de Lancelot, comment il auoyt ploure quant il regarda deuers elle, "et ie scay que il vous congneut, et saichez que cest lancelot du lac, le meilleur cheuallier qui viue." Ainsi parlerent longuement entre elles deux | et font moult grant ioye de le*ur* accointement nouueau. Icelle nuyct ne souffrit oncques la Royne de logres que la dame de mallehault geust sinon auec elle | mais elle y geut a force. Car elle doubtoyt moult de gesir auec si riche dame ; Quant elles furent couchees si

At night the ladies sleep together,

and talk of their new loves,

commencerent a parler de leurs nouuelles amours ; La royne demanda a la dame de mallehault selle a[y]me nulluy par amours, et elle luy dict que nenny. "Saichez, dame, que ie naymay oncques que vne foys, ne de celle amour ne fis ie que penser ;" et ce dit elle de lancelot, quelle auoit tant ayme co*m*me femme pourroit aymer homme mortel | Mais elle nen auoit oncques aultre ioye eue, non pourtant ne dit pas que ce eust il este. La royne pensa quelle feroyt ses amours de elle et de galle-hault, mais elle nen veult parler iusques a ta*n*t quelle scaura de gallehault sil la veult aymer ou non | car autrement ne len requerroit elle pas. Lendemain se leuerent matin elles deux, & allerent au tref du roy, qui gisoit la pour faire a monseigneur gauuain et aux aultres cheualiers compaignie. La royne sesueilla, & dist, "que moult estoyt mauluais qui a ceste heure dormoyt." Lors se tournerent contreual les prez, et dames et damoyselles

the Lady of Mallehault saying that she never loved but one, and then only in thought, (and that was Lancelot).

The Queen thinks she will make the Lady and Galiot fall in love with one another.

Next morning they go to Arthur's tent and wake him, and then return over the meadows

auec elles. Et ils allerent la ou laccointement damours *where the meeting with Lancelot took place,* auoyt este faict, et dict la Royne a la dame de mallehault *and the Queen tells the Lady of Mallehault all about it,* toute laccointance de lancelot | et comme il estoit esbahy deuant elle, et riens ne luy laissa a dire. Puis commenca a louer gallehault, et dit que cestoit le plus *and then praises Galiot as the wisest and best man in the world.* saige homme et le plus vertueulx du monde; "Certes," fait elle, "ie luy compteray lacointance de nous deux quant il viendra, et sachez que il en aura grant ioye. Or allons | car il ne demourra gueres quil ne viengne."

The rubric of the next chapter is as follows:

¶ Comment la premiere acointance fut faicte de *How Galiot became acquainted with the Lady of Melyhalt.* gallehault et de la dame de malehault par le moyen de la royne de logres. Et comment lancelot & gallehault sen alloient esbatre et deuiser auec leurs dames.

It relates how Queen Guinevere requires Galiot to let her dispose of his love as he had disposed of hers. To this he consents, and she commends him to the Lady of Mallehault. Next, they arrange for the promised *parlement de eulx quatre;* and the queen points out to Lancelot the lady who had so many a day kept him in prison, i. e., the Lady of Mallehault. At recognizing his old acquaintance, Lancelot feels somewhat distressed, but is reassured by observing the new love-making between her and Galiot. Seated in a wood, the four "demourerent grant piece, ne oncques ne tindrent parolles, fors tant seullement de accoller & de baiser comme ceulx qui voulentiers le faisoyent."

We next hear of Gawain's recovery, and of the separation of the party of four above spoken of. Galiot takes Lancelot home with him to his own country, whilst the Lady of Mallehault remains for a time with the queen and Arthur. When Lancelot is next spoken of, he is in Galiot's country, where we will now leave him.

NOTES TO THE APPENDIX.

P. xxiii. *Descosse* = *d'Écosse*, of Scotland. In Old French, words are frequently run together; thus we have *labbaye* for *l'abbaye*, *sesmeurent* for *s'émeurent*, etc. Also the letter *s* is often replaced in modern French by an acute or circumflex accent; so that *Escosse* = *Écosse*; *chasteau* = *château*, etc. The word *si* often occurs below with a great variety of meanings, *viz.* I, he; and, also; so, thus; etc.

P. xxiv. *baille*, given, entrusted. *brouyr* (brûler), being burnt. *monstier*, monastery. *gauues*, so in the original throughout; *gaunes* is used in other romances.

P. xxv. *auecques* = *avec*, with.

P. xxvi. *aduision*, vision. *behourdys*, tournament. *naure*, wounded. *deffera* = *desferra*, un-ironed; it means that Lancelot drew the weapons out of the knight's wounds. *deuers*, "Préposition relative au temps et au lieu dont on parle; près, vers, contre, proche; de *versus*." Roquefort. *octroya*, permitted (authorized). *mouille*, *lit.* wetted; insulted.

P. xxvii. *veirent*, saw. *escript* (*écrit*), written. *lassemblee*, the gathering; *i.e.* the war, strife. *rua*, overthrew.

P. xxviii. *mire*, physician. *gue*, ford, pass. *tresues*, a truce; spelt *treues* on p. xxix.

P. xxix. *esbatre*, to divert oneself. In modern French, *s'ébattre*.

P. xxx. *orrions*, shall hear. *deust* = *dût*. *cheoient*, from *cheoir*, to fall. Compare *chûte*. *poilz*, hairs. *esbahy*, amazed. *ortelz*, toes. *chaille*; from *chaloir*, to be anxious about. *dilacion*, delay.

P. xxxi. *paour*, fear. *mire*, physician. *veufue*, old.

P. xxxii. *cheuauche*, rides. *boutte*, buts, pushes. *iecte* (*jeté*), cast. *cuyde*, I believe. *Si maist dieu*, so God aid me. Here *maist* is put for *m'aist*. *oncques*, ever. *ennuyt*, this night, to-night. *lottroyera*, will grant him his request. *conroy*, troops.

P. xxxiii. *derrains* (*derniers*), last. *busines*, trumpets. *Or y perra*, now it will appear. *cuidoit*, believed; from the old verb *quider*. *cheuauchent*, ride. *ia*, already. *tertre*, a small hill.

P. xxxiv. *adresse*, a cross-path. *huy*, just before; *lit.* this day. Lat. *hodiè*. *se pasme*, swoons. *leans*, thither.

P. xxxv. *ores*, now. *huy*, to-day. *preudhomme*, a wise and prudent man. *lottroye*, permits him. *tref*, tent. *nenny*, no! *ains*, before. *guerpiront*, will leave. *deduys*, amusements, diversions.

P. xxxvi. *leans*, there. *gerrez*, will lie. *las*, tired. *Ains*, but.

P. xxxvii. *semondray*, shall ask. *esbahy*, amazed. *tollez*, take away. *creanca*, promised. *lees*, wide, full. *lices*, lists.

P. xxxviii. *emmy le pas*, in the midst of the passage. *hucher*, to cry aloud.

P. xxxix. *lieue*, lifts. *saisine*, disposal. *enseignes*, tokens. *aincoys*, first of all.

P. xl. *oncques mes*, never. *a resiouyr* (*réjouir*), in amusing. *escondiroye*, will refuse. *me poyse*, it troubles me. *pieca*, long ago. *se embronche*, covers his face.

P. xli. *sen esueillerent*, awoke thereat. *Adonc*, then. *riens forfait*, anyway injured.

P. xlii. *ne me mescreez mye que*, do not doubt me more than.

P. xliii. *doint*, gives, were to give.

P. xliv. *mesgnie*, properly the *suite* or household of a prince; see Roquefort s. v. *magnie* and *maignee*. *nef*, a boat. *loue*, advise.

P. xlv. *vous esmayez*, afflict yourself. *courrouce*, wroth, displeased.

P. xlvi. *vergier*, orchard. *aual*, below. *se embroncha*, she veiled herself, or, hid herself. *iouxte*, beside.

P. xlvii. *maintes*, many. *ot*, heard. *len prise mieulx*, esteemed it better. *loe*, praises. *deffera*, dis-ironed, drew the weapons out of. *lestrief*, the stirrup.

P. xlviii. *leans* (*la dédans*), there. *belif.* We find in Cotgrave's French Dictionary, "*Belic*, a kind of red or geueles, in Blazon." *enseignes*, tokens, message.

P. xlix. *mestier*, serviceable. *dillec*, thence. *pourneant*, for nothing, in vain. *voire*, truly. *commanday a dieu*, commended to God, bade farewell.

P. li. *mestier en est*, there is need of it. *greigneur bien*, exceedingly well, very highly.

P. lii. *greigneure*, greater. *anuytoit*, became night. *ie me doibz pener*, I ought to take pains.

P. liii. *ouen*, this year.

The Romans of Lancelot of the Laik.

[PROLOGUE.]

THe foft morow ande The luftee Aperill,
The wynter set, the stormys in exill,
Quhen that the brycht *and* frefch illumynare
Uprifith arly in his fyre chare   4
His hot courß in to the orient,
And frome his fpere his goldine ftremis sent
Wpone the grond, in maner off mefag,
One euery thing to valkyne thar curage, 8
That natur haith set wnder hire mycht,
Boith gyrß, and flour, *and* euery lufty vicht:
And namly thame that felith the affay
Of lufe, to fchew the kalendis of may, 12
Throw birdis fonge with opine wox one hy,
That feffit not one lufaris for to cry,
Left thai forʒhet, throw flewth of Ignorans,
The old wfage of lowis obferuans.   16
And frome I can the bricht face affpy,
It deuit me no langare fore to ly,

[Fol. 1.]
In April, when the fresh luminary upriseth,

and sendeth from his sphere his golden streams,

and when I espy his bright face,

1

THE POET BEWAILS HIS LOT.

<small>I walk forth, bewailing my sad life.</small>

Nore that loue schuld fleuth In to me finde,
Bot walkine furth, bewalinge in my mynde   20
The dredful lyve endurit al to longe,
Sufferans in loue of forouful harmys ftronge,
The fcharpe dais and the hewy ȝerys,
Quhill phebus thris haith paffith al h*is* fperis,   24
Vithoutine hope ore traiftinge of comfort ;
So be such meine fatit was my sort.
Thus in my faull Rolinge al my wo,

<small>The sword of love carves my heart.</small>

My carful hart carwing cañ In two   28
The derdful fuerd of lowis hot diffire ;
So be the morow set I was a-fyre
In felinge of the acceſſ hot *and* colde,
That haith my hart in fich a fevir holde,   32
Only to me thare was noñe vthir eſſ
Bot thinkine qhow I fchulde my lady pleſſ.
The fcharp affay and ek the Inwart peine
Of dowblit wo me neulyng*is* cañ conftrein,   36
Quhen that I have remembrit one my tho*ch*t

<small>My lady knoweth not how I am wobegone.
[Fol. 1 b.]</small>

How sche, quhois bewte al my harm̄ haith wrocht,
Ne knouith not how I ame wo begoñe,
Nor how that I ame of hire f*er*uand*is* oñe ;   40
And in my felf I cañ nocht fynde the meyne
In to quhat wyſſ I fal my wo compleine.

<small>I walked thus in the field, and came to a wellbeseen garden.</small>

Thus in the feild I walkith to *and* froo,
As tho*ch*tful wicht that felt of no*ch*t bot woo,   44
Syne to o gardinge, that weſſ weil befeñ,
Of quiche the feild was al depaynt w*ith* greñ.
The tendyre and the lufty flour*is* new
Up thrōue the greñ vpone thar ftalk*is* grew   48
Aȝhane the fone, and thare levis fpred,
Quharw*ith* that al the gardinge was I-clede ;
That pryapus, in to his tyme before,
In o luftear walkith nevir more ;   52

<small>It was closely environed with leaves.</small>

And al about enweronyt and Iclofit
One fich o wyſſ, that none w*ith*in fuppofit

Fore to be feñ wi*th* ony vicht thare owt ;
So dide the levis clof it[1] all about.   56
Thar was the flour, thar was the queñ alpheft,[2]
Ry*ch*t wering being of the ny*ch*t*is* reft,
Wnclofi*n*g gañe the crownel for the day ;
The bry*ch*t fone illumynit haith the fpray,   60   The sun illumin-
  ed the sprays ;
The ny*ch*t*is* fobir ande the moft fchowr*is*,
As criftoll terys wi*th*hong vpone the flour*is*,
Haith vpwarpith In the lufty aire,
The morow makith soft, ameyne, and faire ;   64

And the byrd*is* thar my*ch*ty voce out-throng,   the birds sang
  till the woods re-
Quhill al the wood refonite of thar fonge,   sounded ;
That gret confort till ony vicht It wer
That pleffith thame of luftenes to here.   68
Bot gladnef til the tho*ch*tful, eue*r* mo
The more he feith, the more he haith of wo.
Thar was the garding wi*th* the flour*is* ourfret,   the garden was
  adorned with
Quich is in pofy fore my lady set,   72   flowers.
That hire Reprefent to me oft befor,
And thane alfo ; thus al day gan be for[3]
Of thocht my goft wi*th* torment occupy,
That I becāme In to one exafy,   76   [Fol. 2.]
  I fell there into
Ore flep, or how I wot ; bot fo befell   an ecstasy or
  sleep,
My wo haith done my livis goft expell,
And in fich wif weil long I can endwr,
So me betid o wondir aventur.   80
As I thus lay, Ry*ch*t to my fpreit vas feñ
A birde, yat was as ony lawrare greñ,   and saw in my
  dream a green
A-licht, and fayth in to hir bird*is* chere ;   bird, who said :
" O woful wrech, that levis in to were !   84
To fchew the thus the god of loue me fent,
That of thi feruice no thing is content,
For in his court yhoue lewith i*n* diffpar,   "The God of
  Love is discon-
And vilfully suftenis al thi care,   88   tent with thee.

---

[1] MS. "clofit."   [2] May we read "alcest" ?
[3] MS. "befor."

	And fchapith no thinge of thine awn remede,	
	Bot clepith ay and cryith apone dede.	
	Yhow callith the bird*is* be morow fro thar bour*is*,	
	Yhoue devith boith the erbis and the flour*is*,	92
	And clepit hyme vnfaithful king of lowe,	
	Yow dewith hyme in to h*is* rigne abufe,	
	Yhow tempith hyme, yhoue doith thi felf no gud,	
You are destitute of wit.	Yhoue are o moñ of wit al deftitude.	96
	Wot yhoue no*ch*t that al liwis creatwre	
	Haith of thi wo i*n* to h*is* hand the cwre?	
Though you call on trees, your lady hears not.	And fet yhoue clep one erbis and one treis,	
	Sche her*is* not thi wo, nore ȝhit fche feis;	100
	For none may know the dirkneſs of thi tho*ch*t,	
	Ne blamyth h*er* thi wo fche knowith no*ch*t.	
	And It is weil accordinge It be so	
	He fuffir harme, that to redreſs h*is* wo	104
	Previdith not; for long ore he be fonde,	
	Holl of his leich, that fchewith not h*is* vound.	
Ovid says it is better to shew, than to conceal love.	And of owid ye autor fchall yhow knaw	
	Of lufe that feith, for to confel or fchow,	108
	The laft he clepith althir-beft of two;	
	And that is futh, and fal be eu*er* mo.	
	And loue alfo haith chargit me to fay,	
[Fol. 2 b.]	Set yhoue prefume, ore beleif, ye affay	112
	Of his f*er*uice, as It wil ryne ore go,	
	Prefwme It not, fore It wil not be so;	
	Al magre thine a f*er*uand fchal yow bee.	
As touching thine adverfity, seek the remedy."	And as tueching thine adu*er*fytee,	116
	Complen and sek of the ramed, the cwre,	
	Ore, gif yhow likith, furth thi wo endure."	
	And, as me tho*ch*t, I anfuerde aȝaiñe	
Then answered I:	Thus to the byrde, in word*is* fchort and plane:	120
	"It ganyth not, as I have harde Recorde,	
	The f*er*uand for to difput wi*th* ye lord;	
"Love knows the reason of my wo."	Bot well he knowith of al my vo the quhy,	
	And in quhat wyſs he hath me fet, quhar I	124

Nore may I not, nore can I not attane,
Nore to hir hienes dare I not complane."
"Ful!" quod the bird, "lat be thi nyſ diſpare,   "Fool," said the bird, "despair not;
For in this erith no lady is ſo fare,   128
So hie eſtat, nore of ſo gret empriſ,
That in hire ſelf haith viſdome ore gentrice,
Yf that o wicht, that worthy is to be
Of lovis court, ſchew til hir that he   132
Seruith hire in lovis hartly wyſ,
That ſchall thar for hyme hating or diſpiſ.
The god of love thus chargit the, at ſchort,   the God of Love charges thee to
That to thi lady yhoue thi wo Report;   136   speak out your love, or else to
Yf yhoue may not, thi plant ſchall yhov vrit.   write thy plaint;
Se, as yhoue cane, be maner oft endit
In metir, quhich that no man haith fuſſpek,
Set oft tyme thai contenyng gret effecc;   140
Thus one fume wyſ yhow ſchal thi wo dwelar.
And, for thir ſedulis and thir billis are
So generall, and ek ſo ſchort at lyte,
And ſwme of thaim is loſt the appetit,   144
Sum trety ſchall yhoue for yi lady fak,   write, then, some treatise for her to
That wnkouth is, als tak one hand and mak,   read;
Of love, ore armys, or of ſum othir thing,
That may hir one to thi Remembryng brynge;   148
Qwich foundith Not one to no hewynes,   [Fol. 3.]
Bot one to gladneſ and to lufteneſ,
That yhoue belevis may thi lady pleſ,   one that may please her and
To have hir thonk and be one to hir eſ;   152   get her thanks.
That ſche may wit in feruice yhow art one.
Faire weil," quod ſche, "thus ſchal yhow the diſpone,   Farewell, and be merry."
And mak thi ſelf als mery as yhoue may,
It helpith not thus fore to wex al way."   156
With that, the bird ſche haith hir leif tak,
For fere of quich I can onone to wak;   Thereon I awoke, and wondered
Sche was ago, and to my ſelf thocht I   what it might mean.
Quhat may yis meyne? quhat may this ſignify?   160

HE RESOLVES TO DO SO.

Is It of troucht, or of Illufioune ?
Bot finaly, as in conclufioune,
Be as be may, I fchal me not discharge,
Sen It apperith be of lovis charg ;   164
And ek myne hart none othir biffynes
Haith bot my ladice feruice, as I gefſ ;

I determined to take in hand this occupation.
Among al vther*is* I fchal one honde tak
This litil occupatioune for hire fak.   168
Bot hyme I pray, the my*ch*ty gode of loue,
That fitith hie in to his fpir abuf,
(At *com*mand of o wyfſ quhois vifioune
My goft haith takin this opvnioune,)   172
That my lawboure may to my lady pleſ
And do wnto hir ladefchip fu*m* eſ,
So that my t*r*auell be no*ch*t tynt, and I
Quhat vther*is* fay fetith nothing by.   176

I know it will but hurt my name, when men hear my feeble negligence.
For wel I know that, be this world*is* faṁe.
It fchal not be bot hurting to my naṁe,
Quhen that thai here my febil negligens,
That empit is, and bare of eloquens,   180
Of difcreffiou*n*e, and ek of Retoryk ;
The metire and the cu*n*ing both elyk
So fere difcording frome p*er*feccioune ;

I submit my poem to the correction of the wise;
Q*uhi*lk I fubmyt to the correccioune   184
Of yai*m* the quhich that is difcret *and* wyfſ,
And ent*er*it is of loue in the feruice ;

[Fol. 3 b.]
Quhich knouyth that no lovare dare wi*th*ftonde,
Quhat loue hyme chargit he mot tak one honde,   188
Deit*h*, or defaṁ, or ony man*er* wo ;
And at this tyme wi*th* me It ftant ry*ch*t fo,

for I dare not oppose Love's command.
As I that dar makine no demande
To quhat I wot It lykith loue *com*mande.   192
Tueching his charg*is*, as w*ith* al deftitut,
W*ith*in my mynd fchortly I conclud
For to fulfyll, for ned I mot do fo.
Thane in my tho*ch*t rolling to and fro   196

Quhare that I myht fum wnkouth mater fynde,
Quhill at ye laft it fell in to my mynd *At last I thought of the story of "Lancelot of the Lake,"*
Of o ftory, that I befor had fene,
That boith of loue and armys can conteñ, 200
Was of o knycht clepit lancelot of ye laik,
The fone of bane was, king of albanak;
Of quhois fame and worfchipful dedis
Clerkis in to diuerß bukis redis, 204
Of quhome I thynk her fum thing for to writ *of whom I here think to write something.*
At louis charge, and as I cane, endit;
Set men tharin fal by experiens
Know my confait, and al my negligens. 208
Bot for that ftory is fo pafing larg, *But because my ignorance cannot comprehend the French romance,*
One to my wit It war fo gret o charg
For to tranflait the romans of that knycht;
It paffith fare my cunyng and my mycht, 212
Myne Ignorans may It not comprehende;
Quharfor thare one I wil me not depend *I shall not tell how he was born;*
How he was borne, nor how his fader deid
And ek his moder, nore how he was denyed 216
Efter thare deth, prefumyng he was ded,
Of al ye lond, nore how he fra that ftede *nor how he was nourished by the Lady of the Lake;*
In fecret wyß wnwyft away was tak,
And nwrift with ye lady of ye lak. 220
Nor, in his 3outh, think I not to tell *nor how he was brought to Arthur's court,*
The auentouris, quhich to hyme befell;
Nor how the lady of the laik hyme had
One to the court, quhare that he knycht was mad; 224
None wift his nome, nore how that he was tak *[Fol. 4.]*
By loue, and was Iwondit to the ftak,
And throuch and throuch perfit to ye hart, *and pierced to the heart by the beauty of Wanore (Guinevere),*
That al his tyme he couth It not aftart; 228
For thare of loue he enterit in feruice,
Of wanore throuch the beute and franchis,
Throuch quhois feruice in armys he has vrocht *for whose service he wrought many wonders;*
Mony wonderis, and perellis he has socht. 232

Nor how he thor, in to his ȝoung curage,
nor how he made a vow to revenge a wounded knight, Hath maid awoue, and in to louis rage,
In the rewenging of o wondit knycht
That cumyne was in to the court that nycht; 236
who had a broken sword in his head, and a truncheon of a broken spear in his body; In to his hed a brokin[1] fuerd had he,
And in his body alſo mycht men see
The tronſione of o brokine ſper that was,
Quhich no man out dedenyt to aras; 240
Nor how he haith the wapnis out tak,
And his awow apone this wis can mak,
That he ſchuld hyme Reweng at his poware
One euery knycht that louith the hurtare 244
Better thane hyme, the quhich that vas Iwond.
Throw quich awoue in armys hath ben founde
a vow which caused the death of many a wight warrior; The deth of mony wereoure ful wicht;[2]
For, fro tho wow was knowing of the knycht, 248
Thare was ful mony o paſage in the londe
By men of armys kepit to withſtond
This knycht, of quhome thai ben al set afyre
Thaim to reweng in armys of deſir. 252
or how he and Sir Kay were sent to defend the lady of Nohalt; Nor how that thane incontynent was fend
He and ſir kay togidder to defend
The lady of nohalt, nor how that hee
Gouernit hyme thare, nore in quhat degre. 256
Nor how the gret paſing vaſſolag
He eſcheuit, thröue the outragouſ curag,
or how he conquered the Sorrowful Castle; In conquiryng of the sorowful caſtell.
Nor how he paſſith doune in the cauis fell, 260
And furth ye keys of Inchantment brocht,
That al diſtroyt quhich that thare vas vrocht.
[Fol. 4 b.] or how he rescued Sir Gawane and his nine fellows; Nore howe that he reſkewit ſir gawane,
With his ix falouſ in to preſone tane; 264
Nore mony vthere diuerſ aduenture,
Quhich to report I tak not in my cwre,

[1] MS. "abrokin."
[2] The MS. wrongly transposes ll. 247 and 248.

LANCELOT'S EARLY DEEDS.

Nor mony affemblay that gawane gart be maid
To wit h*is* name; nor how that he hyme hade 268
Wnwift, and hath the worfchip *and* empri$;
Nor of the kny*cht*is in to mony,[1] diuer$ wy-f$
Throuch his **awoue** that hath thare dethis found;
Nor of the fufferans that by louis wounde 272
He in his trawel fufferith au*er* more;
Nor in the quenis p*rese*ns how tharfor
By camelot, in to that gret Revare,
He was ner dround. I wil It not declare 276
How that he was in louis hewy tho*ch*t
By dagenet in to the court I-bro*ch*t;
Nor how the kny*ch*t that tyme he cane p*er*few,
Nor of the gyant*is* by camelot he flew; 280
Nor wil I not her tell the man*er* how
He flew o kny*ch*t, by nat*ur* of his wow,
Off melyholt; nore how in to that toune
Thar came one hyme o gret confufione 284
Of pupil *and* [of] kny*ch*t*is*, al enarmyt,
Nor how he thar haith kepit hyme wnharmyt;
Nor of his worfchip, nor of h*is* gret prowes,
Nor his defens of armys in the pres. 288
Nor how the lady of melyhalt y*a*t fche
Came to the feild, and pray[i]th hyme that he
As to o lady to hir[2] his fuerd hath ʒold,
Nor how he was in to hir keping hold; 292
And mony vthir nobil deid alfo
I wil report quharfor I lat ourgo.
For quho thai*m* lykith for to fpecyfy,
Of one of thai*m* mycht mak o gret ftory; 296
Nor thing I not of his hye renōwn
My febil wit to makin menfioune;
Bot of the wer*is* that was fcharp *and* ftrong,
Richt p*er*ellou$, and hath enduryt long, 300

nor of the many "assemblies" Gawane held to find out his name;

nor of his suffering caused by love's wound;

nor how he was nearly drowned at Camelot;

nor how he was brought to court by Dagenet;

nor of the giants he slew at Camelot;

nor how he slew a knight of Melyholt;

and there defended himself against a crowd;

whereupon the lady of Melyhalt prayed him to yield his sword to her; and kept him in her power.

Whoever likes, might make of these things a long story.

But I think to tell of the wars between Arthur and Galiot;

---

[1] We should perhaps omit "mony." [2] MS. "his."

THE DEDICATION.

[Fol. 5.]

wherein Lancelot won renown by his defence of Arthur;

and at last made peace between the two princes.

I shall also tell how Venus rewarded him,

My summary must end for the present.

But I pray for the support of a very great poet,

whose name I may not mention;

for our riming is but derision, when his excellence is remembered.

The world knows his eloquence in inditing Latin;

and none can ever gladden the world like him:

to him be the thanks for my success.

Of Arthur In defending of his lond
Frome galiot, sone of the fair gyonde,
That broc*h*t of kny*ch*t*is* o pasing confluens ;
And how lancelot of arthur*is* hol defens   304
And of the ver*is* berith the renow*ñ* ;
And how he be the wais of fortou*n*e
Tuex the two princ*is* makith the accorde,
Of al there mortall wer*is* to concorde ;   308
And how that venus, siting hie abuf,
Reuardith hyme of trauell in to loue,
And makith hyme his ladice grace to have,
And thankfully his *s*eruice cane resave ;   312
This is the mat*er* quhich I think to tell.
Bot stil he mot ryc*h*t w*ith* the lady duell,
Quhill tyme cu*m* eft that we schal of hy*m* spek.
This proceſſ [now] mot closine be*ñ* and stek ;   316
And furth I wil one to my mat*er* go.
Bot first I pray, and I besek also,
One to the most conpilour to support,
Flour of poyet*is*, quhois nome I wil report   320
To me nor to no*ñ* vthir It accordit,
In to our rymyng his na*m* to be recordit ;
For sum fuld deme It of presumpsioune,
And ek our rymyng is al bot derysioune,   324
Quhen that reme*m*brit is his excellens,
So hie abuf that stant in reue*r*ans.
Ye fresch enditing of h*is* laiting toung
Out throuch yis world so wid is yroung,   328
Of eloquens, and ek of retoryk ;
Nor is, nor was, nore neue*r* beith hyme lyk,
This world gladith of h*is* suet poetry.
His saul I blyſſ conseruyt be for-thy ;   332
And yf that ony lusty terme I wryt
He haith the thonk y*er*of, *and* this endit.

EXPLICIT P*RO*LOG*US*, ET INCIPIT P*RI*MUS LIBER.

[BOOK I.]

Quhen [that] tytan, withe his lusty heit,
Twenty dais In to the aryeit   336
Haith maid his courß, and all with diuerß hewis
Aparalit haith the feldis and the bewis;
The birdis amyd the erbis *and* the flouris,
And one the branchis, makyne gone thar bouris, 340
And be the morow finging in ther chere
Welcum the lufty feffone of the ȝere.
In to this tyme the worthi conqueroure
Arthure, wich had of al this worlde the floure   344
Of cheuelry auerding to his crown,
So pafing war his knychtis in renoune,
Was at carlill ; and hapynnit fo that hee
Soiornyt well long in that faire cuntree.   348
In to whilk tyme In to the court thai heire
None awenture, for wich the knyghtis weire
Anoit all at the abiding thare.
For-why, beholding one the fobir ayre   352
And of the tyme the pafing luftynes,
Can fo thir knyghtly hartis to encreß,
That thei fhir kay one to the king haith fende,
Befeiching hyme he wold wichfaif to wende   356
To camelot the Cetee, whare that thei
Ware wont to heryng of armys day be day.
The king forfuth, heryng thare entent,
To thare defir, be fchort awyfment,   360
Ygrantid haith ; and fo the king proponit
And for to pas hyme one[1] the morne difponit.
Bot fo befell hyme [on] that nycht to meit
An aperans, the wich one to his fpreit   364

[Fol. 5 b.]
When Titan, being in Aries, had apparelled the fields,

and birds began to make their bowers;

king Arthur was at Carlisle.

His knights, hearing of no adventure, were annoyed.

They therefore sent Sir Kay to pray the king to go to Camelot.

The king proposed to do so on the morrow.

---

[1] MS. "to pas one hyme one," with first "one" lightly crossed out.

That night he dreamt that his hair all fell off;	It femyth that of al his hed ye hore	
	Of fallith and maid defolat; wharfore	
	The king therof was penfyve in his mynd,	
	That al the day he couth no refting fynde,	368
which made him delay his journey.	Wich makith hyme his Iorneye to delaye.	
	And fo befell apone the thrid day,	
	The bricht fone, pafing in the weft,	
	Haith maid his courſs, and al thing goith to Reft;	372
Again he dreamt, that his bowels fell out, and lay beside him.	The king, fo as the ftory can dewyſs,	
	He thoght aȝeine, apone the famyne wyſs,	
[Fol. 6.]	His vombe out fallith vith his hoil syde	
	Apone the ground, *and* liging hyme befid;	376
	Throw wich anon out of his flep he ftert,	
	Abafit and adred in to his hart.	
He told the queen, who answered, "No man should respect vain dreams."	The wich be morow one to the qwen he told,	
	And fhe aȝeine to hyme haith anfuer ȝolde;	380
	"To dremys, f*ir*, fhuld no man have Refpek,	
	For thei ben thing*is* weyn, of non affek."	
	"Well," q*uo*d the king, "god grant It fo befall!"	
The king next shewed his dream to a clerk,	Arly he roſs, and gert one to hyme call	384
	O clerk, to whome that al his hewynes	
	Tweching his drem fhewith he expreſs,	
who said, "Sir, such things testify nothing."	Wich anfuer yaf and feith one to the kinge;	
	"Shir, no Record lyith to fuch thing;	388
	Wharfor now, fhir, I praye yow tak no kep,	
	Nore traift in to the vanyteis of slep;	
	For thei are thing*is* that afkith no credens,	
	But caufith of fum maner influe*n*s,	392
	Empriſs of thoght, ore fup*er*fleuytee,	
	Or than fum othir cafualytee."	
"Yet," replied he, "I shall not leave it so."	"Ȝit," q*uo*d the king, "I fal no*ch*t leif It so;"	
	And furth he chargit mefinger*is* to go	396
	Throgh al his Realm, w*ith*outen more demande,	
He bade all the bishops and clergy come to Camelot within twenty days.	And bad them ftratly at thei fhulde comande	
	All the bifhopes, and makyng no delay	
	The fhuld appere be the tuenty day	400

At camelot, with al thar hol clergy
That moſt expert war, for to certefye
A mater tueching to his goſt be nyght;
The meſag goith furth with the lettres Right.   404

The king eft ſone, within a litill ſpace,
His Iornay makith haith frome place to place,
Whill that he cam to camelot; and there
The clerkis all, as that the chargit were,   408 *He goes to Camelot, and finds the clerks assembled.*
Aſſemblit war, and came to his preſens,
Of his deſir to viting the ſentens.

To them that war to hyme moſt ſpeciall
Furth his entent ſhauyth he al hall;   412
By whois conſeil, of the worthieſt
He cheſith ten, yclepit for the beſt,   *He discloses all to the ten that are most expert,*
And moſt expert and wiſeſt was ſuppoſit,
To qwhome his drem all hail he haith difcloſſit;   416   [Fol. 6 b.]
The houre, the nyght, and al the cercumſtans;
Beſichyne them that the ſignifycans   *and beseeches them to explain the dreams.*
Thei wald hyme ſhaw, that he mycht reſting fynde
Of It, the wich that occupeid his mynde.   420
And one of them with[1] al ther holl aſſent
Saith, "ſhire, fore to declare our entent   *One of them asks for nine days to advise upon the matter.*
Vpone this matere, ye wil ws delay
Fore to awyſing one to the ix day."   424
The king ther-to grantith haith, bot hee
In to o place, that ſtrong was and hye,   *The king complies, but shuts them up in a strong place.*
He cloſith them, whare thei may no whare get,
Vn to the day, the wich he to them ſet.   428
Than goith the clerkis ſadly to awyſſ
Of this mater, to ſeing in what wyſſ
The kingis drem thei ſhal beſt ſpecefy.
And than the maiſtris of aſtronomy   432   *The masters of astronomy fetch their books,*
The bookis longyne to ther artis ſet;[2]
Not was the bukis of arachell forget,

---

[1] MS. "saith with" (with a very slight scratch through "saith").   [2] So in MS. Read "fet."

	Of nembrot, of danʒhelome, thei two,	
	Of moyſes, *and* of herynes all ſoo ;	436
and calculate the disposition of the planets.	And ſeking be ther calcolaciou*n*e	
	To fynd the planet*is* diſpoſiciou*n*e,	
	The wich thei fond ware wond*er* ewill yſet	
	The ſamyne nyght the king his ſweuen met.	440
	So ner the point ſocht thei have the thing,	
They found the matter heavy for the king, and doubted if they should tell him so.	Thei fond It wond*er* hewy to the king,	
	Of wich thing thei waryng in to were	
	To ſhew the king, for dreid of his danger.	444
	Of ane accorde thei planly haue p*r*oponit	
	No worde to ſhow, and ſo thei them diſponit.	
Being sent for,	The day is cu*m*yng, and he haith fore them ſent,	
	Beſichyne them to ſhewing ther entent.	448
they all spake, "Sir, we can find no evidence."	Than ſpak they all, and that of an accorde ;	
	" Shir, of this thing we can no thing Recorde,	
	For we can noght fynd in til our ſciens	
	Tweching this mater ony ewydens."	452
"Ere we part," quoth the king, "ye shall witness something."	" Now," q*uo*d the king, " and be the glorius lorde,	
	Or we depart ye ſhall ſum thing recorde ;	
	So pas yhe not, nor ſo It fall not bee."	
	" Than," q*uo*d the clerk*is*, " grant ws dais three."	456
[Fol. 7.] He grants them three days more.	The wich he grantid them, and but delay,	
	The term paſſith, no thing wold the ſay,	
	Wharof the king ſtondith heuy cherith,	
	And to the clerk*is* his viſag ſo apperith,	460
	That all thei dred them of the king*is* myght.	
They pray for a further delay of three days.	Than ſaith o clerk, " s*ir*, as the thrid nyght	
	Ye dremyt, ſo [now] giffis ws delay	
	The thrid tyme, and to the thrid day."	464
	By whilk tyme thei fundyng haith the ende	
	Of this mater, als far as ſhal depend	
	To ther ſciens ; yit can thei not awyſ	
	To ſchewing to the king be ony wyſ.	468
They still refuse to declare their thought.	The day is cum, the king haith them beſocht,	
	But one no wyſ thei wald declar ther thoght ;	

INTERPRETATION OF THE DREAMS. 15

Than was he wroth in to his felf and noyt,
And maid his wow that thei fhal[1] ben diftroyt.   472   *The king vows to destroy them;*
His baronis he commandit to gar tak
Fyve of them one to the fir-ftak,
And vther fyue be to the gibbot tone ;
And the furth with the kingis charg ar gone.   476
He bad them in to fecret wyß that thei   *but secretly charges his knights not to harm them.*
Shud do no harm, but only them affey.
The clarkis, dredful of the kingis Ire,
And faw the perell of deth and of the fyre,   480
Fyve, as thei can, has grantit to record ;
That vther herde and ben of ther accorde ;
And al thei ben yled one to the king,
And fhew hyme thus as tueching of this thing.   484   *They yield at last, and say,*
"Shir, fen that we conftrenyt ar by myght
To fhaw that wich[2] we knaw no thing aricht ;
For thing to cum preferuith It allan
To hyme the wich is euery thing certañ,   488
Excep the thing that til our knawleg hee
Hath ordynat of certan for to bee ;
Therfor, fhir king, we your magnificens
Befeich It turne till ws to non offens,   492
Nor hald was nocht as learis, thoght It fall   *"Hold us not as liars, though it happen not as we say.*
Not in this mater, as that we telen fhall."
And that the king haith grantit them, and thei
Has chargit one, that one this wiß fall feye.   496
"Prefumyth, fhir, that we have fundyne so ;
                                                       You must forego all earthly honour;
All erdly honore ye nedis[3] moft for-go,
And them the wich ye moft affy in-tyll   [Fol. 7 b.]
                                                       and those on whom you most rely, will fail you."
Shal failye 3ow, magre of ther will ;   500
And thus we haue in to this matere founde."
The king, quhois hart was al wyth dred ybownd,
And afkit at the clerkis, if thei fynde
By there clergy, that ftant in ony kynde   504

---

[1] MS. "fhat."   [2] MS. "wich that."
[3] MS. "nedift ;" but see l. 518.

THE CLERKS GIVE MYSTERIOUS ADVICE.

The king asks if his destiny can be altered.
Of poſſibilitee, fore to reforme
His deſteny, that ſtud in ſuch a forme;
If in the hewyne Is preordynat
On ſuch o wiſs his honor to tranſlat. 508
The clerk*is* ſaith, "forſuth, and we haue ſene

They reply, that the matter is dark.
O thing whar-of, if we the trouth ſhal meñ,
Is ſo obſcure and dyrk til our clergye,
That we wat not what It ſhal ſignefye, 512
Wich cauſith ws we can It not furth ſay."
"Yis," q*uo*d the king, "as lykith yow ye may,
For wers than this can nat be ſaid for me."

A master says, there is no help but in the true watery lion, and in the leech, and in the flower.
Thane ſaith o maiſtir, " than ſuthly th*us* finde we; 516
Thar is no thing ſal ſucour nor reſkew,
Your worldly honore nedis moſt adew,
But throuch the watrye lyone *and* ek fyne,
On throuch the liche *and* ek the wattir ſyne, 520

God knows what this should mean.
And throuch the conſeill of the flour; god wot
What this ſhude meñ, for mor ther-of we not."
No word the king anſuerid ayane,
For al this reſone thinkith bot i*n* weyne. 524

The king shews no outward grief,
He ſhawith outwart his contenans
As he therof takith no greuans;

but is not rid of anxiety all night.
But al the nyght it paſſid nat his thoght.
The dais courſs w*ith* ful deſir he ſocht, 528
And furth he goith to bring his mynd i*n* reſt

Next day he goes to the forest.
W*ith* mony O knyght vn to the gret foreſt;
The rachis gon wn-copelit for the deire,
That in the wodis makith nois *and* cheir: 532
The knycht*is*, w*ith* the grewhund*is* in aweit,
Secith boith the planis and the ſtreit.

The chase.
Doune goith the hart, doune goith the hynd alſo;
[In to the feld can ruſching to and fro]¹ 536
The ſwift grewhund, hardy of aſſay;
Befor ther hedis no thing goith away.

¹ A line must here be lost, but there is nothing to shew this in the MS. The inserted line is imitated from l. 3293.

GALIOT'S MESSAGE.

The king of hunting takith haith his fport,
And to his palace home he can Refort, 540 *The king returns.*
Ayan the noon; and as that he was set
Vith all his noble knyght*is* at the met, [Fol. 8.]
So cam ther in an agit knyght, *and* hee *As they sit at meat, an aged knight enters,*
Of gret efftat femyt for to bee; 544 *fully armed.*
Anarmyt all, as tho It was the gyf,
And thus the king he faluft, one this wiſ,
" Shir king, one to yow am y fende *The knight's message is that*
    Frome the worthieft that i*n* world is kend, 548 *king Galiot bids Arthur to yield*
That leuyth now of his tyme and age, *to him his kingdom.*
Of manhed, wifdome, *and* of hie curag,
Galiot, fone of the fare gyande;
And thus, at fhort, he bid*is* yow your londe 552
Ye yald hyme our, w*ith*out Impedyment;
Or of hyme holde, and if tribut and rent.
This is my charge at fhort, whilk if youe left
For to fulfill, of al he haith conqueft 556
He fais that he moft tendir fhal youe hald."
By fhort awys the king his anfuer yald; *The king refuses.*
"Shir knyc*h*t, your lorde wondir hie pretendis,
When he to me fic falutatioune send*is*; 560
For I as yit, in tymys that ar gone,
Held neu*er* lond excep of god alone,
Nore neu*er* thinkith til erthly lord to yef
Trybut nor rent, als long as I may lef." 564
"Well," q*uo*d the knyc*h*t, "ful for repentith me; *The knight replies, that his*
Non may recift the thing the wich mone bee. *lord bids him defiance, and will*
To yow, fir king, than frome my lord am I *invade his land in a month;*
With diffyans fent, and be this refone why; 568
His purpos Is, or this day moneth day,
With all his oft, planly to affay
Your lond, w*ith* mony ma*n*ly man of were,
And helmyt knyc*h*tis, boith with fheld *and* fpere; 572 *not to return till he has conquered;*
And neu*er* thinkith to retwrn home whill
That he this lond haith conqueft, at his will;

aud he intends to possess queen Vanour.	And ek vanour the quen, of whome that hee	
	Herith report of al this world that fhee	576
	In fairhed and in wertew doith excede,	
	He bad me fay he think*is* to poffede."	
Arthur returns his defiance.	" Schir," q*uod* the king, " your mefag me behuf*is*	
	Of refone and of curtafy excuff;	580
	But tueching to your lord *and* to his oft,	
	His powar [and] his mefag and his boft,	
	That pretendith my lond for to diftroy,	
	Thar-of as ȝit tak I non anoye ;	584
[Fol. 8 b.]	And fay your lord one my behalf, when hee	
	Haith tone my lond, that al the world fhal see	
	That It fhal be magre myne entent."	
The knight departs, lamenting Arthur's adventurous spirit.	With that the kny*ch*t, w*ith*outen leif, is went,	588
	And richt as he was pafing to the dure,	
	He faith, " a gode !¹ what wykyt aduenture	
	Apperith!" w*ith* that his hors he nome,	
	Two knicht*is* kepit, waiting h*is* outcome.	592
	The knic*h*t is gon, the king he gan Inquere	
	At gawan, and at other kny*ch*t*is* sere,	
Arthur asks Gawane who Galiot is.	If that thei knew or eu*er* hard recorde	
	Of galiot, and wharof he wes lorde ;	596
	And ther was non among his kny*ch*t*is* all	
	Which anfuerd o word in to the hall.	
	Than galygantynis of walys rafe,	
Galygantynis of Wales replies,	That trauelit in diuerſ lond*is* has,	600
	In mony knychtly auentur haith ben ;	
	And to the king he faith, " fir, I haue sen	
	Galiot, which is the fareft knycht,	
that Galiot is the tallest knight by half a foot of all he ever saw ; that he is wise, liberal, humble,	And hieft be half a fut one hycht,	604
	That eu*er* I saw, and ek his me*n* accordith ;	
	Hyme lakid no*ch*t that to a lord recordith.	
	For vifare of his ag is non than hee,	
	And ful of larges and humylytee ;	608

¹ MS. "agodᵉ."

An hart he haith of pafing hie curag,   *courageous, and under xxiv years of age.*
And is not xxiiij ȝer of age,
And of his tyme mekil haith conquerit;
Ten king*is* at his *com*mand ar fterit.   612   *Ten kings obey him.*
He v*it*h his me*n* fo louit is, y gefſ,
That hyme to plefſ is al ther befynes.
Not fay I this, fir, in to ye entent
That he, nor none wnde*r* the firmame*n*t,   616
Shal pouere haue ayane your maieftee;
And or thei fhuld, this y fey for mee,
Rather I fhall kny*ch*tly in to feild
Refaue my deith anarmyt wnde*r* fheld.   620
This fpek y left;"—the king, ayan the morn,
Haith varnit huntar*is* baith with hund *and* horne,   *The king goes again to the chase.*
And arly gan one to the foreft ryd,
With mony manly knyght*is* by h*is* fid,   624
Hyme for to fport and comfort w*ith* the dere,
Set contrare was the fefone of y*e* yere.
His moft huntyng was atte wyld bore;   *He likes boar-hunting best.*
God wot a luftye cuntree was It thoore,   628   [Fol. 9.]
In the ilk tyme! weil long this noble king
In to this lond haith maid his fuiornyng;
Frome the lady was send o mefinger   *A messenger comes from the lady of Melyhalt,*
Of melyhalt, wich faith one this maner,   632
As that the ftory fhewith by recorde:
"TO yow, fir king, as to hir foue*r*an lorde,
     My lady hath me chargit for to fay
How that your lond ftondith i*n* affray;   636
For galiot, fone of the fare gyande,   *to say that Galiot has entered Arthur's land,*
Enterit Is by armys in your land,
And fo the lond and cuntre he anoyth,
That quhar he goith planly he diftroyth,   640
And makith al obeifand to his honde,
That nocht is left wnconqueft i*n* that lond,   *and has conquered all but two castles belonging to his mistress.*
Excep two caftell*is* longing to hir cwre,
Wich to defend fhe may no*ch*t long endure.   644

20 ARTHUR'S READINESS FOR WAR.

Wharfor, fir, in word*is* plan *and* fhort,
Ye mon difpone your folk for to fupport."

The king promises not to delay, and inquires the number of the foe.
"Wel," q*uod* the king, "one to thi lady fay
The neid is myne, I fall It not delay ; 648
But what folk ar thei ne*m*myt for to bee,
That in my lond is cu*m*yne in fich degree ? "

"A hundred thousand," is the reply.
"An hundreth thoufand boith vith fheld *and* fpere
On hors ar armyt, al redy for the were." 652
"Wel," q*uod* the king, "and but delay this ny*ch*t,
Or than to morn as that the day is lycht,

The king says he will set off that very night.
I fhal remuf ; ther fhal no thing me mak
Impedyme*n*t, my Iorney for to tak." 656
Than feith his kny*ch*t*is* al w*ith* one affent.

His knights advise him to wait till he has raised an army.
"Shir, that is al contrare our entent ;
For to your folk this mater is wnwift,
And ye ar here our few for to recift 660
3one power, and youre cuntre to defende ;
Tharfor abid, and for your folk ye send,
That lyk a king and lyk a weriour
Ye may fuften in armys your honoure." 664

"Now," q*uod* the king, "no langer that I 3eme
My crowne, my fepture, nor my dyademe,
Frome that I here, ore frome I wnd*er*ftand,
That ther by fors be entrit in my land 668
Men of armys, by ftrenth of vyolens,

He refuses to wait longer than till the morrow.
If that I mak abid or refydens
In to o place langar than o ny*ch*t,
For to defend my cuntre *and* my ry*ch*t." 672

[Fol. 9 *b*.]
The king that day his mefage haith furth sent
Throuch al his realme, and fyne to reft is went.
Up goith the morow, wp goith the bry*ch*t day,
 Wp goith the sone in to his frefh aray ; 676
Richt as he fpred his bemys frome northeft,

The king arises next morning without delay,
The king wpraß w*ith*outen more areft,
And by his awn confeil and entent
His Iornaye tuk at fhort awyfment. 680

LANCELOT'S LAMENT.

And but dulay he goith frome place to place
Whill that he cam nere whare¹ the lady was,
And in one plane, apone o reuer fyde, *and reaches a plain by the river side,*
He lichtit doune, and ther he can abide; 684
And yit with hyme to batell fore to go
Vij thousand fechteris war thei, and no mo. *having only seven thousand with him.*
This was the lady, of qwhome befor I tolde,
That lancilot haith in to hir kepinge holde; 688 *Lancelot, having been imprisoned by the lady of Melyhalt,*
But for to tell his pafing hewyneffe,
His peyne, his forow, and his gret diftreffe
Of prefone and of loues gret fuppris,
It war to long to me for to dewys. 692
When he remembrith one his hewy charge
Of loue, wharof he can hyme not difcharge.
He wepith and he forowith in his chere,
And euery nyght femyth hyme o yere. 696
Gret peite was the forow that he maad,
And to hyme-felf apone this wiſ he faade: *laments his fate.*

" Qwhat haue y gilt, allace! or qwhat deferuit? *Lancelot's lament;*
That thus myne hart fhal vondit ben and carwit
One by the fuord of double peine and wo? 701
My comfort and my plefans is ago, *his pleasure is gone;*
To me is nat that fhuld me glaid referuit.

I curſ the tyme of myne Natiuitee, 704 *he curses his natal day;*
Whar in the heuen It ordinyd was for me,
In all my lyue neuer til haue eeſ;
But for to be example of difeſ,
And that apperith that euery vicht may see. 708

Sen thelke tyme that I had fufficians
Of age, and chargit thoghtis fufferans,
Nor neuer I continewite haith o day *he has never spent a single day free from anxiety,*
With-out the payne of thoghtis hard aflay; 712
Thus goith my youth in tempeft and penans.

¹ MS. "whare that," with slight scratch through "that."

and is now in prison; [Fol. 10.]	And now my body is In prefone broght ; But of my wo, that in Regard is noght, The wich myne hart felith euer more.	716
and invokes Death.	O deth, allacc ! whi hath yow me forbore That of remed haith the fo long befoght !"	

Thus neueremore he felith to compleine,
This woful knyght that felith not bot peine ;   720
'Thus the smart of love's sorrow pricketh him. So prekith hyme the fmert of loues fore,
And euery day encreffith more and more.
And with this lady takine is alfo,
He is kept by her from the exercise of knighthood ; And kepit whar he may no whare go   724
To haunt knychthed, the wich he moft defirit ;
And, thus his hart with dowbil wo yfirite,
and there we let him dwell. We lat hyme duel here with the lady ftill,
Whar he haith laifere for to compleine his fyll.   728

Meanwhile, Galiot besieged a castle. And galiot in this meyne tyme he laie
By ftrong myght o caftell to affay,
With many engyne and diuerſſ wais fere,
For of fute folk he had a gret powere   732
That bowis bur, and vther Inftrumentis,
His army had pavilions, tents, and iron-wheeled chariots. And with them lede ther palȝonis and ther tentis,
With mony o ftrong chariot and cher
With yrne qwhelis and barris long and fqwar ;   736
Well ftuffit with al maner apparell
That longith to o fege or to batell ;
Whar-with his oft was clofit al about,
That of no ftrenth nedith hyme to dout.   740
When he heard of Arthur's coming, And when he hard the cumyne of the king,
And of his oft, and of his gaderyng,
The wich he reput but of febil myght
Ayanis hyme for to fuften the ficht,   744
His confell holl affemblit he, but were,
he assembled his council, Ten knightis with other lordis fere,
And told theme of the cuming of the king,
And afkit them there confell of that thing.   748

PREPARATION FOR THE BATTLE.

Hyme thoght that it his worſchip wold degrade,
If he hyme felf in propir perſone raide
Enarmyt ayane ſo few menye
As It was told arthur[is] fore to bee ; 752
And thane the kyng-An-hundereth-knychtis cold,
(And ſo he hot, for neuermore he wolde
Ryd of his lond, but In his cumpany
O hundyre knyghtis ful of chiuellry). 756
He faith, "ſhir, ande I one hond [may] tak,
If It you pleſſ, this Iorney ſhal I mak."
Quod galiot, "I grant It yow, but ye
Shal firſt go ryd, yone knychtis oft and see." 760
With-outen more he ridith our the plan,
And ſaw the oſt and is returnyd ayañ ;
And callit them mo than he hade ſen, for why
He dred the repreſe of his cumpany. 764
And to his lord apone this wys faith hee,
"Shir, ten thouſand y ges them for to bee."
And galiot haith chargit hyme to tak
Als fell folk, and for the feld hyme mak. 768
And ſo he doith and haith them wel Arayt ;
Apone the morne his banaris war diſplayt.
Up goth the trumpetis with the clariounis,
  Ayaine the feld blawen furth ther ſownis, 772
Furth goth this king with al his oſt anon.
Be this the word wes to king arthur gone,
That knew no thing, nor wiſt of ther entent,
But ſone his folk ar one to armys went ; 776
But arthur by Report hard saye
How galiot non armys bur that day,
Wharfor he thoght of armys nor of ſheld
None wald he tak, nor mak hyme for the feld. 780
But gawane haith he clepit, was hyme by,
In qwhome Rignith the flour of cheuelry ;
And told one what maner, and one what wyſſ
He ſhuld his batelles ordand and dewys ; 784

who thought it would degrade him, to fight in proper person against so few.

[Fol. 10 b.]
The king of a hundred knights (Maleginis) undertakes the exploit;

who reconnoitres Arthur's host, and says it is 10,000 strong: whereon Galiot charges him to take the same number.

Galiot's host set out.

Arthur's host don their armour.

Arthur, hearing that Galiot is unarmed, will not arm himself;

but calls Gawane, and tells him how to order his battalions.

Befeching hyme, [hyme] wifly to for-see
A3aine thei folk, wich was far mo than hee.
He knew the charg and paffith one his way
Furth to his horf, and makith no dulay ; 788
The clariou*n*is blew and furth goth al onoñ,
And our ye watt*er* and the furd ar goñe.
Within o playne vpone that other fyd
Ther gawan gon his batellis to dewide, 792
As he wel couth, and set them i*n* aray,
Syne with o manly contynans can fay,
" Ye falowis wich of the round table beñ,
Through al this erth whois fam is hard *and* fen, 796
Reme*m*brith now It ftondith one the poynt,
For why It lyith one your fperis poynt,[1]
The well-fare of the king and of our londe ;
And fen the fucour lyith in your honde, 800
And hardement is thing fhall moft awaill
Frome deth ther men of armys in bataill,
Lat now your ma*n*hed and your hie curage
The pryd of al thir multitude affuage ; 804
Deth or defence, non other thing we wot."
This frefch king, that maleginis was hot,
With al his oft he cu*m*myne our the plañ,
And gawan fend o batell hyme agañ ; 808
In myde the borde,[2] and feftinit in the ftell
The fperithis poynt, that bitith fcharp *and* well ;
Bot al to few thei war, and my*ch*t no*ch*t left
This gret Rout that cu*m*myth one fo faft. 812
Than haith f*i*r gawan fend, them to fupport,
One othir batell with one kny*ch*tly forte ;
And fyne the thrid, and fyne the ferde alfo ;
And fyne hyme-felf one to the feld can go, 816
When that he fauch thar latt*er* batell fteir,
And the ten thoufand cu*m*myne al thei veir ;

---

[1] At the bottom of this page appears for the first time a catchword, which is—" The wel fare."   [2] Or " berde."

GAWANE DEFEATS MALEGINIS.

Qwhar that of armes prewit he so well,
His ennemys gane his mortall [ftrokis] fell. 820
He goith ymong them in his hie curage, *He goes among them in his courage,*
As he that had of knyghthed the wfage,
And couth hyme weill conten in to on hour;
Aȝaine his ftrok refiftit non armour; 824
And mony knycht, that worth ware and bolde, *and many other of Arthur's knights perform wonders.*
War thore with hyme of arthuris houfhold,
And knyghtly gan one to the feld them bere,
And mekil wroght of armys In to were; 828
Sir gawan than vpone fuch wyfs hyme bure,
This othere goith al to difcumfitoure; *Maleginis goeth to discomfiture, and 7,000 of his men flee.*
Sewyne thoufand fled, and of the feld thei go,
Whar-of this king in to his hart was wo, 832
For of hyme felf he was of hie curage.
To galiot than fend he in mefag,
That he fhuld help his folk for to defende;
And he to hyme hath xxx^{te} thousand sende; 836 *Galiot sends him 30,000 more.*
Whar-of this king gladith in his hart,
And thinkith to Reweng all the fmart
That he to-for haith fuffirit and the payne. [Fol. 11 b.]
And al his folk returnyt Is ayayne 840 *His folk return across the field as thick as hail.*
Atour the feld, and cummyne thilk as haill;[1]
The fwyft horfs goith firft to the affall.
This noble knyght that feith the grete forfs
Of armyt men, that cummyne vpone horfs, 844
To-giddir femblit al his falowfchip,
And thoght them at the fharp poynt to kep,
So that thar harm fhal be ful deir yboght.
This vthere folk with ftraucht courfs hath focht 848
Out of aray atour the larg felld;
Thar was the ftrokis feftnit in the fhelde,
Thei war Refauit at the fperis end.
So arthuris folk can manfully defend; 852 *Arthur's folk receive them manfully,*

[1] MS. "thilk as (Rayne) haill," as if it were at first intended to find a rime to "ayayne."

GAWANE'S VALIANT DEEDS.

<table>
<tr><td></td><td>The formeſt can thar lyues end conclude,</td><td></td></tr>
<tr><td></td><td>Whar ſone aſſemblit al the multitude.</td><td></td></tr>
<tr><td></td><td>Thar was defens, ther was gret aſſaill,</td><td></td></tr>
<tr><td></td><td>Richt wonderfull and ſtrong was ye bataill,</td><td>856</td></tr>
<tr><td>but sustain much pain,</td><td>Whar arthuris folk fuſtenit mekil payn,</td><td></td></tr>
<tr><td></td><td>And knychtly them defendit haith aȝaine.</td><td></td></tr>
<tr><td>and cannot endure against so many.</td><td>Bot endur thei mycht, apone no wyſs,</td><td></td></tr>
<tr><td></td><td>The multitude and ek the gret fupprriſs;</td><td>860</td></tr>
<tr><td></td><td>But gawan, wich that ſetith al his payn</td><td></td></tr>
<tr><td></td><td>Vpone knyghthed, defendid ſo aȝaine,</td><td></td></tr>
<tr><td></td><td>That only in the manhede of this knyght</td><td></td></tr>
<tr><td></td><td>His folk reIoſit them of his gret myght,</td><td>864</td></tr>
<tr><td></td><td>And ek abaſit hath his ennemys;</td><td></td></tr>
<tr><td></td><td>For throw the feld he goith in ſuch wyſs,</td><td></td></tr>
<tr><td></td><td>And in the preſs ſo manfully them feruith,</td><td></td></tr>
<tr><td>Gawane carves helmets in two, and smites heads off shoulders;</td><td>His ſuerd atwo the helmys al to-kerwith,</td><td>868</td></tr>
<tr><td></td><td>The hedis of he be the ſhouderis ſmat;</td><td></td></tr>
<tr><td></td><td>The horſs goith, of the maiſter deſolat.</td><td></td></tr>
<tr><td></td><td>But what awaleth al his beſynes,</td><td></td></tr>
<tr><td></td><td>So ſtrong and ſo inſufferable vas the preſs?</td><td>872</td></tr>
<tr><td>but his men recross the ford to ȝo to their lodges.</td><td>His folk are paſſit atour the furdis ilkon,</td><td></td></tr>
<tr><td></td><td>Towart ther bretis and to ther luges gon;</td><td></td></tr>
<tr><td></td><td>Whar he and many worthy knyght alſo</td><td></td></tr>
<tr><td></td><td>Of arthuris houſs endurit mekill wo,</td><td>876</td></tr>
<tr><td></td><td>That neuer men mar in to armys vroght</td><td></td></tr>
<tr><td></td><td>Of manhed, ȝit was It al for noght.</td><td></td></tr>
<tr><td>[Fol. 12.]</td><td>Thar was the ſtrenth, ther was the paſing myght</td><td></td></tr>
<tr><td>Gawane fights alone till night,</td><td>Of gawan, wich that whill the dirk nyght</td><td>880</td></tr>
<tr><td></td><td>Befor the luges faucht al hyme alon,</td><td></td></tr>
<tr><td></td><td>When that his falowis entrit ware ilkon,</td><td></td></tr>
<tr><td></td><td>On arthuris half war mony tan and ſlan;</td><td></td></tr>
<tr><td>when Galiot's folk return home.</td><td>And galotis folk Is hame returnyd aȝaine,</td><td>884</td></tr>
<tr><td></td><td>For it was lait; away the oſtis ridith,</td><td></td></tr>
<tr><td></td><td>And gawan ȝit apone his horſs abidith,</td><td></td></tr>
<tr><td></td><td>With ſuerd in hond, when thei away var gon,</td><td></td></tr>
<tr><td></td><td>And so for-wrocht hys lymmys ver ilkon,</td><td>888</td></tr>
</table>

And wondit ek his body vp and doune,
Vpone his horß Right thore he fel in fwoune ;   *Gawane swoons upon his horse.*
And thei hyme tuk *and* to his lugyne bare,
Boith king and qwen of hyme vare i*n* difpare ;   892 *The king and queen fear he has brought himself to confusion.*
For thei fuppofit, throw marwellis that he vroght,
He had hyme-felf to his confufiou*n*e broght.
   [T]his [1] was nere by of melyhalt, the hyll,
Whar lanfcclot ʒit was w*it*ℎ the lady ftill.   896
The kny*ch*ti*s* of the court [can] pafing home ;
This ladiis kny*ch*ti*s* to hir palice com,
And told to hir, how that the feld was vent,
And of gawan, and of his hardyme*n*t,   900 *The lady of Melyhalt hears of Gawane's deeds;*
That merwell was his manhed to behold ;
And fone thir tithing*is* to the kny*ch*t vas told,   *and Lancelot also,*
That was with wo and hewynefs oppreft ;
So noyith hyme his fuiorne and his reft,   904
And but dulay one for o kny*ch*t he send,   *who sends for a knight to take a message to the lady;*
That was moft fpeciall with the lady kend.
He comyne, and the kny*ch*t vn to hyme faid,
"Difplef ʒow not, fir, be ʒhe not ill paid,   908
So homly thus I yow exort to go,
To gare my lady fpek o word or two
With me, that am a carful pr*e*fonere." [2]
"Sir, your co*m*mande y fhall, w*ith*outen were,   912
Fulfill ;" and to his lady paffit hee
In lawly wyf befiching hir, that fhe
Wald grant hyme to pas at his requeft,
Vnto hir kny*ch*t, ftood wnd*er* hir areft ;   916
And fhe, that knew al gentillef aright,
Furth to his chamber paffit wight [3] the licht.   *who comes to his chamber.*
A nd he arof and faluft Curtafly   [Fol. 12 *b.*]
   The lady, and faid, "madem, her I,   920 *Lancelot beseeches her to appoint his ransom,*
Your prefoner, befekith yow that ʒhe
Wold merfy and compaffione have of me,

---
   [1] See note to this line.
   [2] MS. "presone*r*ere."   [3] Read "with" (?).

And mak the ranſone wich that I may yeif;
I waiſt my tyme in preſoune thus to leife.   924
For why I her on þe report be told,
That arthur, with the flour of his houſholde,
Is cummyne here, and in this cuntre lyis,
And ſtant In danger of his ennemyis,   928
And haith aſſemblit; and eft this ſhalt bee
Within ſhort tyme one new aſſemblee.
Thar-for, my lady, y youe grace beſech,
That I mycht pas, my Ranſon for to fech;   932
preſuming that some of Arthur's knights will pay it. Fore I preſume thar longith to that ſort
That louid me, and ſhal my nede ſupport."

She replies that she does not want a ransom, but has imprisoned him for his guilt. "Shire knycht, It ſtant nocht in ſich dugree;
It is no ranſone wich that cauſith me   936
To holden yow, or don yow ſich offens;
It is your gilt, It is your wiolens,
Whar-of that I deſir no thing but law,
Without report your awñ treſpas to knaw."   940

"Madem, your pleſance may ye wel fulfill
Of me, that am in preſone at your will.
He prays for pardon, Bot of that gilt, I was for til excuſſ,
For that I did of werrey nede behwſſ,   944
It tuechit to my honore and my fame;
I mycht nocht lefe It but hurting of my nam,
And ek the knycht was mor to blam than I.
But ye, my lady, of your curteſſy,   948
Wold ȝe deden my Ranſoune to reſaue,
and begs for liberty: Of preſone ſo I my libertee mycht haue,
Y ware ȝolde euermore [to be] your knyght,
Whill that I leif, with al my holl mycht.   952
And if ſo be ye lykith not to ma
or at least to be allowed to go to the next battle, My ranſone, [madem,] if me leif to ga
To the aſſemble, wich ſal be of new;
under a promise to return at night. And as that I am feithful knycht and trew,   956
At nycht to yow I enter ſhall aȝaine,
But if that deth or other lat certañ,

BUT AT LAST GRANTS HIS BOON. 29

Throw wich I [may] have fuch Impediment,
That I be hold,[1] magre myne entent." 960 [Fol. 13.]
"Sir knycht," quod fhe. "I grant yow leif, withthy
Your name to me that ȝe wil fpecify."
She consents, if he will specify to her his name.
"Madem, as ȝit, futly I ne may
Duclar my name, one be no maner way ; 964
But I promyt, als faft as I haue tyme
He refuses for the present.
Conuenient, or may vith-outen cryme,
I fhall ;" and than the lady faith hyme tyll,
"And I, fchir knycht, one this condifcione will 968
Grant yow leve, fo that ye oblift bee
She grants him leave, under the proposed condition.
For to Return, as ye haue faid to me."
Thus thei accord, the lady goith to reft,
The fone difcending clofit in the veft ; 972
The ferd day was dewyfit for to bee
Betuex the oftis of the affemblee.

And galiot Richt arly by the day,
Ayane the feld he can his folk aray ; 976
And fourty thoufand armyt men haith he,
Galiot assembles 40,000 fresh men.
That war not at the othir affemble,
Commandit to the batell for to gon ;
"And I my-felf," quod he, "fhal me difpone 980
On to the feild aȝaine the thrid day ;
Whar of this were we fhal the end affay."

And arthuris folk that come one euery fyd,
He for the feld can them for to prouide, 984
Arthur also provides his men for the field.
Wich ware to few aȝaine the gret affere
Of galiot ȝit to fuften the were.
The knychtis al out of the cete roſ
Of melyholt, and to the femble gois. 988
The knights of Melyhalt join him.
And the lady haith, in to facret wyſ,
The lady secretly provides Lancelot with a red courser, and a shield and spear, both red also.
Gart for hir knycht and prefoner dewyſ
In red al thing, that ganith for the were ;
His curfeir red, fo was boith fcheld *and* fpere. 992

---

[1] MS. "behoid."

LANCELOT ENCOURAGES HIMSELF.

He rides towards the field, and halts in a plain by the river-side.

Lancelot is encouraged, seeing the blithe morn, the mead, the river, the green woods, and the knights and banners.

[Fol. 13 b.]

Casting his eyes aside, he sees the queen looking over a parapet.

Love catches him by the heart.

He counsels his heart to help itself at need,

to forego cowardice,

And he, to qwham the prefone hath ben fmart,
With glaid defir apone his curfour ftart ;
Towart the feld anon he gan to ryd,
And in o plan houit one reu*er* syde.   996
This kny*ch*t, the wich that long haith ben i*n* cag,
He grew in to o frefch *and* new curage,
Seing the morow bly*th*full and amen,
The med, the Reuer, and the vodis gren,   1000
The kny*ch*t*is* in [ther] armys them arayinge,
The baner*is* ayaine the feld difplayng,
His ȝouth in ftrenth and in p*ro*fperytee,
And fyne of luft the gret aduerfytee.[1]   1004
Thus in his tho*ch*t reme*m*bryng at the laft,
Eft*er*ward one fyd he gan his Ey to caft,
Whar our a bertes [2] lying haith he sen
Out to the feld luking was the qwen ;   1008
Sudandly with that his goft aftart
Of loue anone haith caucht hyme by the hart ;
Than faith he, " How long fhall It be so,
Loue, at yow fhall wirk me al this wo ?   1012
Apone this wyf*s* to be Infortunat,
Hir for to f*er*ue the wich thei no thing wate
What fufferance I in hir wo endure,
Nor of my wo, no*r* of myne aduenture ?   1016
And I wnworthy ame for to attane
To hir p*re*sens, nor dare I noght complane.
Bot, hart, fen at yow knawith fhe is here,
That of thi lyue and of thi deith is ftere,   1020
Now is thi tyme, now help thi-felf at neid,
And the dewod of eu*er*y point of dred,
That cowardy be none In to the señ,
Fore and yow do, yow knowis thi peyne, I weyn ;   1024
Yow art wnable eu*er* to attane
To hir mercy, or cum be ony mayne.

---

[1] May we read " diuerfytee " ?   [2] MS. " abertes."

THE RED KNIGHT'S TRANCE.

Tharfor y red hir thonk at yow differue,   *and to deserve her thanks or die.*
Or in hir presens lyk o knycht to sterf."   1028
With that confusit with an hewy thocht,   *Confused with a heavy thought,*
Wich ner his deith ful oft tyme haith hyme focht,
Deuoydit was his spritis and his goft,
He wist not of hyme-felf nor of his oft ;   1032
Bot one his horſs, als ftill as ony fton.   *he [sits] on his horse as still as stone.*
When that the knychtis armyt war ilkon,
To warnnyng them vp goith the bludy fown,   *The bugles are blown, and the knights are ready on horseback, 20,000 in number.*
And euery knyght vpone his horſs is bown ;   1036
Twenty thoufand armyt men of were.
The king that day he wold non armys bere ;
His batellis ware devyfit euerilkon,
And them forbad out our the furdis to gon.   1040 *They are forbidden to cross the fords, but cannot be restrained.*
Bot frome that thei ther ennemys haith sen,
In to fuch wys thei couth them noght fuſten ;
Bot ovr thei went vithouten more delay,   [Fol. 14.]
And can them one that oyer sid affay.   1044
The red knycht ftill in to his hewy thoght   *The red knight still halting by the ford, a herald seizes his bridle, and bids him awake.*
Was hufyng ȝit apone the furd, *and* noght
Wift of hime felf ; with that a harrold com,
And fone the knycht he be the brydill nom,   1048
Saying, "awalk ! It is no tyme to flep ;
Your worfchip more expedient vare to kep."
No word he fpak, fo prikith hyme the fmart
Of hevynes, that ftood vnto his hart.   1052
Two fcrewis cam with that, of quhich [that] on   *Two shrews next approach ; one takes his shield off his neck, the other casts water at his ventayle, which causes him to wink, and arouse himself.*
The knychtis fheld rycht frome his hals haith ton ;
That vthir watter takith atte laft,
And in the knychtis wentail haith It caft ;   1056
When that he felt the vatter that vas cold,
He wonk, and gan about hyme to behold,
And thinkith how he fum-quhat haith myfgon.
With that his fpere In to his hand haith ton,   1060
Goith to the feild withouten vordis more ;   *He goes to the field, and sees the first-conquest king.*
So was he vare whare that there cam before,

O manly man he was in to al thing,
And clepit was the ferft-conquest king.   1064
The Red knycht with [the] fpuris fmat the fted,
The tother cam, that of hyme hath no drede ;

They meet.

With ferß curag ben the knychtis met,
The king his fpere apone the knycht hath set,   1068
That al in peciß flaw in to the felde ;

The red knight, though shieldless, overthrows his foe.

His hawbrek helpit, fuppos he had no fcheld.
And he the king in to the fcheld haith ton,
That horß and man boith to the erd ar gon.   1072

The shrew restores his shield.

Than to the knycht he cummyth, that haith tan
His fheld, to hyme deliuerith It ayane,
Befiching hyme that of his Ignorance,
That knew hyme nat, as takith no grewance.   1076
The knycht his fche[l]d but mor delay haith tak,
And let hyme go, and no thing to hyme fpak.
Than thei the¹ wich that fo at erth haith fen

The men of the first-conquest king come to the rescue.

Ther lord, the ferft-conqueft king, y men,   1080
In haift thei cam, as that thei var agrevit,
And manfully thei haith ther king Releuit.

[A]nd Arthuris folk, that lykith not to byde,
In goith the spuris in the ftedis syde ;   1084

[Fol. 14 b.]

To-giddir thar affemblit al the oft :
At whois meting many o knycht was loft.

The battle was right cruel to behold.

The batell was richt crewell to behold,
Of knychtis wich that haith there lyvis ȝolde.   1088
One to the hart the fpere goith throw the fcheld,
The knychtis gaping lyith in the feld.
The red knycht, byrnyng in loues fyre,
Goith to o knycht, als fwift as ony vyre,   1092
The wich he perfit throuch and throuch the hart ;

The red knight loses his spear, but draws his sword, and roams the field like a lion.

The fpere is went ; with that anon he ftart,
And out o fuerd in to his hond he tais ;
Lyk to o lyone in to the feld he gais,   1096

---

¹ MS. "thei," altered to "thee," which is still wrong.

In to his Rag fmyting to and fro
Fro fum the arm, fro fum the nek in two,
Sum in the feild lying is in fwoun,
And sum his fuerd goith to the belt al douñe.　　1100　Some he cleaves to the belt.
For qwhen that he beholdith to the qwen,
Who had ben thore his manhed to haue sen,
His doing in to armys and his myght,
Shwld fay in world war not fuch o wight.　　1104
His faloufchip siche comfort of his dede　　　　　His fellows take comfort from his deeds,
Haith ton, that thei ther ennemys ne dreid;
But can them-self ay manfoly conten
In to the ftour, that hard was to fuften;　　1108
For galyot was O pafing multitude　　　　　　though Galiot's host was a surpassing multitude.
Of prewit men in armys that war gude,
The wich can with o frefch curag affaill
Ther ennemys that day In to batell;　　1112
That ne ware not the vorfchip and manhede　　Had it not been for the manhood of the red knight, Arthur's folk had been in peril.
Of the red knycht, in perell and in dreid
Arthuris folk had ben, vith-outen vere;
Set thei var good, thei var of fmal powere.　　1116
And gawan, wich gart bryng hyme-felf befor　　Gawane is led to the parapet,
To the bertes, set he was vondit sore,
Whar the qwen vas, and whar that he mycht see
The manere of the oft and affemble;　　1120
And when that he the gret manhed haith sen
Of the red knycht, he faith one to the qwen,　　and saith to the queen, that none ever did better than yon red knight.
"Madem, 3one knyght in to the armys Rede,
Nor neuer I hard nore faw in to no fted　　1124
O knycht, the wich that in to fchortar fpace
In armys haith mor forton nore mor grace;
Nore bettir doith boith with fper and fcheild,
He is the hed and comfort of our feild."　　1128　[Fol. 15.]
"Now, fir, I traift that neuer more vas fen　　The queen prays for Lancelot.
No man in feild more knyghtly hyme conten;
I pray to hyme that euery thing hath cure,
Saif hyme fro deth or wykit aduenture."　　1132

The field was perilous on both sides,	The feild It was ry*ch*t pe*r*ellus and ftrong
	On boith the fydis, and continewit long,
from early morn till the sun had gone down.	Ay from the fone the varld*is* face gan licht
	Whill he was gone *and* cu*m*yne vas the nycht; 1136
	And than o forß thei my*ch*t It not afftart,
	On eu*e*ry fyd behouit them depart.
Every knight then returns home, and the red knight privily goes back to the city.	The feild is don and ham goith eu*e*ry kny*ch*t,
	And prevaly, unwift of any wicht, 1140
	The way the red kny*ch*t to the cete taiis,
	As he had hecht, *and* in hi*s* chambre gais.
	When arthure hard how the kny*ch*t Is gon,
	He blamyt fore his lordis eu*e*rilk-one; 1144
	And oft he haith remembrit in his thoght,
Arthur, seeing the multitude of Galiot's men, recalls his dream, saying,	What multitud that galiot had broght;
	Seing his folk that ware so ewil arayt,
	In to his mynd he ftondith al affrayt, 1148
	And faith, "I traift ful futh It fal be founde
	My drem Richt as the clerk*is* gan expounde;
"My men now fail me at need."	For why my men failʒeis now at neid,
	My-felf, my londe, in p*e*rell and in dreide." 1152
Galiot tells his council	And galiot vpone hie worfchip set,
	And his confell anon he gart be fet,
	To them he faith, "with arthur weil ʒe see
	How that It ftant, and to qwhat degre, 1156
	Aʒanis ws that he is no poware;
that there is no honour in conquering Arthur,	Wharfor, me think, no worfchip to ws ware
	In conqueryng of hyme, nor of his londe,
	He haith no ftrenth, he may ws not vithftonde. 1160
	Wharfor, me think It beft is to delay,
and proposes a twelvemonth's truce.	And refput hyme for a tuelmoñeth day,
	Whill that he may affemble al his myght;
	Than is mor worfchip aʒanis hyme to ficht;" 1164
	And thus concludit thoght hyme for the beft.
	The very kny*ch*t*is* paffing to there Reft;
	Of melyholt the ladeis kny*ch*t*is* ilkone
	Went home, and to hir p*r*esens ar thei gon; 1168

THE LADY VISITS LANCELOT. 35

At qwhome ful fone than gan fcho to Inquere, *The lady of Melyholt asks her knights who hath won most honour.*
And al the maner of the oft*is* till spere ;
How that It went, and in what mane*r* wyſ,
Who haith moſt worſchip, *and* who is moſt to pryſ?
" Madem," q*uod* thei, " O knyc*h*t was In the feild, [Fol. 15 *b*.]
Of Red was al his armour and his ſheld, *They reply, that a red knight had exceeded all others.*
Whois manhed can al otheris to exced,
May nan report in armys half his deid ; 1176
Ne wor his worſchip, ſhortly to conclud,
Our folk of help had ben al deſtitud.
He haith the thonk, the vorſchip in hyme lyis,
That we the feld defendit in ſich wyſ." 1180
The lady thane one to hir-felf haith thoc*h*t, *The lady wonders if her prisoner is meant.*
" Whether Is ʒone my p*re*ſonar, ore noght?
The futhfaſtneſ that ſhal y wit onon."
When euery wight vn to ther Reſt war gon, 1184
She clepith one hir cwfynes ful nere *She calls her cousin,*
Wich was to hir moſt fpeciall and ·dere,
And faith to hir, " qwheyar if yone bee
Our preſoner, my conſell Is we see." 1188
With that the maden In hir hand hath ton *who takes a torch, and they go to the stable,*
O torche, and to the ſtabille ar thei gon ;
And fond his ſted lying at the ground, *and find his steed wounded.*
Wich wery was, ywet w*ith* mony wounde. 1192
The maden faith, " vpone this horſ is fen,
He in the place quhar strok*is* was hath beñ ;
And ʒhit the horſ It is noc*h*t wich that hee
Furt*h* w*ith* hyme hade ;"—the lady ſaid, " p*er* dee,
He vſyt haith mo horſ than one or two ;
I red one to his armys at we go." *Next they view his armour,*
Tharwith one to his armys ar thei went ;
Thei fond his helm, thei fond his hawbrek rent, 1200 *and find his hauberk rent, and his shield fruſhed all to naught.*
Thei fond his ſcheld was fruſchit al to noc*h*t ;
At ſchort, his armour In sich wyſ vas vroc*h*t
In eue*r*y place, that no thing was left haill,
Nore neue*r* eft accordith to bataill. 1204

THE LADY IS LOVE-SMITTEN.

They think he has well used his armour.
Than faith the lady to hir cufyneſs,
"What fal we fay, what of this mater geſs?"
"Madem, I fay, thei have nocht ben abwfyt;
He that them bur fchortly he has them vfyt." 1208
"That may ȝe fay, fuppos the beft that lewis,
Or moft of worfchip in til armys prewis,
Or ȝhit haith ben in ony tyme beforn,
Had them in feld in his maft curag born." 1212

They next visit the knight himself,
"Now," quod the lady, "will we paſs, and see
The knycht hyme-felf, and ther the futh may we

[Fol. 16.]
Knaw of this thing." Incontynent them[1] boith
Thir ladeis vn to his chambre goith. 1216

who was now asleep.
The knycht al wery fallyng was on flep;
This maden paffith In, *and* takith kep.

The lady's cousin observes his breast and shoulders bloody, his face hurt, and his fists swollen.
Sche fauch his breft with al his fchowderis bare,
That bludy war and woundit her and thare; 1220
His face was al to-hurt and al to-fchent,
His newis fwellyng war and al to-Rent.
Sche fmylyt a lyt, and to hir lady faid,
"It femyth weill this knycht hath ben affaid." 1224

The lady next observes him,
The lady fauch, and rewit in hir thoght
The knychtis worfchip wich that he haith vroght.

and is smitten to the heart by the dart of love,
In hire Remembrance loues fyre dart
With hot defyre hir fmat one to the hart; 1228
And then a quhill, with-outen wordis mo,
In to hir mynd thinking to and fro,
She ftudeit fo, and at the laft abraid

and prays her cousin to draw aside, while she kisses the knight.
Out of hir thocht, and fudandly thus faid, 1232
"With-draw," quod fhe, "one fyd a lyt[2] the lyght,
Or that I paſs that I may kyſs the knyght."

Her cousin reproves her,
"Madem," quod fche, "what is It at ȝe men?
Of hie worfchip our mekill have ȝe fen 1236
So fone to be fupprifit with o thoght.

lest the knight should awake.
What is It at ȝhe think? prefwm ȝe noght
That if yon knycht wil walkin, and perfaif,

[1] "then" (?). [2] MS. "alyt."

He fhal yarof no thing bot ewill confaif; 1240
In his entent Ruput yow therby
The ablare to al lych̄tneſs and foly?
And blam the more al vther*is* in h*is* mynd,
If your gret wit in fich defire he fynde?" 1244
"Nay," q*uod* the lady, "no thing may I do   The lady replies.
For fich o knych̄t may be defam me to."
"Madem, I wot that for to loue yone knych̄t,   Her cousin next argues the point;
Confidir his fame, his worfchip, and h*is* mych̄t; 1248
And to begyne as worfchip wil dewyſs,
Syne he ayaine mych̄t lowe yow one fuch wyſs,
And hold yow for his lady and his loue,
It war to yow no maner of Reprwe. 1252
But quhat if he appelit be and thret   "What if he loves another?"
His hart to lowe, and ellis whar y-fet?
And wel y wot, madem, if It be so,
His hart hyme sal not fuffir to loue two, 1256
For noble hart wil have no dowbilneſs;   [Fol. 16 *b*.]
If It be fo, ȝhe tyne yowr low, I geſs;
Than is your-felf, than is your loue Refufit,
Your fam is hurt, your gladneſs is conclufit. 1260
My confell is, therfore, you to abften
Whill that to yow the werray Rych̄t be fen
Of his entent, the wich ful fon ȝhe may
Have knawlag, If yow lykith to affay." 1264
So mokil to hir lady haith fhe vroght   She persuades the lady to return to her chamber, without further delay.
That at that tyme fhe haith Returnyt h*ir* thoch̄t.
And to hir chambre went, w*ith*outen more,
Whar loue of new affaith hir ful sore. 1268
So well long thei fpeking of the knych̄t,
Hir cufynace hath don al at fhe mych̄t   Her cousin labours to expel her love for Lancelot from her thoughts, but her labour is in vain.
For to expel that thing out of hir thoch̄t;
It wil not be, hir labour Is for noch̄t. 1272
Now leif we hir In to hir neweft pan,
And to arthur we wil retwrn agañ.

EXPLICIT P*RIM US* LIBER, INCIPIT SECUND*US*.

[BOOK II.]

Night.

The clowdy nyght, wndir whois obfcure
The reft and quiet of euery criatur　　1276
Lyith fauf, quhare the goft w*ith* befyneß
Is occupiit, w*ith* thoghtfull hewynes;
And, for that thoc*ht* furth fchewing vil h*is* myc*ht*,
Go fare-wel reft and quiet of the nyc*ht*.　　1280

Arthur cannot rest.

Artur, I meyne, to whome that reft is noc*ht*,
But al the nyc*ht* fupprifit is with thoc*ht*;
In to his bed he turnyth to and fro,
Remembryng the apperans of his wo,　　1284
That is to fay, his deith, his confufioune,
And of his realme the opin diftruccioune.
That in his wit he can no thing p*r*owide,
Bot tak his forton thar for to abyd.　　1288

The sun goeth up.

Vp goith the fon, vp goith the hot morow;
The thoghtful king al the nyc*ht* to forow,

[Fol. 17.]

That fauch the day, vpone his feit he ftart,

Arthur goeth forth.

And furth he goith, diftrublit in his hart.　　1292
A quhill he walkith in his penfyf goft,

He hears that a clerk has arrived,

So was he ware thar cu*m*myne to the oft
O clerk, with whome he was aqwynt befor,
In to his tyme non bett*er* was y-bore;　　1296
Of qwhois com he gretly vas Reiofit,
For in to hyme fum comfort he fuppofit;

between whom and himself there was a hearty affection.

Betuex them was one hartly affeccioune.
Non ord*er*is had he of Relegioune,　　1300
Fam*us* he was, and of gret excellence,

He was expert in the seven sciences,

And ryc*ht* expe*r*t in al the vij. fcience;
Contemplatif and chaft in goue*r*nance,

and was named Amytans.

And clepit was the maift*er* amytans.　　1304

The king befor his palʒoune one the gren,
That knew hyme well, *and* haith his cu*m*myn feñ,
Velcu*m*myt hyme, and maid hyme ry*ch*t gud chere,   *Arthur welcomes him.*
And he agan, agrewit as he were,   1308
Saith, " nothir of thi falofing, nor the,   *He recks nothing of Arthur's salutation.*
Ne rak I no*ch*t, ne charg I no*ch*t," quo*d* hee.
Than quo*d* the king, " maifte*r*, *and* for what why   *The king inquires what trespass he has committed.*
Ar ʒe agrewit? or quhat treffpas have I   1312
Co*m*mytit, fo that I fhal yow difples?"
Quod he, " no thing It is ayane myn eſs,   *He replies, "It is not against me, but against thyself.*
But only co*n*trare of thi-felf alway;
So fare the courſs yow paffith of the way.   1316
Thi fchip, that goth apone the ftormy vall,   *Thy ship is almost drowned in the whirlpool.*
Ney of thi careldis in the fwelf it fall,
Whar fhe almoft is in the p*e*rell drent;
That is to fay, yow art fo far myfwent   1320
Of wykitneſs vpone the vrechit dans,
That yow art fallyng in the storng¹ vengans
Of goddis wreth, that fhal the fon deuour;   *That is, God's wrath shall soon devour thee.*
For of his ftrok approchit now the hour   1324
That boith thi Ringe, thi ceptre, *and* thi crovñ,
Frome hie eftat he fmyting fhal adoune.
And that accordith well, for in thi tho*ch*t
Yow knawith not hyme, the wich that haith the wro*ch*t,   *Because thou knowest Him not, who set thee up in this high estate,*
And fet the vp in to this hie eftat
From powert; for, as the-felwyne wat,
It cu*m*myth al bot only of his myght,
And not of the, nor of thi eld*er*is Richt   1332
To the difcending, as in heritage,
For yow was not byget in to spoufag.   *though not begotten in spousage.* [Fol. 17 b.]
Wharfor yow aucht his biding to obferf,
And at thy my*ch*t yow fhuld hyme pleſs *and* ferf;   1336
That dois yow nat, for yow art fo confuffit
With this fals warld, that thow haith hyme Refufit,

¹ So in MS. Is it necessary to alter it to " strong " ?

THE TYRANNY OF KINGS.

  And brokine haith his reul and ordynans,
  The wich to the he gave in gouernans. 1340

He made thee king, He maid the king, he maid the gouernour,
  He maid the fo, and fet in hie honour
  Of Realmys and of [diuerß] peplis fere;
  Efter his loue thow fhuld them Reul *and* ftere, 1344
  And wnoppreffit kep in to Iuftice,
  The wykit men and pwnyce for ther wice.
  Yow dois no thing, bot al in the *contr*are,

and thou sufferest thy people to fare ill. And fuffrith al thi puple to forfare; 1348
  Yow haith non Ey but one thyne awn delyt,
  Or quhat that plefing fhall thyne appetyt.
  In the defalt of law and of Iuftice,
  Wndir thi hond is fufferyt gret fuppriß 1352
  Of fadirleß, and modirleß alfo,
  And wedwis ek fuftenit mekill wo.

The poor are oppressed. With gret myfchef oppreffit ar the pure;
  And thow art cauß of al this hol Iniure, 1356
  Whar-of that god a raknyng fal craf
  At the, and a fore Raknyng fal hafe;
  For thyne eftat is gewyne to Redreß
  Thar ned, and kep them to ry*ch*twyneß; 1360
  And thar is non that ther complant*is* her*is*;
  The my*ch*ty folk, and ek the flattereris
  Ar cheif with the, and doith this oppreffiou*n*;

If they complain, it is their confusion. If thai complen, It is ther confuffiou*n*e. 1364
  And daniell faith that who doith to the pure,
  Or fader*l*eß, or modirleß, EnIure,
  Or to the puple, that ilke to god doth hee;
  And al this harme fuftenit Is throw the. 1368
  Yow fufferith them, oppreffith *and* anoyith;
  So yow art cauß, throw the thei ar diftroyth;
  Than, at thi my*ch*t, god fo diftroys yow.

What wilt thou do, when God destroys sinners off the visage of the earth? What fhal he do a3ane? quhat fhal yow, 1372
  When he diftroys by vengance of his fuerd
  The fynar*is* fra the vysag*is* of the Erde?

ARTHUR ASKS ADVICE.

Than vtraly yow fhall diftroyt bee;
And that Richt weill apper*is* now of thee, 1376
For yow allon byleft art folitere;
And the wyſ salamon can duclar,
'Wo be to hyme that is byleft alone,
He haith no help;' so Is thi forton goñe; 1380 [Fol. 18.]
For he is callit, w*ith* quhom that god is no*ch*t,
Allone; and fo thi wykitneſ haith wro*ch*t
That god hyme-felf he is bycu*m*myn thi fo,
Thi pupleis hart*is* haith thow tynt alfo; 1384
Thi wykitneſ thus haith the maid alon,
That of this erth thi fortone Is y-goñ.
Yow mone thi lyf, yow mone thi vorfchip tyne,
And eft to deth that neue*r* fhal haf fyne." 1388
" Maister," q*uo*d he, " of yowre beneuolens,
Y yow befech that tueching my*n* offens,
ȝhe wald wichfaif your confell to me If
How I fal mend, and ek her-eftir leif." 1392
" Now," q*uo*d the maifter, " and I have me*r*well qwhy
Yow afkith confail, and wil in non affy,
Nor wyrk thar-by; and ȝhit yow may In tym,
If yow lykith to amend the cryme." 1396
" Ȝhis," faith the king, " and futhfaftly I will
Ȝour ordynans in eue*r*y thing fulfyll."
" And if the lift at confail to abide,
The remed of thi harme to p*r*ouyde— 1400
Firft, the begyning is of fapiens,
To dreid the lord and his mag*n*ificens;
And what thow haith in contrar hyme ofendit,
Whill yow haith my*ch*t, of fre defir amend it;[1] 1404
Repent thi gilt, repent thi gret trefpaſ,
And remembir one goddis richwyfneſ;
How for to hyme that wykitneſ anoyt,
And how the way of fynaris he diftroit; 1408

Sidenotes:
Solomon saith, 'Wo to him who is left alone! He hath no help.'
Thou hast lost thy people's hearts,
and shalt come to death that hath no end."
Arthur asks how he shall amend,
and promises to fulfil his bidding.
The master replies, "Thou must first dread the Lord.
Repent thy guilt.

[1] MS. "amendit."

	And if ye lyk to ryng wnde*r* his peß,	
	Ye wengans of his my*ch*ty hond yow feß,	
	This fchalt yow do, if yow wil be pe*r*fit.	
	Firſt, mone yow be penitent and contrit	1412
	Of euery thing that tuechith thi confiens,	
	Done of fre will, or ȝhit of neglygens.	
Thy need requireth full contrition.	Thi neid requirith ful contretioune,	
	Princepaly with-out conclufioune;	1416
	With humble hart and goftly byfyneß,	
	Syne fhalt yow go deuotly the confeß	
Confess to some holy confessor.	Ther-of vnto fum haly confeffour,	
	That the wil confail tueching thin arour;	1420
	And to fulfill his will and ordynans,	
Do penance, and amend all wrong."	In fatiffaccione and doing of penans,	
	And to amend al wrang and al Iniure,	
	By the ydone til euery Creature;	1424
[Fol. 18 *b.*]	If yow can In to thi hart fynde,	
	Contretioune well degeft In to thi mynd.	
	Now go thi weie, for if it leful were,	
	Confeffioune to me, I fhuld It here."	1428
Arthur tries to remember every sin done since his years of innocence,	Than arthur, Richt obedient *and* mek,	
	In to his wit memoratyve can feik	
	Of euery gilt wich that he can pens,	
	Done frome he paffith the ȝer*is* of Innocens;	1432
	And as his maifter hyme commandit had,	
and made his confession with lamentable cheer.	He goith and his confeffione haith he maad	
	Richt deuotly with lementable chere;	
	The mane*r* wich quho lykith for to here	1436
	He may It fynd In to the holl romans,	
	Of confeffione o pafing *ce*rcumftans.	
	I can It not, I am no confeffour,	
	My wyt haith ewill confat of that labour,	1440
	Quharof I wot I aucht repent me fore.	
	The king wich was confeffit, what is more,	
	Goith and til his maif*ter* tellith hee,	
	How euery fyne In to his awn degree	1444

He shew, that mycht occuryng to his mynde.
"Now," quod the maiftere, "left thow aght behynde *"Leftest thou aught behind,"*
Of albenak the vorfchipful king ban, *quoth the master, "about Ban, king*
The wich that vas in to my feruice flan, 1448 *of Albanak, and his disinherited*
And of his wif difherift eft alfo? *wife?"*
Bot of ther fone, the wich was them fro,
Ne fpek¹ y not;"—the king in his entent
Abafyt was, and furthwith is he went 1452
Aȝane, and to his confeffour declarith; *The king again confesses, and re-*
Syne to his maifter he ayane Reparith, *turns,*
To quhome he faith, "I aftir my cunyng
Your ordinans fulfillit in al thing; 1456
And now right hartly y befeich and prey,
ȝhe wald withfchaif fum thing to me fay,
That may me comfort in my gret dreid, *prays for comfort,*
And how my men ar falȝet in my Neid, 1460
And of my dreme, the wich that is fo dirk." *and inquires about his dream.*
This maifter faith, "and thow art bound to virk *The master saith, "If thou art*
² A T my confail, and if yow has maad *bound to work by my counsel,*
Thi confeffione, as yow before hath faid, 1464
And in thi conciens thinkith perfeuere,
As I prefume that thow onon fhalt here
That god hyme-felf fhal fo for yᵉ prouide,
Thow fhal Remayne and In thi Ring abyd. 1468 *thou shalt abide in thy kingdom.*
And why thi men ar falȝet At this nede, *[Fol. 19.]*
At fhort this is the cauſ, fhalt yow nocht dred,
Fore thow to gode was frawart and perwert;
Thi ryngne and the he thocht for to fubwart; 1472
And yow fal knaw na power may recift,
In contrar quhat god lykith to affi[f]t.
The vertw nore the ftrenth of victory *Strength of victory cometh from*
It cummyth not of man, bot anerly 1476 *God only.*

¹ MS. apparently has "srpek;" but a comparison with line 1543 shews that the apparent *r* is due to the meeting of two slight flourishes belonging to the *s* and *p*.

² This line (though it should not) begins with an illuminated letter.

Of hyme, the wich haith euery ftrinth; *and* than,
If that the waiis pleffit hyme of man,
He fhal have forſ aӡane his ennemys.
A-ryght agan apone the famyne vyſ, 1480

Whoso displeases Him shall be subject to his enemies, as we read in the Bible concerning the Jews.

If he difpleſ vn to the lord, he fhall
Be to his fais a fubiet or a thrall,
As that we may In to the bible red,
Tueching the folk he tuk hyme-felf to led 1484
In to the lond, the wich he them byhicht.
Ay when thei ӡhed in to his ways Richt,
Ther fois gon befor there fuerd to nocht;

When they wrought against Him, they were so full of fear that the sound of a falling leaf made a thousand flee.

And when that thei ayanis hyme hath vrocht, 1488
Thei war fo full of radur and diffpare,
That of o leif fleing in the air,
The found of It haith gart o thoufand tak
At onys apone them-felf the bak, 1492
And al ther manhed vterly foryhet;
Sich dreid the lord apone ther hartis set.
So fhalt yow know no powar may withftond,
Ther god hyme-felf hath ton the cauſ on hond. 1496

Thine own offence is the reason why thy people fail thee.

And ye quhy ftant in thyne awn offens,
That al thi puple falӡhet off defens.
And fum ar falӡeing magre ther entent;
Thei ar to quhom thow yewyne hath thi rent, 1500
Thi gret Reuard, thi richeſ and thi gold,
And cheriffith and held in thi houfhold.
Bot the moft part ar falӡheit the at wyll,

Thou hast shewn some of them unkindness,

To quhome yow haith wnkyndneſ fchawin till; 1504
Wrong and inIure, and ek defalt of law,
And pwnyfing of qwhich that thei ftand aw;
And makith feruice but reward or fee,
Syne haith no thonk bot fremmytneſ of the. 1508
Such folk to the cummyth bot for dred,
Not of fre hart the for to help at nede.
And what awalith owthir fheld or fper,
Or horſ or armoure according for ye were, 1512

UNJUST KINGS ARE PUNISHED. 45

Vith-outen man them for to ftere and led ? [Fol. 19 b.]
And man, yow wot, that vantith hart is ded, *and a man that wanteth heart is dead.*
That in to armys feruith he of noght ;
A cowart oft ful mekil harm haith vroght. 1516
In multitude nore ȝhit in confluens
Of fich, is nowther manhed nore defens.
And fo thow hath the rewlyt, that almoft *Thou hast so conducted thyself as*
Of al thi puple the hartis ben ylost ; 1520 *to lose all thy people's hearts.*
And tynt richt throw thyne awn myfgouernans
Of auerice and of thyne errogans.
What is o prince ? quhat is o gouernoure *What is a prince without honour ?*
Withouten fame of worfchip and honour ? 1524
What is his mycht, fuppos he be A lorde,
If that his folk fal nocht to hyme accorde ?
May he his Rigne, may he his holl Empire *Can he by himself sustain his kingdom, by*
Suften al only of his owne defyre, 1528 *serving his own appetite?*
In ferwyng of his wrechit appetit
Of awerice and of his awn delyt,
And hald his men, wncherift, in thraldome ?
Nay! that fhal fone his hie eftat confome. 1532 *His oppression of his people consumes his high*
For many o knycht[1] therby is broght ydoune, *estate, and makes other kings war*
All vtraly to ther confufioune ; *on them.*
For oft it makith vther kingis by
To wer on them In traft of victory ; 1536
And oft als throw his peple is diftroyth,
That fyndith them agrewit or anoyth ;
And god alfo oft with his awn fwerd, *God also punishes their vices."*
Punyfith ther wyfis one this erd. 1540
Thus falith not o king but gouernans,
Boith realme and he goith one to myfchans."

AS thai war thus fpeking of this thinge, *Meanwhile, the king of a hundred*
Frome galiot cam two knychtis to the king ; 1544 *knights and the first-conqueft*
That one the king of hundereth knychtis was ; *king come from Galiot,*
That other to nome the fyrst-conqueft king[2] has,

[1] "king" (?).
[2] MS. "kinghe," a spelling due to confusion with "knight." See l. 1533.

At firſt that galyot conquerit of one.
The nereſt way one to the king thei gon, 1548
And vp he roſ. as he that wel couth do
Honor, to quhome that It afferith to ;
And ʒhit he wiſt not at thei kingis were ;
So them¹ thei boith and vyth rycht knyghtly cher 1552
Reuerendly thei faluſt hyme, and thane

and the former delivers his message, to the effect that
[Fol. 20.]

The king of hunder knyghtis he began
And ſaid hyme, "fir, to ʒow my lord ws fende,
Galiot, whilk bad ws ſay he wende, 1556
That of this world the vorthieſt king wor ʒhe,
Greteſt of men and of awtoritee.

Galiot wonders at the feebleness of Arthur's folk,

Wharof he has gret wonder that ʒhe ar
So feble cummyne In to his contrare, 1560
For to defend your cuntre and your londe,
And knowith well ʒhe may hyme nocht withſtonde.
Wharfor he thinkith no worſchip to conquere,
Nore in the weris more to perfyuere ; 1564
Confiddir yowr wakneſ and yowr Indegens,
Aʒanis hyme as now to mak defens.

and is willing to grant a year's truce,

Wharfore, my lord haith grantit by vs here
Trewis to yhow and refput for o ʒhere, 1568

if Arthur will return to fight against him in a year's time ;

If that yhow lykith by the ʒheris ſpace
For to retwrn ayane In to this place,
Her to manteine yhour cuntre and withſtond
Hyme with the holl power of yhour lond. 1572
And for the tyme the trewis ſhal endure,
Yhour cuntre and yhour lond he will aſſurre ;
And wit ʒhe ʒhit his powar is nocht here.
And als he bad ws ſay yhow by the yhere, 1576

and desires to have the red knight in his household.

The gud knycht wich that the Red armys bure
And in the feild maid the diſcumfiture,
The whilk the flour of knychthed may be cold,
He thinkith hyme to haue of his houſhold." 1580

¹ "then" (?).

" Well," quod the king, " I have hard quhat yhe fay,
But if god will, and ek if that I may,
In to fich wyſ I think for to withſtond,
Yhour lord ſhall have no powar of my londe." 1584
Of this meſag the king Reioſing haſ, *Arthur rejoices at the truce,*
And of the trewis wich that grantit was,
Bot anoyt ȝhit of the knycht was he,
Wich thei awant to have in fuch dogre. 1588
Ther leif thei tuk; and when at thei war gon,
¹This maifter faith, " how lykith god difpone! *which the master attributes to God's providence, and exhorts him, saying,*
    Now may yhow ſe *and* futh is my recorde;
For by hyme now is makith this accord; 1592
And by non vthir worldly providens,
Sauf only grant of his bynewolans,
To ſe if that the lykith to amend,
And to prouid thi cuntre to defend. 1596
Wharfor yow ſhalt in to thi lond home fair,
And gowerne the as that I ſhall declaire.
Firſt, thi god with humble hart yow ſerfe, *[Fol. 20 b.] "First, serve God with humble heart, and let the wand of law pass through the land.*
And his comand at al thi mycht obſerf; 1600
And fyne, lat paſ the ilk bleſſit wonde
Of lowe with mercy Iuſtly throw thi londe;
And y beſeich—to quhome yow fal direke
The rewle vpone, the wrangis to correk— 1604
That yow be nocht in thi electioune blynde;
For writin It Is and yow fal trew It fynde.
That, be thei for to thonk or ellis blame,
And towart god thi part ſhal be the fam; 1608
Of Ignorans ſhalt yow nocht be excuſit,
Bot in ther werkis forly be accuſit,
For thow ſhuld euer cheſ apone fich wyſ
The miniſteris ² that rewll haith of Iuſtice:— 1612 *Thus shalt thou choose the ministers of justice.*
Firſt, that he be deſcret til wnderſtond
And lowe and ek the mater of the londe;

¹ The initial T is illuminated.   ² MS. "mifteris."

HOW TO CHOOSE JUDGES.

   And be of mycht and ek Autoritee,
   (For puple ay contempnith low degre,)   1616
   And that of trouth he folow furth the way;
   That is als mych as he louyth trewth alway,
   And haitith al them the wich fal pas therfro.
   Syne, that he god dreid and lowe al-so.   1620

Avoid avaricious and wrathful men.
   Of auerice be-war with the defyre,
   And of hyme full of haftynes and fyre;
   Be-war thar-for of malice and defire,
   And hyme alfo that lowith no medyre;   1624
   For al this abhominable was hold,
   When Iuftice was in to the tymis olde.
   For qwho that is of an of thir by-know,
   The left of them fubuertith all the low,   1628
   And makith It w[n]Iustly[1] to procede;

Eschew unfit men, for this shall be thy meed in the day of judgment.
   Efchew tharfor, for this fal be thi meid
   Apone the day when al thing goith aright,
   Whar none excufſ hidyng fchal ye lyght;   1632
   But he the Iug, that no man may fuffpek,
   Euery thing ful Iuftly fal correk.
   Be-war thar-with, as before have I told,
   And chefſ them wyfly that thi low fhal hold.   1636
   And als I will that it well oft be sen,
   Richt to thi-self how thei thi low conten;

Be diligent to inquire how judgment is given.
   And how the Right, and how the dom is went,
   For to Inquer that yow be delygent.   1640

[Fol. 21.]
   And punyfſ for, for o thing fhal yow know,
   The most trefpas is to fubuert the low,
   So that yow be not in thar gilt accufit,
   And frome the froit of bliffit folk refufit.   1644

Visit every chief town throughout the bounds of thy kingdom.
   And pas yow fhalt to euery chef toune,
   Throw-out the boundis of thi Regioune
   Whar yow fall be, that Iuftice be Elyk
   With-out diuifione baith to pur and ryk.   1648

---

[1] MS. "w Iustly."

And that thi puple have [ane] awdiens
With thar complantis, and alſo thi preſens;
For qwho his eris frome the puple ſtekith,
And not his hond in ther ſupport furth rekith, 1652
His dom ſall be ful grewous & ful hard,
When he ſal cry and he ſal nocht be hard.
Wharfor thyne eris ifith to the pwre, *Give thine ears to the poor.*
Bot in redreſſ of ned, & not of inIure; 1656
Thus ſall thei don of Reſſone & knawlag.

But kingis when thei ben of tender ag, *Kings, while minors, may be excused;*
Y wil not ſay I traſt thei ben excuſit,
Bot ſchortly thei ſall be far accuſit, 1660
When ſo thei cum to yheris of Reſone, *but, when of age, they must punish those that have wrested justice.*
If thei tak not full contriſioune,
And pwnyſſ them that hath ther low myſgyit.
That this is trouth it may not be denyit; 1664
For vther ways thei ſal them not diſcharg,
[Excep thei pwnyſſ them that have the charg]¹
One eſtatis of ther realm, that ſhold
With-in his ȝouth ſe that his low be hold.² 1668
And thus thow the, with mercy, kep alway *Temper justice with mercy.*
Of Iuſtice furth the ilk bleſſit way.

And of thi wordis beis trew and ſtable, *Be true and stable in thy words.*
Spek not to mych, nore be not vareable. 1672
O kingis word ſhuld be o kingis bonde,
And ſaid It is, a kingis word ſhuld ſtond;
O kingis word, among our faderis old,
Al-out more precious & more ſur was hold 1676
Than was the oth or ſeel of any wight;
O king of trouth fuld be the werray lyght, *A king should be the very light of truth.*
So treuth and Iuſtice to o king accordyth.
And als, as thir clerkis old recordith, 1680

³ In tyme is larges and humilitee
Right well according vnto hie dugre,

¹ A blank space here occurs, just sufficient to contain one line.
² MS. "behold."
³ The initial I is illuminated; rather because there is here a change of subject than because it begins a new sentence.

	And pleffith boith to god and man al-so ;	
[Fol. 21 b.]	Wharfor I wil, incontinent thow go,	1684
	And of thi lond in euery part abide,	
	Whar yow gar fet and clep one euery fid	
	Out of thi cuntreis, and ek out of thi tovnis,	
Invite thy dukes, earls, great barons, thy poor knights, and thy bachelors, and welcome them severally.	Thi dukis, erlis, and thi gret baronis,	1688
	Thi pur knychtis, and thi bach[e]leris,	
	And them refauf als hartly as afferis,	
	And be them-felf yow welcum them ilkon :	
	Syne, them to glaid and cheris, thee difpone	1692
	With fefting and with humyll contynans.	
	Be not penfyve, nore proud in arrogans,	
Keep company not with the rich man only, but with the poor worthy man also.	Bot with them hold in gladnes cumpany ;	
	Not with the Rich nor myghty anerly,	1696
	Bot with the pure worthi man alfo,	
	With them thow fit, with them yow ryd and go.	
	I fay not to be our fameliar,	
	For, as the moft philofephur can duclar,	1700
Yet remember that familiarity breeds contempt.	To mych to oyf familiaritee	
	Contempnyng bryngith one to hie dugre ;	
	Bot cherice them with wordis fair depaynt,	
	So with thi pupelle fal yow the aquaynt.	1704
Choose out of each district an aged knight to be thy counsellor.	Than of ilk cuntre wyfly yow enquere	
	An agit knycht to be thi confulere,	
	That haith ben hold in armys Richt famus,	
	Wyfs and difcret, & no thing Inwyus ;	1708
	For there is non that knowith fo wel, I-wyfs,	
	O worthy man as he that worthi Is.	
When thou hast sojourned long in a place, then provide thee with plenty of horses, armour, gold, silver, and clothing;	When well long haith yow fwiornyt in a place,	
	And well acqueynt the vith thi puple has,	1712
	Than fhalt thow ordand & prowid the	
	Of horfs and ek of armour gret plente ;	
	Of gold, and filuer, tressore, and cleithing,	
	And euery Riches that longith to o king ;	1716
and, before leaving, distribute gifts liberally.	And when the lykith for to tak thi leif,	
	By largefs thus yow thi reward geif,	

First to the pure worthy honorable,
That is til armys and til ma*n*hed able ; 1720
(Set he be pur, ȝhit worfchip in hyme bidith) ;
If hyme the horſ one wich thi-felwyne Ridith, *Give to the poor worthy man the horse thou thyself ridest.*
And bid hyme that he Rid hyme for yhour fak ;
Syne til hyme gold and filu*er* yow betak ; 1724
The horſ to hyme for worfchip and prowes,
The trefor for his fredome and larges.
If moft of Riches and of Cherifing ; [Fol. 22 *a*.]
Eftir this gud kny*ch*t berith vitneſing. 1728
Syne to thi te*n*nand*is* & to thi wawafouris *Give to thy tenants and vavasours easy hackneys, palfries, and coursers.*
If effy haknays, palfrais, and curfouris,
And robis fich as plefand ben and fair ;
Syne to thi lord*is*, wich at my*ch*ty aire, 1732
As duk*is*, erlis, princ*is*, and ek king*is*, *Give to thy lords things strange and uncouth.*
Yow if them ftrang, yow if them vncout*h* thing*is*,
As diuerſ iowell*is*, and ek p*r*eciouſ ftonis,
Or halk*is*, hundis, ordinit for the nonis, 1736
Or wantone horſ that can no*ch*t ftand in ftāble ;
Thar gift*is* mot be fair and delitable.
Thus, firft vn to the vorthi pur yow if
Giftis, that may the*r* pouerte Releif ; 1740
And to the rich ift*is* of plefans,
That thei be fair, fet no*ch*t of gret fubft*a*ns ;
For riches afkith no thing bot delyt,
And powert haith ay ane appetyt 1744
For to support ther ned and Indigens :
Thus fhall yow if and makith thi difpens.
And ek the quen, my lady, fhalt alfo *So, too, shall the queen give to maidens and ladies,*
To madenis and to ladeis, quhar ȝhe go, 1748
If, and cheriſ one the famyne wyſ ;
For in to largeſ al thi welfar lyis. *for all thy welfare lies in liberality.*
And if thy gift*is* with fich *con*tinans
That thei be fen ay gifyne v*ith* plefans ; 1752
The wyſ man fais, and futh it is app*r*ouit.
Thar is no thonk, thar is no ift alowit,

Remember that the giver should be as glad in his cheer as the receiver.	Bot It be ifyne In to fich manere, (That is to fay, als glaid in to his chere), As he the wich the ift of hyme Refauith; And do he not, the gifar is diffauith. For who that iffis, as he not if wald, Mor profit war his ift for to with-hald; His thonk he tynith, and his ift alfo.	1756 1760
Give with both hand and heart at once;	Bot that thow ifith, if with boith two, That is to fay, vith hart and hand atonis; And fo the wyfman ay ye ift difponis. Beith larg and iffis frely of thi thing;	1764
for liberality is the treasure of a king.	For largeſs is the trefour of o king, And not this other Iowellis nor this gold That is in to thi trefory with-holde.	1768
[Fol. 22 b.] Whoso gives liberally, his treasury increases.	Who gladly iffith, be vertew of larges His trefory encrefis of Richeſs, And fal aȝane the mor al-out refawe.	
For the receiver shall place his goods at the king's disposal,	For he to quhome he ȝewith fall hawe, Firft his body, fyne his hart with two, His gudis al for to difpone also	1772
who shall gain, moreover, both worſhip and praise.	In his feruice; and mor atour he fhall Have O thing, and that is beft of all; That is to fay, the worfchip and the loſs That vpone larges in this world furth goſs. And yow fhal knaw the lawbour & the preſs In to this erth about the gret Richeſs	1776 1780
Is there any labour except for meat and clothing? All the remnant is for fame.	Is ony, bot[1] apone the cauſs we see Of met, of cloth, & of profperitee? All the remanant ftant apone the name Of purches, furth apone this worldis fame. And well yow wot, in thyne allegians Ful many Is, the wich haith fufficians Of euery thing that longith to ther ned; What haith yow more, qwich [haith] them al to lede,	1784 1787

[1] MS. "Is ony bout bot;" "bout" being defaced.

For al thi Realmys and thi gret Riches,
If that yow lak of worſchip the encreſſ?
Well leſſ, al-out; for efter thar eſtate
Thei have vorſchip, and kepith It al-gat; 1792
And yow degradith al thyne hie dugree,
That ſo ſchuld ſhyne In to nobelitee,
Throuch wys and throw the wrechitneſſ of hart.
And knowis yow not what ſall be[1] thi part, 1796   *Knowest thou not what shall be thy part, when thou passest away from this world?*
Out of this world when yow ſal paſſ the courſſ?
Fair well, I-wyſſ! yow neuer ſhall Recourſſ
Whar no prince more ſhall the ſubiet[2] have,
But be als dep in to the erd y-grave, 1800
Sauf vertew only and worſchip wich abidith;   *Virtue and honour will alone remain.*
With them the world apone the laif dewidith;
And if he, wich ſhal eftir the ſucced,   *And if thy successor be liberal,*
By larges ſpend, of quhich that yhow had dreid, 1804   *he will be commended of the world;*
He of the world comendit is and priſit,
And yow ſtant furth of euery thing diſpiſit;
The puple faith and demyth thus of thee,
"Now is he gone, a werray vrech was hee, 1808
And he the wich that is our king and lord
Boith wertew haith & larges in accorde;
Welcum be he!" and ſo the puple foundith.
Thus through thi viſſ his wertew mor aboundith, 1812   [Fol. 23 a.]
And his vertew the more thi wice furth ſchawith.   *and his virtue will abound through thy vice.*
Wharfor ȝhe, wich that princes ben y-knawith,
Lat not yhour vrechit hart so yhow dant,
That he that cummyth next yhow may awant 1816
To be mor larg, nore more to be commendit;
Beſt kepit Is the Riches well diſpendit.   *Riches well spent are the best kept.*
O ȝhe, the wich that kingis ben, fore ſham
Remembrith yhow, this world hath bot o naam 1820
Of good or ewill, efter ȝhe ar gone!
And wyſly tharfor cheſſith yhow the ton

[1] MS. has "by."   [2] MS. has "ſubeiᶜt."

	Wich moſt accordith to nobilitee,	
	And knytith larges to yhour hie degre.	1824
	For qwhar that fredome In O pr*i*nce Ri*n*gnis,	
	It bryngith In the victory of king*is*,	
	And makith realmys and puple boith to dout,	
	And ſubect*is*[1] of the cuntre al about.	1828

Whoso will be a conqueror, let him not reck to give largely.

	And qwho that thinkith ben o co*n*querour,	
	Suppos his largeſƷ ſumquhat pas myſour,	
	Ne rak he nat, bot frely iffith ay ;	
	And as he wynyth, beis var al-way	1832
	To mych nor ƷHit to gredy that he hold,	
	Wich ſal the hart*is* of the puple colde.	

Both love and fear spring from liberality.

	And low and radour cu*m*myth boith two	
	Of larges ; Reid and Ʒhe ſal fynd It ſo.	1836
	Alex*ander* this lord the warld that wan,	
	Firſt w*ith* the ſuerd of larges he began,	

Alexander gave so liberally,

	And as he wynith ifith largely,	
	He rakith No thing bot of cheuelry ;	1840
	Wharfor of hyme ſo paſſith the Renown,	

that many cities desired to have such a lord,

	That many o cetee, and many o ſtrang towñ	
	Of his worſchip that herith the Recorde,	
	Diffirith ſo to haveing ſich o lorde ;	1844

and offered themselves peaceably to him, though they were manly men of war.

	And offerith them w*ith*-outen ſtrok of ſpere,	
	Suppos that thei war manly men of were,	
	But only for his gentilleſƷ that thei	
	Have hard ; and ſo he louit was al-way	1848
	For his larges, humilitee, and manhed,	
	W*ith* his awn folk, that neue*r*more, we Reid,	

[Fol. 23 *b.*]

	For al his weris nor his gret trawell,	
	In al his tym that thei hyme onys faill ;	1852
	Bot in his worſchip al thar beſynes	
	Thei ſet, and lewith in to no diſtres ;	
	Whar-throw the ſuerd of victory he berith.	

Many princes bear the palm of

| | And many prince full oft the palm werith, | 1856 |

[1] Or "ſubett*is*."

As has ben hard, by largeß, of before,
In conqueringe of Rignis & of glore. — *victory, through liberality;*
And wrechitnes Richt fo, in the contrar,
Haith Realmys maid ful defolat & bare, 1860 — *while miserliness hath made realms desolate.*
And king*is* broght doun from ful hie eftat;
And who that Red ther old buk*is*, wat
The vicis lef, the wertew have in mynde,
And takith larges In his awn kynd; 1864
A-myd ftanding of the vicis two,
Prodegalitee and awerice alfo. — *Choose the mean between prodigality and avarice.*
Wharfor her-of It nedith not to more,
So mych ther-of haith clerk*is* vrit to-fore. 1868
Bot who the wertw of larges & the law — *Whoso chooses to be liberal,*
Sal cheß, mot ned confidir well & knaw
In to hyme-felf, and thir thre wnd*er*ftande,
The fubftans firft, the powar of his land, 1872 — *must understand three things; the amount he has, to whom he giveth, and the fit time for giving.*
Whome to he iffith, and the cauß wharfore,
The nedful tyme awatith eue*r*more.
Kepith thir thre; for qwho that fal exced
His rent, he fallith fodandly in nede. 1876
And fo the king, that on to myft*er* drowis, — *(1) The king that becomes indigent overthrows his subjects.*
His subiett*is* and his puple he our-thrawis,
And them difpolȝeith boith of lond and Rent;
So is the king, fo is the puple fchent. 1880
For-quhi the woice It fcrik[i]th vp ful ewyne — *For the voice of the oppressed shrieketh up ceaselessly to heaven;*
W*ith*-out abaid, and paffith to the hewyne,
Whar god hyme-felf refauith ther the crye
Of the oppreffioune and the teranny, 1884
And vith the fuerd of wengans dou*n* y-fmytith, — *and God smiteth down with the sword of vengeance.*
The wich that caruith al to for, and bitith,
And hyme diftroyth, as has ben hard or this
Of euery king that wirkith fich o mys. 1888
For ther is few efchapith them, It fall
Boith vpone hyme & his fucceffione fall; — *For God hath given the king the wand of justice:*
For he forfuth haith ifyne hyme the wond
To Iuftefy and Reull in pece his lond, 1892 [Fol. 24 a.]

	The puple all fubmytit to his cure;	
	And he aȝan one to no creatur	
	Save only fhall vn to his gode obey..	
	And if he paffith fo far out of the wey,	1896
and if he oppresses them whom he should rule,	Them to oppreſs, that he fhuld reul & gid,	
	Ther heritag, there gwdis to dewide,	
	Ye, wnder whome that he moft nedis ftond,	
God shall stretch His mighty hand for correction.	At correccioune fal ftrek his mychty hond,	1900
	Not euery day, bot fhal at onys fall	
	On hyme, mayhap, and his fuccefcione all.	
Herein, alas! is the blindness of kings.	In this, allace! the blyndis of the kingis,	
	And Is the fall of princis and of Rygnis.	1904
	The moft wertew, the gret Intellegens,	
The blessed token of a king's wisdom is for him to restrain his hand from his people's riches.	The bleffit tokyne of wyfdom and prudens	
	Iff, in o king, for to reftren his honde	
	Frome his pupleis Riches & ther lond.	1908
	Mot euery king have this wice in mynd	
	In tyme, and not when that he ned fynde!	
	And in thi larges beith war, I pray,	
(2) Choose a *fitting time*. (3) Take care *to whom* you give.	Of nedful tyme, for than is beft alway.	1912
	Awyſs the ek quhome to that thow falt if,	
	Of there fam, and ek how that thei leif;	
Let not the virtuous and the vicious stand in the same degree.	And of the wertws and wicious folk alfo,	
	I the befeich dewidith well thir two,	1916
	So that thei ftond nocht in[to] o degree;	
	Difcreccioune fall mak the diuerfitee,	
	Wich clepith the moder of al vertewis.	
Beware of flattery.	And beith war, I the befeich of this,	1920
	That is to fay of flatry, wich that longith	
	To court, and al the kingis larges fongith.	
	The vertuouſs man no thing thar-of refauith,	
	The flattereris now fo the king diffauith	1924
	And blyndith them that wot no thing, I-wyſs,	
	When thei do well, or quhen thei do o myſs;	
	And latith kingis oft til wnderftonde	
	Thar vicis, and ek ye faltis of ther lond.	1928

In to the realme about o king Is holde
O flatterere were than is the ſtormys cold, *A flatterer is worse than a storm or a pestilence.*
Or peſtelens, and mor the realme anoyith ;
For he the law and puple boith diſtroyith. 1932
And in to principall ben ther three thing*is*, *[Fol. 24 b.] Three things make flatterers in favour.*
That cauſſith flattereris ſtonding w*it*h the king*is*;
And on, It is the blyndit Ignorans *First, the blind ignorance of kings.*
Of king*is*, wich that hath no goue*r*nans 1936
To wnde*r*ſtond who doith ſich o myſ ;
But who that fareſt ſchewith hym, I-wyſ,
Moſt ſuffiſith and beſt to his pleſans.
Wo to the realme that havith ſich o chans ! 1940
And ſecundly, quhar that o king Is *Secondly, where a king is vicious himself.*
Weciuſ hyme-ſelf, he cheriſſith, ywys,
Al them the wich that one to vicis foundith,
Whar-throw that vicis and flattery ek aboundith. 1944
The thrid, is the ilk ſchrewit harrmful wice, *Thirdly, where the king is so foolish, that he knows their flattery, yet withdraws from reproving them.*
Wich makith o king w*it*hin hyme-ſelf ſo nyce,
That al thar flattry and ther gilt he knowith
In to his wit, and ʒhit he hyme w*it*h-drowith 1948
Them to repreſ, and of ther vicis he wot ;
And this It is wich that diſſemblyng hot,
That in no way accordith for o king.
Is he not ſet abuf apone his Ri*n*gne, 1952
As ſoue*r*ane his puple for to lede ?
Whi ſchuld he ſpare, or quhom of ſchuld he dred *Why should a king spare to say the truth ?*
To ſay the treuth, as he of Right is hold ?
And if ſo ware that al the king*is* wold, 1956
When that his leg*is* comytit ony wyce,
As beith not to ſchamful, nore to nyce,
That thei preſume that he is negligent,
But als far as he thinkith that thei myſ-went, 1960 *He should reprove without dissembling, as it is fitting.*
But diſſemblyng reprewith as afferis ;
And pwnice them quhar pwnyſing Requeris,
Sauf only m*er*cy in the tyme of ned.
And ſo o king he ſchuld his puple led, 1964

WISE KINGS MAKE A WISE PEOPLE.

<blockquote>

That no trefpaſs, that cummyth in his way,
Shuld paſs his hond wne-pwniſt away;
Nore no good deid in to the famyn degree,
Nore no wertew, fuld wn-Reuardid bee.   1968

Then flattery, that now is high, should be low.
Than flattry fhuld, that now is he, be low,
And wice from the kingis court with-drow;
His miniſteris that fhuld the Iuſtice reull,
Shuld kep well furth of quiet & reull,   1972
That now, god wat, as It conferwit Is,
The ſtere is loft, and al is gon amys;

[Fol. 25 a.]
And vertew fhuld hame to the court hyme dreſs,
That exillith goith in to the wildernes.   1976

If a king thus stood like his own degree, his people would be virtuous and wise.
Thus if o king ftud lyk his awn degree,
Wertwis and wyſs than fhuld his puple bee,
Only fet by vertew hyme to pleſs,
And fore adred his wifdom to difpleſs.   1980
And if that he towart the vicis draw,
His folk fall go on to that ilk law;
What fhal hyme pleſs that wil nocht ellis fynd,
Bot ther-apon fetith al ther mynde.   1984

Thus the rule of his people and kingdom standeth only in the king's virtue.
Thus only in the wertew of o king
The reull ftant of his puple & his ringne,
If he be wyſs and, but diffemblyng, fchewis,
As I have faid, the vicis one to fchrewis.   1988
And fo thus, ſir, It ftant apone thi will
For to omend thi puple, or to ſpill;
Or have thi court of vertewis folk, or fullis;

Since thou art wholly master of the schools, teach them, and they shall gladly learn."
Sen yow art holl maifter of the fcoullis   1992
Teichith them, and thei fal gladly leir,
That is to fay, that thei may no thing heir[1]
Sauf only wertew towart thyn eſtat;
And cheriſs them that wertews ben algait.   1996
And thinkith what that wertew is to thee;
It pleffith god, vphaldith thi degree."

</blockquote>

[1] Or, "leir." MS. apparently has "leir," corrected to "heir."

THE WATER-LION MEANS GOD.

"Maifter," quod he, " me think rycht profitable
Yowr confeell Is, and wonder honorable 2000
For me, and good ; rycht well I have confauit,
And in myne hartis Inwartneſs refauit.
I fhal fulfill and do yowr ordynans
Als far of wit as I have fuffifans ; 2004
Bot y befeich yow, in til hartly wyſs,
That of my drem ȝhe fo to me dewyſs,
The wich fo long haith occupeid my mynd,
How that I fhal no maner fucour fynd 2008
Bot only throw the wattir lyon, & fyne
The leich that is without medyfyne ;
And of the confell of the flour ; wich ayre
Wonderis lyk that no man can duclar." 2012
"Now, fir," quod he, " and I of them al thre,
What thei betakyne fhal I fchaw to the,
Such as the clerkis at them fpecifiit ;
Thei vfit no thing what thei fignefiit. 2016
The wattir lyone Is the god werray,
God to the lyone is lyknyt many way ;
But thei have hyme In to the wattir feñ,
Confufit were ther wittis al, y weñ ; 2020
The wattir was ther awn fragelitee,
And thar trefpas, and thar Inequitee
In to this world, the wich thei ftond y-clofit ;
That was the wattir wich thei have fuppofit, 2024
That haith there knowlag maad fo Inperfyt ;
Thar fyne & ek ther worldis gret delyt,
As clowdy wattir, was euermore betweñ,
That thei the lyone perfitly hath nocht feñ ; 2028
Bot as the wattir, wich was yer awn fynne,
That euermor thei ftond confufit In.
If thei haith ftond in to religioñ clen,
Thei had the lyone Not in watter fen, 2032
Bot clerly vp in to the hewyne abuf,
Eternaly whar he fhal not remufe.

Arthur considers his counsel profitable.

He beseeches him to expound his dream,

how he shall only find help through the water-lion, the leech, and the flower.

The master's explanation.
[Fol. 25 b.]

The water-lion is the very God.

The water is men's fragility ;

whereby they see not the lion perfectly.

Had men been always religious, they had seen the lion not in water, but clearly.

	And euermore in vatter of fyne vas hee,	
	For-quhi It is Impoffeble for to bee;[1]	2036
The world is enclosed in the darkness of their sin.	And thus the world, wich that thei ar In,	
	Y-clofit Is in dyrknes of ther fyne;	
	And ek the thikneſſ of the air betwen	
	The lyone mad in vattir to be fen.	2040
	For It was nocht bot ftrenth of ther clergy	
	Wich thei have here, and It is bot erthly,	
	That makith them there refouns dewyſſ,	
	And fe the lyone thus in erthly wyſſ.	2044
The lion is God's Son, Jesu Christ.	This is the lyone, god, and goddis sone,	
	Ihesu crift, wich ay in hewyne fal wonne.	
	For as the lyone of euery beft is king,	
	So is he lord and maifter of al thing,	2048
	That of the bleffit vyrgyne vas y-bore.	
	Ful many a natur the lyone haith, quhar-fore	
	That he to god refemblyt is, bot I	
	Lyk not mo at this tyme fpecify.	2052
	This is the lyone, thar-of have yow no dred,	
	That fhal the help and comfort In thi ned.	
	The fentens here now woll I the defyne	
The leech without medicine is also God.	Of hyme, the lech withouten medyfyne,	2056
	Wich is the god that euery thing hath vroght.	
[Fol. 26 a.]	For yow may know that vther Is It noght,	
Not as surgeons,	As furgynis and feficianis, wich that delith	
	With mortell thingis, and mortell thingis helyth,	2060
whose art is in medicine,	And al thar art is in to medyfyne,	
	As it is ordanit be the mycht dewyne,	
and in plaisters, drinks, and various anointments; who know the quality of the year, and the disposition of the planets.	As plafteris, drinkis, and anouyntmentis[2] feir,	
	And of the qualyte watyng of the yher;	2064
	And of the planetis difpoficioune,	
	And of the naturis of compleccyoune,	
	And in the diuerſſ changing of hwmowris.	
	Thus wnder reull lyith al there cwris;	2068

---

[1] "see" (?). [2] MS. "anonytmētis," or "anouytmētis."

And yhit thei far as blynd man In the way,
Oft quhen that deith thar craft lift to affay.
Bot god, the wich that is the foueran lech,
Nedith no maner medyfyne to fech ; 2072
For ther is no Infyrmyte, nore wound,
Bot as hyme lykith al is holl and found.
So can he heill Infyrmytee of thoght, *But God can heal infirmity of thought,*
Wich that one erdly medefyne can noght ; 2076
And als the faul that to confufioune goith, *and also the soul that goeth to confusion.*
And haith with hyme and vther parteis boith,
His dedly wound god helyth frome the ground ;
On to his cure no medyfyne is found. 2080
This Is his mycht that neuer more fhall fyne,
This is the leich withouten medyfyne ;
And If that yhow at confeffioune hath ben,
And makith the of al thi fynnis clen, 2084
Yow art than holl, and this ilk famyn is he *He shall be thy leech in all necessity.*
Schall be thi leich In al neceffitee.

Now of the flour y woll to the difcern :
This is the flour that haith¹ the froyt etern, 2088
This is the flour, this fadith for no fchour,
This is the flour of euery flouris floure ;
This is the flour, of quhom the froyt vas born, *The flower is she of whom the eternal fruit was born,*
This ws redemyt efter that we war lorn ; 2092
This Is the flour that euer fpryngith new,
This is the flour that changith neuer hew ;
This is the vyrgyne, this is the bleffit flour *the virgin that bore the Saviour,*
That Ihefu bur that is our salweour, 2096
This flour wnwemmyt of hir wirginitee ;
This is the flour of our felicitee,
This is the flour to quhom ve fhuld exort,
This is the flour not feffith to fupport 2100 *that ceaseth not to support us caitiffs,*
In prayere, confell, and in byffynes,
Vs catifis ay In to our wrechitnes

[Fol. 26 b.]

---

¹ The word, though indistinct, is almost certainly "haith."
Stevenson has "high ;" but this gives no sense.

ARTHUR IS COMFORTED.

On to hir sone, the quich hir confell herith;
This is the flour that al our gladneß fterith, 2104
Throuch whois prayer mony one is fawit,
That to the deth eternaly war refawit,
Ne war hir hartly fuplicatioune.
This is the flour of our faluatioune, 2108
Next hir sone, the froyt of euery flour;
This is the fam that fhal be thi fuccour,
If that the lykith hartly Reuerans
And feruice ȝeld one to hir excellens, 2112
Syne worfchip hir with al thi byffyneß;
Sche fal thi harm, fche fall thi ned redreß.
Sche fall fice confell if one to the two,
The lyone and the fouerane lech alfo, 2116
Yow fall not Ned yi drem for to difpar,
Nor ȝhit no thing that is in thi contrare.
Now—quod the maifter—yow may well wnderftand
Tueching thi drem as I have born on hande; 2120
And planly haith the mater al declarith,
That yhow may know of wich yow was difparith.
The lech, the lyone, and the flour alfo,
Yow worfchip them, yow ferve them euermo; 2124
And ples the world as I have faid before;
In gouernans thus ftondith al thi glore.
Do as yow lift, for al is in thi honde,
To tyne thi-felf, thi honore, and thi londe, 2128
Or lyk o prince, o conquerour, or king,
In honore and in worfchip for to Ringe."

"Now," quod the king, "I fell that the fupport
Of yhour confell haith don me fich comfort, 2132
Of euery raddour my hart is In to eß,
To ȝhour command, god will, y fal obeß.
Bot o thing is yneuch wn to me,
How galiot makith his awant that he 2136
Shall have the knycht, that only by his honde
And manhed, was defendour of my londe;

through whose prayer are many saved.

She shall so counsel the lion and the leech, that thou need not despair.

Do now as thou list, for all is in thy hand.

The king replies,

that his heart is eased from fear;

but inquires if Galiot will win over the red knight, and what is his name.

ARTHUR AGAIN BECOMES MOURNFUL. 63

If that fhall fall y pray yhow tellith me,
And quhat he hecht, and of quhat lond is hee?" 2140
"What that he hecht yow fhall no foryer know,
His dedis fall her-efterwart hyme fchaw ;   *The master evades reply.*
Bot contrar the he fhall be found no way.
No more thar-of as now y will the fay."[1] 2144
With that the king haith at his maiftir tone   [Fol. 27 a.]
His leve, one to to his cuntre for to goñe ;   *The king and the host return home.*
And al the oft makith none abyde,
To paffing home anone thei can prowid ; 2148
And to fir gawane thei haith o lytter maad,
Ful fore ywound, and hyme on with them haade.
[T]he king, as that the ftory can declar,
Paffith to o Cete that was Right fair, 2152   *The king sojourns twenty-four days at Cardole, in Wales.*
And clepit cardole, In to walis, was,
For that tyme than It was the nereft place,
And thar he foiornyt xxiiijti days
In ryall fefting, as the auttore fays. 2156
So difcretly his puple he haith cherit,
That he thar hartis holy haith conquerit.
And fir gawan, helyt holl and found   *Sir Gawan is healed in fifteen days.*
Be xv dais he was of euery wounde ; 2160
Right blyth therof in to the court war thei.
And fo befell, the xxiiij[2] day,
The king to fall in to o hewynes,   *The king becomes mournful, as he sits at the mess.*
Right ate his table fiting at the meß ; 2164
And fir gawan cummyth hyme before,   *Gawan rebukes him.*
And faid hyme, "fir, yhour thoght is al to fore,
Confidering the diuerß knychtis fere
Ar of wncouth and ftrang landis here." 2168
The king anfuert, as in to matalent,   *The king answers in "matalent,"*
"Sir, of my thocht, or ȝhit of myne entent,
Yhe have the wrang me to repref, for-quhy
Thar lewith none that fhuld me blam, for I 2172

---

[1] At the bottom of the page is the catch-word, "With that the king."   [2] MS. "xxviij," altered to "xxiiij."

that he was thinking of the worthiest knight living;	Was thinkand one the worthieft that lewyt, That al the worfchip In to armys prewyt; And how the thonk of my defens he had, And of the wow that galiot haith mad. 2176 But I have fen, when that of my houfhold Thar was, and of my falowfchip, that wold, If that thei wift, quhat thing fhuld me plefſ, Thei wald nocht leif for trawell nor for eſſ. 2180 And fum tyme It prefwmyt was & faid,
that he once had the flower of knighthood in his household, but now this flower is away.	That in my houfhold of al this world I had The flour of knychthed and of chevalry; Bot now thar-of y fe the contrarye, 2184 Sen that the flour of knychthed is away."
[Fol. 27 b.]	"Schir," quod he, "of Refone futh yhe fay; And if god will, In al this warld fo Round He fal be foght, if that he may be found." 2188
Gawan departs to seek Lancelot.	Than gawan goith with o knychtly chere, At the hal·dure he faith In this maner: "In this pafag who lykith for to wend? It is o Iorne moft for to comend 2192 That In my tyme In to the court fallith, To knyghtis wich that chewellry lowith Or trawell In to armys for to hant; And lat no knycht fra thyne-furth hyme awant 2196
All the knights rise to go with him.	That it denyith;"—with that onon thei roſſ, Al the knychtis, and frome the burdis goſſ. The king that fauch In to his hart was wo,
Arthur reproves him.	And faid, "fir gawan, nece, why dois yow fo? 2200 Knowis yow nocht I myne houfhold fuld encreſſ, In knychthed, and in honore, and largeſſ? And now yow thinkith mak me diffolat Of knychtis, and my houſſ tranfulat, 2204 To fek o knycht, and It was neuer more Hard fich o femble makith o before."
Gawan explains.	"Sir," quod he, "als few as may yhow pleſſ; For what I said was no thing for myne eſſ, 2208

Nor for defir of faloufchip, for-why
To paſ alone, but cumpany, think I;
And ilk knycht to paſ o fundry way;
The mo thei paſ the fewar efchef thay, 2212
Bot thus fhal pas no mo bot as yhow left."
"Takith," quod he, "of quhom ʒhe lykith beft, *Arthur assigns him forty companions.*
Fourty in this pafag for to go;"
At this command and gawan chefit fo 2216
Fourty, quhich that he louit, & that was
Richt glaid in to his falowfchip to pas.

[A]nd furth thei go, and al anarmyt thei *These knights arm themselves,*
Come to the king, withouten more delay, 2220
The relykis brocht, as was the maner tho, *and bring the relics, whereon to swear to shew the truth.*
When any knyghtis frome the court fuld go.
Or when the paſſit, or quhen thei com, thei fwor
The trouth to fchaw of euery aduentur. 2224
Sir gawan knelyng to his falowis fais,
"Yhe lordis, wich that in this feking gais,
So many noble and worthi knychtis ar ʒhe,
Me think in wayne yhour trauel fhuld nocht be, 2228
For aduentur is non so gret to pref, [Fol. 28 a.]
As I fuppone, nor ʒhe fal It effchef,
And if ʒhe lyk as I that fhal dewyſ,
Yhour oth to fwer In to the famyne wyſ 2232
Myne oith to kep;"—and that thei vndertak,
How euer fo that he his oith mak
It to conferf, and that thei have all fworñ.
Than gawan, wich that was the king beforn, 2236
On kneis fwore, "I fal the futh duclar *Gawane swears not to return till he has found Lancelot, or evidence of him.*
Of euery thing when I agan Repar,
Nor neuer more aʒhane fal I returñ,
Nore in o place long for to fuiorñ 2240
Whill that the knycht or verray evydens
I have, that fhal be toknis of credens."
His faloufchip abafit of that thing,
And als therof anoyt was the king, 2244

Arthur reproves him for forgetting the coming day of battle.	Sayng, "Nece, yow haith al foly vroght And wilfulneß, that haith no*ch*t in thi thoght The day of batell of galot and me."	
Gawane says it must be so. Gawane and his fellows lace their helms, and take their leave.	Q*uod* gawan, "Now non other ways ma be." Thar-w*ith* he and his falowfchip alfo Thar halmys lafit, on to ther horß thei go, Syne tuk ther lef, and frome the court the fare, Thar names ware to long for to declar. Now fal we leif hyme and h*is* cumpany, That in thar feking paffith biffely ;	2248 2252
The story returns to the lady of Melyhalt.	And of the lady of melyhalt we tell, W*ith* whome the kny*ch*t mot ned alway duell.	2256
	¹[O] day fhe mayd hyme on to h*ir* pr*e*fens fet, And on o fege be-fid hir haith hyme fet, "S*ir*, in keping I have yow halding long," And thus fche faid, "for gret trefpas & wrong, Magre my ftewart, in worfchip, and for-thi 3he fuld me thonk ;"—"madem," q*uod* he, "and I Thonk yhow fo that eu*er*, at my mycht, Whar-fo I paß that I fal be yhour kny*ch*t."	 2260 2264
She inquires Lancelot's name.	"Grant mercy, f*ir*, bot o thing I 3ow pray, What that 3he ar 3he wold wi*ch*sauf to fay."	
He refuses to tell.	"Madem," q*uod* he, "yhour mercy afk I, quhy That for to fay apone no wyß may I."	2268
She vows to keep him in thrall till the day of combat; [Fol. 28 b.]	"No! wil 3he not? non oy*er* ways as now 3he fal repent, and ek I mak awow One to the thing the wich that I beft love, Out frome my keping fal 3he not Remuf Befor the day of the affemblee, Wich that, o 3her, is n*e*reft for to bee ; And if that 3ow haith pleffit for to fay, 3he had fore me deliu*er*it ben this day ;	 2272 2276
and to go to the court to try and learn it.	And I fal knaw, quhey*er* 3he wil or no, For I furt*h*-w*ith* one to the court fal go,	

¹ Room is here left in the MS. for an illuminated letter, and a small "o" inserted as a note.

Whar that al thithing*is* goith & cu*m*yth foñ."
"Madem," q*uod* he, " yhour plefance mot be doñe." 2280
W*ith* that the kny*ch*t one to his chalm*er* goith,   *The knight retires.*
And the lady hir makith to be wroith
Aʒanis hyme, but futhly vas fche not,
For he al-out was mor in to hir thoght. 2284
Than fchapith fhe aʒane the ferd day,
And richly fche gan hir-felf aray ;
Syne clepit haith apone her cufynes,
And faith, "y will one to the court me dreβ ; 2288   *Before going to the court,*
And malice I have fchawin on to ʒhon kny*ch*t,
For-quhy he wold no*ch*t fchew me quhat he hicht,
Bot fo, I-wyβ, It is no*ch*t in my tho*ch*t,
For worthyar non In to this erth is wro*ch*t. 2292
Tharfor I pray, and hartly I requer   *she prays her cousin to take care of him.*
ʒhe mak hyme al the cu*m*pany and chere,
And do hyme al the worfchip and the eβ,
Excep his honore, wich that may hym pleβ ; 2296
And quhen I cum deliu*er*ith hyme als fre
As he is now ;"—" ne have no dred," q*uod* fche.
[T]he lady p*a*rtit, and hir lef hath ton,
And by hir Iorne to the court Is gon. 2300
The king hapnit at logris for to bee,   *The lady meets Arthur at Logris ;*
Wich of his realme was than the chef cete ;
And haith hir met, and In til hartly wyβ
Refauit her, and welcu*m*myt oft-fyβ ; 2304
And haith hir home one to his palice bro*ch*t,   *who brings her home to his palace ;*
Whar that no dante nedith to be focht,
And maid hir cher w*ith* al his ful entent.
Eft fupir one to o chalm*er* ar thei went, 2308
The king and fche, and ek the quen al thre ;
Of hir tithand*is* at hir than afkit hee,
And what that hir one to the court had bro*ch*t ?   *and inquires what has brought her.*
" S*ir*," q*uod* fche, " I come [1] not al for no*ch*t ; 2312

[1] MS. "conne."

<table>
<tr><td>She says she has a friend who has made a challenge, [Fol. 29 a.]</td><td>I have o frend haith o dereyne ydoo,
And I can fynd none able kny*ch*t tharto;
For he the wich that in the *con*trar Is
Is hardy, ftrong, and of gret kyne, I-wyſs;
Bot, It is faid, If I my*ch*t have w*ith* me
3our kny*ch*t, quich in the last affemble</td><td>2316</td></tr>
<tr><td>which the red knight could best maintain.</td><td>Was in the feld, and the red armys bur,
In his manhed y my*ch*t my cauſs aſſur;
And yhow, fir, richt hartly I exort
In to this ned my myf*ter* to fupport."</td><td>2320</td></tr>
<tr><td>Arthur replies that Gawane is gone to seek him.</td><td>"Madem, by faith one to the quen I aw
That I beft loue, the kny*ch*t I neu*er* faw
In nerneſs by which that I hyme knew;
And ek gawane Is gan hyme for to few
W*ith* other fourty kny*ch*t*is* In to cumpany."
The lady fmylit at ther fanteſsy;
The quen thar-w*ith*-prefumyt wel that fche</td><td>2324

2328</td></tr>
<tr><td>The queen asks the lady if she knows where he is.</td><td>Knew quhat he was, and faid, "madem, If 3he
Knowith of hyme what that he is, or quhar,
We 3how befech til ws for to declar."</td><td>2332</td></tr>
<tr><td>She replies no, and proposes to return.</td><td>"Madem," q*uod* fche, "now be the faith that I
Aw to the king and yhow, as for no why
To court I cam, but of hyme to Inquere;
And fen of hyme I can no tithing*is* here,
Nedlyng*is* to-morn homwart mon I fair."</td><td>2336</td></tr>
<tr><td>Arthur prays her to stay.</td><td>"Na," q*uod* the king, "madem, our fon It waire;
3he fal remayne her for the qwenys fak;
Syne fhal 3he of our beft kny*ch*t*is* tak."</td><td>2340</td></tr>
<tr><td></td><td>"Sir," q*uod* fche, "I pray 3ow me excuſs,
For-quhy to paſs nedis me behuſs;
Nor, fen I want the kny*ch*t which I have fo*ch*t,
Wtheris w*ith* me to have defir I no*ch*t,
For I of otheris have that may fuffice."
Bot 3hit the king hir prayt on fich wyſs,</td><td>2344</td></tr>
<tr><td>She remains till the third day.</td><td>That fche remanit whill the thrid day;
Syne tuk hir leif to pafing hom hir way.</td><td>2348</td></tr>
</table>

THE LADY AGAIN SENDS FOR LANCELOT. 69

It nedis not the fefting to declar   *She is sumptuously entertained,*
Maid one to hir, nor company nor fare;
Sche had no kny*ch*t, fche had no damyfeill,
Nor thei richly rewardit war and well.   2352
Now goith the lady homwart, and fche   *and returns home.*
In her entent defyrus Is to fee
The flour of kny*ch*thed and of chevelry;
So was he pryfit and hold to euery wy.   2356
The lady, which one to hir palace come,   [Fol. 29 *b.*]
   Bot of fchort time remanith haith at home   *Soon after, she sends for Lancelot,*
When fche gart bryng, w*ith*outen Recidens,
W*ith* grete effere this kny*ch*t to hir p*rese*ns,   2360
And faid hyme; "fir, fo mekil have I focht
And knowith that be-for I knew no*ch*t,
That If yhow lyk I wil yhour Ransone mak."   *and proposes to ransom him,*
"Madem, gladly, wil ȝhe wichfauf to tak   2364
Efte*r* that as my powar may atteñ,
Or that I may p*r*owid be ony meñ."
"Now, fi*r*," fho faid, "forfut*h* It fal be so,
Yhe fal have thre, and chef' yhow on of tho;   2368   *on one of three conditions.*
And if yhow lykith them for to refuſ,
I can no mor, but ȝhe fal me excuſ,
Yhe ned*is* mot fuften yhour aduentur
Contynualy In ward for til endur."   2372
"Madem," q*uod* he, "and I yhow hartly pray,
What that thei fay¹ ȝhe wald w*ich*fauf to fay?"
"[T]he firft," q*uod* fche, "who hath in to the cheñ   *Either he must tell whom he loves,*
Of low yhour hart, and if ȝhe may dereñ?   2376
The next, yhour nam, the which ȝe fal not lye?   *or declare his name,*
The thrid, if eu*er* ȝhe think of cheualry   *or say if he expects again to equal his former exploits.*
So mekil worfchip to atten in feild
Apone o day in armys wnd*er* fcheld,   2380
As yat ȝhe dyd the famyne day, when ȝhe
In red armys was at the affemblee?"

---

¹ So MS. We should probably read "bee."

>   "Madem," quod he, "is thar non vther way
>   Me to redem, but only thus to fay   2384
>   Of thing*is*, which that Rynyth me to blam,
>   Me to awant my lady or hir name?
>   But If that I moft fchawin furth that one,
>   What su*er*te fchal I have for to gone   2388
>   At libertee out of this dang*er* free?"
>   "Schir, for to dred no myft*er* is," quod fhee;
>   "As I am trew and fai*th*full woman hold,
>   ȝhe fal go fre quhen one of thir is told."   2392
>   "Madem, yhour will non vther ways I may,
> He refuses to tell I mone obey; and to the firft y fay,
> his lady's name,   ¹[I]s, to declar the lady of myne hart,
>   My goft fal rather of my breft aftart"—   2396
>   Whar-by the lady fayndit al for no*ch*t
>   The lowe quhich long hath ben In to h*is* tho*ch*t—
> or his own;   "And of my nam, fchortly for to fay,
>   It ftondith fo that one no wyſ I may.   2400
> [Fol. 30 a.]   Bot of the thrid, madem, I fe that I
>   Mon fay the thing that tuechith velany;
> but declares that For fut*h* it is I traft, and god before,
> he trusts to do
> more than ever   In feld that I fal do of armys more   2404
> before; and re-
> quires his liberty. Than eu*er* I did, if I *com*mandit bee.
>   And now, madem, I have my libertee,
>   For I have faid I neu*er* thocht to fay."
>   "Now, fir," quod fche, "when-eu*er* ȝhe wil ye may; 2408
> She begs of him   Bot o thing Is, I yhow hartly raquer,
> a boon;
>   Sen I have hold yhow apone fuch maner
>   Not as my fo, that ȝhe vald grant me till.
>   "Madem," quod he, "It fal be as ȝhe will."   2412
>   "Now, fir," quod fche, "it is no thing bot ȝhe
> that he will re-   Remañ wit*h* ws wn to the affemble,
> main with her
> till the day of   And euery thyng that In yhour myft*er* lyis
> battle;
>   I fall gar ordan at yhour awn dewyſ;   2416

¹ A space is here left for an illuminated letter.

And of the day I fhall yow certefy
Of the affemble ʒhe fal not pas therby."
"Madem," quod he, "It fal be as yhow lift."
"Now, fir," quod fche, "and than I hald It beft, 2420
That ʒhe remañ lyk to the famyne dogre
As that ʒhe war, yat non fal wit that ʒhe
Deliuerit war ; and in to facret wyſ
Thus may ʒhe be ; and now yhe fal dewyſ 2424
What armys that yhow lykyth I gar mak."
"Madem," quod he, "armys al of blak."
With this, this knycht is to his chalmer goñ ;
The lady gan ful prewaly diffpone 2428
For al that longith to the knycht, in feild ;
Al blak his horſ, his armour, and his fcheld,
That nedful is, al thing fche well prewidith ;
And in hir keping thus with hir he bidith. 2432
Suppos of love fche takyne hath the charg,
Sche bur It clos, ther-of fche vas not larg,
Bot wyfly fche abftenit hir diffir,
For ellis quhat, fche knew, he was afyre ; 2436
Thar-for hir wit hir worfchip haith defendit,
For in this world thar was nan mor commendit,
Boith of difcreccioune and of womanhed,
Of gouernans, of nurtur, and of farhed. 2440
This knycht with hir thus al this whil mon duell,
And furth of arthur fumthing wil we tell—
[T]hat walkyng vas furth in to his Regiounis,
And foiornyt in his ceteis and his townis, 2444
As he that had of vifdome fufficyans.
He kepit the lore of maifter amytans
In ryghtwyfnes, In fefting and larges,
In cherifing cumpany and hamlynes ; 2448
For he was biffy and was deligent,
And largly he iffith, and difpent
Rewardis, boith one to the pur & riche,
And holdith feft throw al the ʒher eliche. 2452

ARTHUR'S LIBERALITY.

In al the warld paffing gan his name,
He chargit not bot of encreſs and fame,
And how his puples hart*is* to empleſs ;
Thar gladnes ay was to his hart moft eſs.　　2456
He rakith not of riches nor treffour,
Bot to difpend one worfchip & honour ;
He ifith riches, he ifith lond and rent,
He cheriffyth them w*ith* word*is* eloquent,　　2460

and thus gains his people's love. So that thei can them vtraly p*ro*pone
In his f*er*uice thar lyves to difpone :
So gladith theme his homely c*on*tynans,
His cherifyng, his wordis of plefans,　　2464
His cumpany, and ek his mery chere,
His gret rewardis, and his ift*is* fere.
Thus hath the king non vthir befynes
Bot cherifing of kny*ch*t*is* and largeſs,　　2468
To mak hyme-felf of honour be c*om*mend ;
And thus the ȝher he drywith to the ende.

EXPLICIT SECUNDA P*A*R*S*, INCIPIT T*ER*CIA P*A*R*S*.

[BOOK III.]

The long dirk pafag¹ of the vinter, & the lycht
  Of phebus comprochit with his mycht;   2472
The which, afcending In his altitud,
Awodith saturñ with his ftormys Rude;
The foft dew one fra the hewyne doune valis²
Apone the erth, one hillis and on valis,   2476
And throw the fobir & the mwft hwmouris
Vp nurifit ar the erbis, and in the flouris
Natur the erth of many diuerſ hew
Our-fret, and cled with the tendir new.   2480
The birdis may them hiding in the grawis
Wel frome the halk, that oft ther lyf berevis;
And scilla hie afcending in the ayre,
That euery vight may heryng hir declar   2484
Of the feffone the paffing luftynes.
This was the tyme that phebus gan hym dreſ
In to the rame, and haith his courſ bygown,
Or that the trewis and the ȝher vas Rown,   2488
Which was y-fet of galiot and the king
Of thar affemble, and of thar meting.
Arthur haith a xv dais before
Affemblit al his barnag and more   2492
That weryng wnder his fubieccioune,
Or louith hyme, or longith to his crown;
And haith his Iornay tone, without let,
On to the place the wich that was y-fet,   2496
Whar he hath found befor hyme mony o knycht
That cummyng war with al thar holl mycht,

The sun ascends in his altitude.

The soft dew falls down from heaven.

Nature decks the earth with various hues. The birds may hide [Fol. 31 a.] *them from the hawk in the groves, and Scilla may ascend in the air.*

The time of combat between Galiot and the king drew near.

Arthur goes to the appointed place.

---

¹ So MS. Should we read "pasith"?
² So MS. It should be "falis."

Al enarmyt both with spere & scheld,
And ful of lugis plantith haith the feld, 2500
Hyme In the wer for to support and serf
At al ther mycht, his thonk for to differf.
And gawan, which was in the seking ȝhit
Of the gud knycht, of hyme haith got no wit, 2504
Remembrith hyme apone the kingis day,
And to his falowis one this wys can say:
" To ȝhow is knowin the mater, in what wyß
How that the king hath with his ennemys 2508
A certan day, that now comprochit nere,
And one to ws war hewynes to here
That he var in to perell or in to dreid,
And we away and he of ws haith neid ; 2512
For we but hyme no thing may eschef,
And he but ws in honore well may lef ;
For, be he lost, we may no thing withstond,
Our-self, our honore we tyne, & ek our lond. 2516
Tharfor, I red we pas on to the king,
Suppos our oth It hurt in to sum thing,
And in the feld with hyme for til endur,
Of lyf or deth and tak our aduentur." 2520
Thar-to thei ar consentit euerilkon,
And but dulay the have thar Iorney toñe.
When that the king them saw, in his entent
Was of thar com Right wonder well content ; 2524
For he preswmyt no thing that thei wold
Have cummyne, but one furth to yer seking hold.
And thus the kinghis oft assemblit has
Aȝane the tyme, aȝaine the day that vas 2528
Y-statut and ordanit for to bee,
And euery thing hath set in the dogre.
  [A]nd galiot, that haith no thing forȝhet
The termys quhich that he befor had set, 2532
Assemblit has, apone his best maner,
His folk, and al his other thingis fere,

That to o weryour longith to prouid,
And is y-come apone the tothir fyde.   2536
Whar he befor was one than vas he two,   *doubling his army and artillery;*
And al his vthir artilȝery also
He dowblith hath, that merwell was to fen ;
And by the rewere lychtit one the greñ,   2540 *and pitches on the green by the river.*
And ftronghar thane ony wallit toune
His oft y-bout yclofit in Randoune.
Thus war thei cummyne apone ather fyd
Be-for the tyme, them-felf for to prowid.   2544 *Before the truce is ended,*
Or that the trewis was complet & rwn,
Men mycht have fen one euery fid begwn
Many a fair and knychtly Iuperty   *many combats are seen between lusty men;*
Of lufty men, and of ȝong chevalry,   2548
Difyrus In to armys for to pruf ;
Sum for wynyng, fum caufith vas for luf,
Sum In to worfchip to be exaltate,
Sum caufit was of wordis he & hate,   2552
That lykit not ydill for to ben ;
A hundereth pair at onis one the gren.   *a hundred pair at once.*
Thir lufty folk thus can thar tyme difpend,
Whill that the trewis goith to the ende.   2556
The trewis paft, the day is cummyne onoñe,   *The truce past,*
One euery fyd the can them to difpone ;
And thai that war moft facret & moft dere
To galiot, at hyme the can enquere,   2560 *Galiot's friends inquire who shall fight on his side on the morrow.*
" Who fal affemble one yhour fyd to-morñe ?
To-nycht the trewis to the end is worne."
He anfuerit, " As yhit one to this were
I ame awyfit I wil none armys bere,   2564
Bot If It ftond of more Neceffitee ;   *[Fol. 32 a.]*
Nor to the feld will pas, bot for to fee
Yhone knycht, the which that berith fich o fame."
Than clepit he the conqueft king be name,   2568 *He commands the first-conquest king to take 30,000 men.*
And hyme commandit xxx thoufand tak
Aȝaine the morne, and for the feld hyme mak.

DEEDS OF SIR ESQUYRIS.

And gawane haith, apone the toyer syde,
Confulit his Eme he fchuld for them prowid,   2572
And that he fchuld none armys to hyme tak
Whill¹ galiot will for the feld hyme mak.
" I grant," quod [he²], " wharfor ȝhe mone difpone

Gawane leads Arthur's forces.

Yhow to the feld with al my folk to-morne,   2576
And thinkith in yhour manhed and curage
For to recift ȝhone folkis gret owtrag."

The day comes.

[T]he nycht is gone, vp goith the morow gray,
The brycht fone fo cherith al the day :   2580
The knychtis gone to armys than, in haft ;
One goith the fcheildis and the helmys laft ;

Arthur's men cross the ford.

Arthuris oft out our the furrde thai ryd.
And thai agane, apone the toyer syd,   2584

Galiot's men assemble in a vale.

Affemblit ar apone o lufty greyne,
In to o waill, whar fone thar mycht be feyne
Of knychtis to-gedder many o pair
In to the feld affemblyng her & thair,   2588
And ftedis which that haith thar mafter lorne ;³
The knychtis war done to the erth doune borne.

Sir Esquyris, a manly knight,

Sir efquyris, which was o manly knycht
In to hyme-felf, and hardy vas & wycht ;   2592
And in till armys gretly for to pryß,
Ȝhit he was pure, he prewit wel oft-fyß ;

at that time of Galiot's company,

And that tyme was he of the cumpanee
Of galiot, bot efterwart was hee   2596
With arthur ; and that day In to the feild
He come, al armyt boith with fpere and fcheld,
With ferß defir, as he that had na dout,

attacks a band,

And is affemblit ewyne apone a rowt ;   2600
His fpere is gone, the knycht goith to the erd,
And out onon he pullith haith o fwerd ;

and proves his manhood.

That day In armys prewit he rycht well
His ftrenth, his manhed ; arthuris folk thai fell.   2604

---

¹ MS. " Wihill."   ² Omitted in MS.
³ MS. has " borne." We should read " lorne," as in line 2092

DEEDS OF SIR GWYANS.

Than galys gwynans, w*ith* o manly hart,   *Than Galys Gwy-*
Which broye*r* was of ywane the baſtart,   *nans, brother of Ywan,*
He cu*m*myne Is onone one to the ſtour
For co*n*quering In armys of honour,   2608   [Fol. 32 b.]
And cownte*r*it w*ith* eſquyris hath so   *encounters him,*
That [1] horſ and man, al four, to erth thai go;   *and horse and man go all four to earth.*
And ſtill o quhill lying at the ground.
W*ith* that o p*ar*t of arthur*is* folk thei found   2612
Till gwyans, and haith hyme ſone reſkewit.   *Arthur's folk res-*
Aȝanis them til eſquyris thei ſewyt   *cue Gwyans;*
Of galiot*is* well xxx[ti] knyc*h*t*is* & mo;   *thirty knights of*
Gwyans goith done, and vthir vij alſo,   2616   *Galiot's arrive, and rescue Es-*
The wich war tone & eſqwyris relewit.   *quyris.*
Than ywane the anterus, aggrewit,   *Next Ywan*
W*ith* kyn*n*iſme*n* one to the melle foc*h*t.   *comes to the mêlée.*
The hardy knyc*h*t*is*, that one thar worſchip thoc*h*t, 2620
Cownte*r*it them In myddis of the ſcheld,
Whar many o knyc*h*t was born doñ i*n* the feld;
Bot thei wich ware on galiot*is* pa*r*t,   *Galiot's men give*
So wnde*r*takand nor of ſo hardy hart   2624   *way.*
Ne ware thei not as was i*n* ye co*n*trare.
Si*r* galys gwyans was reſqwyt thare   *Gwyans is again*
W*ith* his falowis, and eſqwyris don bore.   *rescued.*
Thar al the batell*is* cam, w*ith*outen more,   2628
On ather p*ar*t, and is aſſemblit ſo
Whar fyfty thouſand war thei, & no mo.   *50,000 men are assembled.*
In o plane beſyd the gret Riwere   *30,000 on Galiot's*
Xxx thouſand one galiot*is* half thei vare;   2632   *side approach the river,*
Of arthuris x thouſand and no mo   *and 10,000 on*
Thei ware, and ȝhit thai co*n*tenit them ſo   *Arthur's.*
And in the feld ſo manly haith borñ,
That of thar fois haith the feld forſworñ.   2636
The co*n*queſt king, wich the pe*r*ell knowith
Ful manly one to the feld he drowith;
The lord ſi*r* gawan, coue*r*it w*ith* h*is* ſcheld,   *Gawane puts the conquest-king to flight.*

[1] MS. has "than."

SIR GAWANE'S INTREPIDITY.

	He ruschit in myddis of the feld, 2640
	And haith them so in to his com assayt,
	That of his manhed ware thei al affrait ;
	No langer mycht thei contrar hyme endur,
Galiot, full of anger and grief, sends out a new band.	Bot fled, and goith one to discumfiture. 2644
	And galiot, wich haith the discumfit sen,
	Fulfillit ful of anger and of ten,
	Incontinent he send o new poware,
[Fol. 33 a.]	Whar-with the feldis al our-couerit ware 2648
	Of armyt stedis both in plait and maill,
	With knychtis wich war reddy to assaill.
Gawane draws his men together, and shews them comfortable words.	Sir gawan, seing al the gret suppris
	Of fois cummyng In to sich o wys, 2652
	Togiddir al his cumpany he drew,
	And confortable wordis to them schew ;
	So at the cummyng of thar ennemys
They receive the foe in manly wise.	Thei them resauf, in so manly wys, 2656
	That many one felith deithis wound,
	And wnder horß lyith sobing one the ground.
	This vther cummyth in to gret desir,
	Fulfillit ful of matelent and Ire, 2660
	So freschly, with so gret o confluens,
	Thar strong assay hath don sich vyolens,
	And at thar come arthuris folk so led,
	That thai war ay abaysit and adred. 2664
	Bot gawan, wich that, by this vorldis fame,
	Of manhed and of knychthed bur the name,
	Haith prewit [hym] well be experiens ;
	For only In til armys his defens 2668
Gawane encourages his fellows,	Haith maid his falowis tak sich hardyment,
	That manfully thei biding one the bent.
	Of his manhed war merwell to raherß ;
	The knychtis throw the scheldis can he perß, 2672
	That many one thar dethis haith resauit ;
	None armour frome his mychty hond them sauit,
though their foes are three to one;	Зhit ay for one ther ennemys wor thre.

SIR YWAN RESCUES GAWANE.

Long mycht thei nocht endur in such dugree; 2676
The press it wos so creuell & so strong,
In gret anoy and haith continewit longe,
That, magre them, thei nedis most abak *yet his men are forced to retreat to their tents.*
The way one to thar lugis for to tak. 2680
Sir gawan thar sufferith gret myschef,
And wonderis in his knychthed can he pref;
His faloufchip haith merwell that hym saw,
So haith his fois that of his fuerd stud aw. 2684
King arthur, that al this whill beheld *Arthur beholds the peril of the field, and sends Sir Ywan to help them,*
The danger and the perell of the feld,
Sir ywan with o falowschip he sende,
Them In that ned to help & to defend, 2688
Qwich fond them In to danger and in were, [Fol. 33 b.]
And enterit nere In to thar tentis were.
Sir gawan fechtand was one fut At erde, *who finds Sir Gawane fighting on foot with only his sword.*
And no defend, but only in his swerde, 2692
Aȝanis them both with spere and scheld.
Of galowa the knycht goith to the erde.[1]
Thar was the batell furyous and woud[2] *The battle was furious and wood.*
Of armyt knychtis; to the grownde thai ȝhud. 2696
Sir ywane, that was a noble knyght,
He schew his strenth, he schew thar his gret mycht,
In al his tyme that neuer of before
Off armys, nore of knychthed, did he more: 2700
Sir gawan thar reskewit he of fors, *Sir Ywan rescues Sir Gawane,*
Magre his fois, and haith hyme set one hors
That frome the first conquest king he wan;
Bot sir gawan so ewill was wondit than, 2704 *who was so evilly wounded, that he was the worse thereof evermore.*
And in the feld supprisit was so sore,
That he the wers thar-of was euermore.
Thar schew the lord sir ywan his curage,
His manhed, & his noble wassolage; 2708
And gawan, in his doing, wald nocht irk;

---
[1] Read "felde"? [2] MS. "woid," but the "i" is undotted, and is therefore perhaps meant for the first stroke of a "u."

END OF THE FIRST DAY'S BATTLE.

Darkness parts the combatants.

So al the day enduring to the dyrk
Sal them, magre of thar defyre, *conftren*
On ayar half fore [to] de*part* in twen. 2712
And when that gawan of his horß vas toñ,
The blud out of his noiß & mouth is goñ,
And largly fo paffith euery wounde,

Sir Gawane swoons,

In fwonyng thore he fell one to the ground: 2716
Than of the puple petee was to here
The lemytable clamour, and the chere;

so that the king despairs of his "niece's" life, and laments over him.

And of the king the forow and the care,
That of his nec*is* lyf was in diffpare. 2720
" Far well," he fais, " my gladnes, & my delyt,
Apone kny*ch*thed far well myne appetit,
Fare well of manhed al the g*r*et curage,
Yow flour of armys and of vaffolage, 2724
Gif yow be loft!"—thus til his tent hyme bro*ch*t

The surgeons are sought,

W*i*th wofull hart, and al the furry3enis focht,
Wich for to cum was reddy at his neid;
Thai fond the lord was of his lyf *in* dreid, 2728
For wondit was he, and ek wondit fo,

who found he had two broken ribs, but no mortal wound.

And in his fyd ware brokyne Ribys two.
Bot no*ch*t for-thi the king thai maid beleif

[Fol. 34 a.]

That at that tyme he fhuld the deith efchef. 2732
[O]ff melyhalt the ladyis kny*ch*t*is* were
In to the feld, and can thir thithing*is* here,

The lady of Mely-halt's knights tell her how the battle went,

And home to thar lady ar thai went,
Til hir to fchewing efte*r* thar entent, 2736
In euery poynt, how that the batell ftud
Of galiot, and of his multitud;

and how Gawane bare him in the field, and of his wounds.

And how gawan hyme in the feld hath borñ,
Throw quhoys fwerd fo many o kny*ch*t vas lorñ, 2740
And of the kny*ch*tly wonde*r*is that he wro*ch*t,
Syne how that he one to his tent vas bro*ch*t.
The lady hard, that lowit gawan so,

She weeps for him.

She gan to wep, in to¹ hir hart vas wo. 2744

---

¹ MS. " in in"; but "in to" is clearly meant.

LANCELOT'S LAMENT FOR GAWANE. 81

Thir tythyng*is* one to lancelot ar goñ,   *Lancelot requests to see the lady;*
Whar-of that he was wond*er* wo-bygone,
And for the lady haftely he sent,
And fche til hyme, at his co*m*mand, Is went: 2748
He faluft hir, and faid, "madem, Is trew   *and inquires if Gawane is really likely to die.*
Thir tithing*is* I her report of new
Of the affemble, and meting of the oft,
And of f*ir* gawan, wich that fhuld be loft?   2752
If that be fwth, adew the flour of armys,
Now neue*r*more recoue*r*yt be the harmys!   *He laments over him,*
In hyme was manhed, curteffy, and trouth,
Befy trawell In knyc*h*thed, *e*y but fleuth,   2756
Humilyte, [and] gentrice, and cwrag;
In hyme thar was no man*er* of outrage.
Allace! knyc*h*t, allace! what fhal yow fay?   *first apostrophizing himself,*
Yow may complen, yow may bewail the day   2760
As of his deith, and gladfchip aucht to fes,
Baith menftrafy and fefting at the des;
For of this lond he was the holl comfort,
In tyme of ned al knyc*h*thed to fupport!   2764
Allace! madem, and I durft fay at ʒhe   *and next blaming the lady for not having allowed him to be present in the battle.*
Al yhour beheft not kepit haith to me,
Whar-of that I was in to full belef
Aʒañe this day that I fchuld have my lef,   2768
And noc*h*t as cowart thus fchamfully to ly
Excludit in to cage frome chewalry,
Whar othir knyc*h*tis anarmyt on thar ftedis
Hawnt*is* ther ʒhouthhed in to knyc*h*tly dedis."   2772
"S*ir*," q*uo*d fche, "I red yhow not difplef,
ʒhe may In tyme her-eft*er* cum at es;   [Fol. 34 *b*.]
For the thrid day Is ordanit, & fhal be   *She promises he shall go to the next battle,*
Of the oft*is* a new affemble,   2776
And I have gart ordan al the gere
That longith to ʒour body for to were,
Boith horß and armour In the famyne wyß   *saying that his sable armour is ready.*
Of fable, ewyne aftir ʒhour awn dewyß;   2780

	And yhe fal her remayne one to the day ;	
	Syne may ʒhe paſſ, fore well ʒhe knaw the way."	
	"I will obey, madem, to yhour entent."	
	With that ſche goith, and to hir reſt is went:	2784
In the morn she takes her leave, to go to the court.	One the morn arly vp ſche roſſ	
	Without delay, and to the knycht ſche gois,	
	And twk hir lef, and ſaid that ſcho vald fare	
	On to the court, with-outen any mare.	2788
He kneels, and thanks her often.	Than knelit he, and thankit hir oft-ſys,	
	That ſche ſo mych hath done hyme of gentriſſ,	
	And hir byhecht euer, at his myght,	
	To be hir awn trew & ſtedfaſt knycht.	2792
She goes unto the king,	Sche thonkith hyme, and ſyne ſche goith her way	
	On to the king, with-owten more delay,	
	Whar that in¹ honour with king & qwen ſche fall	
	Rycht thonkfully reſauit be with-all.	2796
	Eft to ſir gawan thai hir led, & ſche	
	Ryght gladly hyme deſyrit for to ſee,	
and finds Sir Gawane quite different from what had been told her.	And ſche hyme fond, and ſche was glad tharfore,	
	All vthir ways than was hir told before.	2800
	The knycht, the wich in to hir keping vas,	
The lady's cousin cherishes Lancelot in her best manner.	Sche had commandit to hir cuſſynece,	
	Wich cheriſt hyme apone hir beſt manere,	
	And comfort hyme, and maid hym rycht gud chere.	2804
	[T]he days goith, ſo paſſith als the nycht,	
The third day, the maiden goes to his chamber, and fastens on his armour.	The thrid morow, as that the ſone. vas lycht,	
	The knycht onon out of his bed aroſſ,	
	The maden ſone one to his chalmer goſſ,	2808
	And ſacretly his armour one hyme ſpent.	
	He tuk his lef, and ſyne his way he went	
He goes to the same green, beside the river, as before.	Ful prewaly, rycht to the ſamyne greñ	
	One the rewere, whar he befor had ben,	2812
	Ewyne as the day [he] the firſt courſſ hath maad.	
	Alone rycht thar he howit, and abaade,	

¹ MS. "with;" which is crossed out, and "in" inserted above, rather minutely written.

THE QUEEN BEHOLDS THE BLACK KNIGHT. 83

Behalding to the bertes, whar the qwen
Befor at the affemble he had sen 2816
Rycht fo the fone fchewith furth his lycht,
And to his armour went is euery wycht;
One athir half the Iufting is bygon,
And many o fair and knych[t]ly courß is rown. 2820
The blak knycht ȝhit howyns on his fted,
Of al thar doing takith he no hed,
Bot ay, apone the befynes of thocht,
In beholding his ey departit nocht. 2824
To quhom the lady of melyhalt beheld,
And knew hyme by his armour & his fcheld,
Qwhat that he was; and thus fche faid one hycht:
"Who is he ȝone? who may he be, ȝhone knycht, 2828
So ftill that hovith and fterith not his Ren,
And feith the knychtis rynyng one the gren?"
Than al beholdith, and in princypale
Sir gawan beholdith moft of all; 2832
Of melyha[l]t the lady to hyme maid
Incontinent, his couche and gart be had
Be-fore o wyndew thore, as he mycht se
The knycht, the oft, and al the affemble. 2836
He lukith furth, and fone the knycht hath fen,
And, but delay, he faith one to the qwen,
"Madem, if ȝhe remembir, fo it was
The red knycht in to the famyne place 2840
That wencuft al [at] the firft affemble;
Whar that ȝone knycht howis, howit hee."
"ȝha," quod the qwen, "rycht well remembir I;
Qwhat is the cauß at ȝhe inquere, & quhy?" 2844
"Madem, of [al] this larg warld is he
The knycht the wich I moft defir to fee
His ftrenth, his manhed, his curag, and his mycht,
Or do in armys that longith to o knycht." 2848
[B]y thus, arthur, with confell well awyfit,
Haith ordanit his batellis, and devyfit:

[Fol. 35 a.]

He abides there alone, looking towards the parapet where he saw the queen.

The jousting begins.

The black knight still halts on his steed.

The lady beholds him and knows him; but yet inquires who he is,

thus calling the attention of Gawane,

who saith to the queen:
"Madam, remember that the red knight halted where yon knight halts."

"Why do you inquire?" she replies.

"He is the knight, madam, whom I most defire to see."

Arthur arranges his lines of battle.

THE ORDER OF BATTLE.

King Ydrus leads the first;

The firft of them led ydrus king, & he
O worthy man vas nemmyt for to bee. 2852

Harwy the Reweyll, an aged knight, the second.

The fecund led harwy the Reweyll,
That in this world was knycht that had moft feill
For to prowid that longith to the were,
One agit knycht, and well couth armys bere. 2856

[Fol. 35 b.]
King Angus, a cousin of Arthur, leads the third.

[T]he thrid feld [he] deliuerit in the hond
Of angus, king of ylys of fcotlande,
Wich cufing was one to king arthur nere,
One hardy knycht he was, without were. 2860

King Ywons the fourth.

The ferd batell led ywons the king,
O manly knycht he was In to al thing.
And thus dewyfit ware his batellis fere,

In every company are 15,000.

In euery feld xv thoufand were. 2864

The lord Sir Ywan leads the rearguard.

[T]he fift[1] batell the lord fir ywan lede,
Whois manhed was in euery cuntre dred,
Sone he was one to wryne the kyng,
Forwart, ftout, hardy, wyfs, and ʒhing; 2868
Xx thoufand in his oft thai paft,
Wich ordanit was for to affemble laft.

Galiot's armies.

[A]nd galiot, apone the tothir fyde,
Rycht wyfly gan his batellis to dewid. 2872

Malenginys leads the first line;

The firft of them led malenginys the king,
None hardyar In to this erth lewyng;
He neuer more out of his cuntre Raid,
Nor he with hyme one hundereth knychtis hade. 2876

the first-conquest king the second; Walydeyne the third;

[T]he fecund the first-conqueft king led,
That for no perell of armys vas adred;
The thrid, o king clepit walydeyne,
He led, and was o manly knycht, but weyne. 2880

Clamedeus the fourth;

[T]he ferd, king clamedeus has,
Wich that lord of far ylys was.

and King Brandymagus the fifth.

The fift[2] batell, whar xl thoufand were,
King brandymagus had to led and ftere, 2884

---

[1] MS. "firft." See 1. 2870.   [2] MS. "firft."

O manly kny*ch*t, and prewit well oft-fyſ,
And in his confell wond*er* fcharp & wyſ.
Galiot non armys bur that day,
Nor as o kny*ch*t he wald hyme-felf aray, 2888
But as o fer*u*and in o habariowne,
O prekyne hat, and ek o gret trownfciown̄
In til his hond, and one o curfour fet,
The beft that was in ony lond to get. 2892
Endlong the rewar men my*ch*t behold & fee,
Of kny*ch*t*is* weryne mony one affemble;
And the blak kny*ch*t ftill he couth abyde,
W*ith*out remowyng, one the Riwer fyde, 2896
Bot to the bartes to behold and fee
Thar as his hart defyrit moft to bee:
And quhen the lady of melyhalt haith fen̄
The kny*ch*t fo ftond, fche faid one to the qwen̄, 2900
"Madem, It is my confell at ȝhe send
One to ȝone kny*ch*t, ȝour-felf for to *com*mend,
Befeiching hyme that he wald wnd*er*tak
This day to do of armys, for ȝour fak." 2904
The quen anfuerit as that hir lykit no*ch*t,
For othir thing was more In to hir tho*ch*t,
"For well ȝhe fe the p*er*ell how disio[i]nt,
The adwentur now ftondith one the point 2908
Boith of my lord his honore, and h*is* lond,
And of his men, in[1] dang*er* how thai ftond:
Bot ȝhe, and ek thir vthere ladice may,
If that yhow lykith, to the kny*ch*t gar fay 2912
The mefag; is none that wil yhow let,
For I tharof fal no*ch*t me ent*er*met."
On to the quen fcho faith, "her I,
If fo it pleſ thir vthir ladice by, 2916
Am for to fend one to the kny*ch*t content;"
And al the ladice can thar-to affent,

Galiot bore no arms;

but was arrayed as a servant in a habergeon with a "prekyne" hat, and a truncheon in his hand.

The black knight still remains looking towards the parapet.

The lady says to the queen—
[Fol. 36 a.]
"Madam, pray commend yourself to yon knight."

The queen replies

that the lady and the rest may send a message, but that she will not herself take part in it.

---

[1] Stevenson reads "the"; but "the" is crossed out, and "in" written over it.

	Befeching hir the mefag to dewyſ,	
	As fche that was moſt prudent & moſt wyſ.	2920
The lady sends a discreet maiden,	Sche grantit, and o madeñ haith thai tone,	
	Difcret, apone this mefag for till gone ;	
and Sir Gawane a squire, with two spears,	And fir gawan a fqwyar bad alfo,	
	With two fperis one to the knycht to go.	2924
	The lady than, withouten more dulay,	
	Haith chargit hir apone this wyſ to fay:	
to say that all the ladies, the queen alone excepted, commend them to the black knight,	"Schaw to the knycht, the ladice euer-ilkone	
	Ben In the court, excep the quen allon,	2928
	Til hyme them haith recommandit oft-fyſ,	
	Befeching hyme of knychthed and gentriſ,	
	(Or if It hapyne euermore that he fhall	
	Cum, quhar thai may, owther an or all,	2932
	In ony thing awail hyme or fupport,	
	Or do hyme ony plefans or comfort,)	
and pray him to essay some deed of arms.	He wold wichfaif for loue of them this day	
	In armys fum manhed to affay ;	2936
	And fay, fir gawan hyme the fperis fent ;	
	Now go, this is the fek of our entent."	
The damsel and squire	The damyfell fche hath hir palfray tone,	
	The sqwyar with the fperis with hir goñ ;	2940
[Fol. 36 b.]	The nereſt way thai paſ one to ye knycht,	
repeat the message.	Whar fche repete hir mefag haith ful rycht :	
Sir Lancelot, finding the queen not in the message,	And quhen he hard, and planly wnderſtude,	
	How that the quen not in the mefag ȝude,	2944
was not content,	He fpak no word, bot he was not content ;	
	Bot, of fir gawan, glaid in his entent,	
	He afkit quhar he was, and of his fair ?	
	And thai to hyme the maner can duclair ;	2948
but asks the squire to hold the two spears ready for him.	Than the fqwyar he prayth that he wold	
	Paſ to the feld, the fperis for to hold.	
	He faw the knychtis femblyng her and thare,	
	The ſtedis Rynyng with the fadillis bare ;	2952
	His fpuris goith in to the ſtedis syde,	
	That was ful fwyft, and lykit not to byd ;	

And he that was hardy, ferß, and ſtout,
Furth by o ſyd affemblyng on a rout   2956   He attacks a company of a hundred knights, slays the nearest,
Whar that one hund*er*eth kny*ch*t*is* was, & mo ;
And w*ith* the firſt has Recount*er*it so,
That frome the deth not helpith hy*m* h*is* ſcheld,
Boith horß and man is lying in the feld ;   2960
The ſpere is gone, and al in pecis brak,
And he the trunſcyoune in h*is* hand hath tak   and with the stump of his spear bereaves two or three of their saddles.
That two or thre he haith the ſadill*is* reft,
Whill in his hond ſchortly no thing is left.   2964
Syne, to the ſquyar, of the feld is goñ,
Fro hyme o ſpere In to his hond haith ton,   He takes a new spear from the squire, and overthrows three knights.
And to the feld returnyt he a3ayne :
The firſt he met, he goith one the plan,   2968
And ek the next, and fyne the thrid alſo ;
Nor in his hond, nore in his ſtrak was ho.
His e*n*nemys that veryng In affray
Befor his ſtrok, and makith rovm alway ;   2972
And in ſich wyß ay in the feld he vro*ch*t,
Whill that his ſperis gon var al to no*ch*t ;
Whar-of ſ*ir* gawan berith vitneſing
Throw al this world that thar vas non levyng,   2976
In ſo ſchort tyme ſo mych of armys wro*ch*t.
His ſperis gone, out of the feld he ſocht,   His spears gone, he returns to his first position.
And paſſit is one to the Rewere syde,
Ry*ch*t thore as he was wont for to abyde ;   2980
And ſo beholdyne In the famyne plañ,   [Fol. 87 a.]
As to the feld hyme lykit no*ch*t a3añ.
Sir gawan ſaw, and faith on to the quen,   Sir Gawane says to the queen :
"Madem, yhone knycht diſponit [not],[1] I weyñ,   2984   "Madam, yon knight thinks himself despised, because you so specially excepted yourself in the message ;
To help ws more, fore he ſo is awyſit ;
As I p*re*ſume, he thinkith hyme diſpiſit
Of the meſag that we gart to hyme mak ;
Yhowre-ſelf yhe have ſo ſpecialy out-tak,   2988

---

[1] "not" seems required.

THE SECOND MESSAGE TO THE BLACK KNIGHT.

He thinkith ewill contempnit for to bee,
Confidering how that the neceffitee
Moſt prinſpally to yhowr ſupporting lyis.
Tharfor my conſell is, yhow to dewyſ,   2992
And ek ʒhowre-felf in yhowr trefpas accuſ,

ask him mercy, therefore, and excuse your guilt.

And afk hyme mercy, and yhour gilt excuſ.
For well it oucht o prince or o king
Til honore and til cheriſ in al thing   2996
O worthi man, that is in knychthed prewit.
For throw the body of o man efchevit
Mony o wondir, mony one aduenture,
That merwell war til any creature.   3000
And als oft-tyme is boith hard & fen,

For often, by one knight's prowess, have 40,000 been worsted by 5,000.

Quhar xl thoufand haith difcumfit ben
Vith v thoufand, and only be o knycht;
For throw his ftrenth, his vorfchip, & his mycht,   3004
His falowfchip fich comfort of hym tais
That thai ne dreid the danger of thar fays.
And thus, madem, I wot, withouten were,

If yon knight will continue to help the king,

If that ʒhone knycht this day will perfywere   3008
With his manhed for helping of the king,
We fal have cauſ to dred in to no thing.
Our folk of hyme thai fal fich comfort tak,
And fo adred thar ennemys fal mak,   3012
That fur I am, onys or the nycht,

yon folk shall perforce take to flight."

Of forſ ʒhone folk fal tak one them the flycht:
Wharffor, madem, that ʒhe have gilt to mend,
My confell is one to ʒhon knycht ʒe fend."   3016

She consents to send a message.

"Sir," quod fche, "quhat pleffith yhow to do
ʒhe may dewyſ, and I confent thar-to."
Than was the lady of melyhalt content,
And to fir gawan in-to-contynent   3020

[Fol. 37 b.]

Sche clepit the maid, wich that paffit ar;

A maiden is therefore sent to say,

And he hir bad the mefag thus duclar.
"Say [to][1] the knycht, the quen hir recommendith,

---

[1] "to" seems required.

SIR GAWANE SENDS HIM TEN SPEARS MORE.

And fal correk in quhat that fche offendith 3024
At his awn will, how fo hyme lift dewyſ;
And hyme exortith, in moft humyll wyſ, — *that the queen humbly exhorts him*
As euer he will, whar that fche can or may,
Or powar haith hir charg, be ony way, 3028
And for his worfchip and his hie manhede,
And for hir luf, to helpen in that ned — *to help in that need to preserve the king's honour, and to deserve her thanks.*
The kingis honore, his land fore to preferf,
That he hir thonk for euer may deferf." 3032
And four fquyaris chargit he alfo
With thre horſ and fperis x to go — *Sir Gawane also sends four squires with three horses and ten spears.*
Furth to the knycht, hyme prayng for his fak,
At his raqueft thame in his ned to tak. 3036

[T]he maden furth with the fqwyaris is went
One to the knycht, and fchawith yar entent.
Tho mefag hard, and ek ye prefent feñ, — *The message heard, he inquires about the queen,*
He anfwerit, and afkith of the qwen·; 3040
"Sir," quod fche, [" sche]¹ in to ȝhone bartiis lyis, — *and is told that from yon parapet she can witness his deeds.*
Whar that this day yhour dedis fal dewyſ,
Yhowr manhed, yhour worfchip, and affere,
How ȝhe conteñ, and how yhe armys bere; 3044
The quen hir-felf, and many o lady to,
Sal Iugis be, and vitnes how yhe do."
Than he, whois hart ftant in o new aray,
Saith, "damyceyll, on to my lady fay, 3048 — *He returns a message that he is the queen's knight.*
How euer that hir lykith that it bee,
Als far as wit or powar is in me,
I am hir knycht, I fal at hir command
Do at I may, withouten more demand. 3052
And to fir gawan, for his gret gentriſ,
Me recommend and thonk a thoufand fyſ."
With that o fper he takith in his hond,
And fo in to his fterapis can he ftond 3056 — *He stands in his stirrups; and seems to increase a foot in height.*
That to fir gawan femyth that the knycht

---

¹ A second "sche" is here required.

THE BLACK KNIGHT'S CHARGE.

Encrefyng gon o larg fut one hycht;
And to the ladice faith he, and the qwen,
"3hon is the knycht that euer I have fen   3060
In al my tyme moft knychtly of affere,
And in hyme-felf gon fareft armys bere."

[Fol. 38 a.]
Greatly encouraged,

[T]he knycht that haith Remembrit in his thocht
The qwenys chargis, & how fche hym befocht,   3064
Curag can encrefing to his hart;
His curfer lap, and gan onon to ftart;
And he the fqwaris haith reqwyrit fo,
That thai with hyme one to the feld wald go.   3068

without delay he crosses over the river to the field;

Than goith he one, withouten mor abaid,
And our the reuar to the feld he raid;
Don goith his fpere onone In to the Reft,
And in he goith, withouten mor areft,   3072

and goes in wherever he sees most peril.

Thar as he faw moft perell and moft dred
In al the feld, and moft of help[1] had ned,
Whar femblyt was the firft-conqueft king
With mony o knycht that was in his leding.   3076

He overthrows two knights.

The firft he met, doune goith boith horß & man;
The fper was holl, and to the next he Rañ
That helpit hyme his hawbrek nor his fcheld,
Bot throuch and throuch haith perfit in the feld.   3080

Sir Kay, Sir Sygramors, Sir Gresown, Sir Ywan, Sir Brandellis, and Gahers, all six in a race spur across the field with stretched spears,

Sir kay, the wich haith this encontyr fen,
His horß he ftrekith our the larg gren,
And fir fygramors ek the defyrand,
With fir grefown cummyth at yar honde,   3084
Son of the duk, and alfua fir ywan
The baftart, and fir brandellis onan,
And gaherß, wich that broyir was
To gawan; thir fex in a Raß   3088
Deliuerly com prekand our the feldis
With fperis ftraucht, and couerit with thar fcheldis;
Sum for love, fum honor to purcheß,

and 100 knights after them.

And aftir them one hundereth knychtis was,   3092

[1] MS. "held."

SIX KNIGHTS FOLLOW HIM. 91

In famyne will, thar manhed to affay.
On his v falowis clepit than fir kay,
And faith them, "firis, thar has ȝhonder ben — *Sir Kay exhorts them*
A courß that neuer-more farar was fen   3096
Maid be o knycht, and we ar cummyn ilkon
Only ws one [his] worfchip to difpone ;
And neuer we in al our dais mycht
Have bet axampil than iffith ws ȝone knycht 3100
Of well doing ; and her I hecht for me — *to keep near the black knight,*
Ner hyme al day, if that I may, to bee, — *and follow his guidance all day.*
And folow hyme at al [my] mycht I fall,
Bot deth or vthir adwentur me fall.   3104
With that thir fex, al in one affent,
With frefch curag In to the feld Is went.
The blak knychtis fpere in pecis goñe,   *[Fol. 38 b.]*
Frome o fqwyar oñe vthir haith he toñe,   3108 *With a second spear, the black knight seeks the field, closely followed by the six.*
And to the feld onone he goith ful rycht ;
Thir fex with hyme ay holdith at yar mycht.
And than bygan his wonderis in the feld ;
Thar was no helme, no hawbryk, nore no fcheld, 3112
Nor yhit no knycht fo hardy, ferß, nore ftout, — *No knight nor armour can withstand him.*
No ȝhit no maner armour mycht hald owt
His ftrenth, nore was of powar to withftond ;
So mych of armys dyde he with his honde,   3116
That euery wight ferleit of his deid, — *Every wight wonders at his deeds.*
And al his fois ftondith ful of dreid.
So befely he can his tyme difpend,
That of the fperis wich fir gawan fend,   3120
Holl of them all thar was not lewit oñe ; — *He uses up all Gawane's spears.*
Throw wich but mercy to the deyth is gon
Ful many o knycht, and many o weriour,
That couth fuften ful hardely o ftour.   3124
And of his horß fupprifit ded ar two, — *Two horses of his are killed, and he fights on foot.*
One of his awn, of gawanis one alfo,
And he one fut was fechtand one the gren,
When that fir kay haith with his falowis feñ ; 3128

SIR KAY ASKS WHO THE BLACK KNIGHT IS.

<small>The squire brings him a fresh horse;</small>
The fqwyar with his horſſ than to hym brocht;
Magre his fois he to his courfeir focht
Deliuerly, as of o mychty hart,
<small>he leaps into the saddle without stirrups.</small>
Without fteropis in to his fadill ftart,   3132
That euery wycht beholding mervell has
Of his ftrenth and deliuer befynes.
<small>Sir Kay asks who he is,</small>
Sir kay, feing his horſſ, and how that thai
War cled in to fir gawanis aray,   3136
Afkith at the fquyar if he knewith
What that he was, this knycht? & he hym fchewith
<small>but the squire cannot tell.</small>
He wift no thing quhat that he was, nore hee
Befor that day hyme neuer faw with Ee.   3140
Than afkith he, how and one quhat wyſſ
On gawanis horſſ makith hyme fich feruice?
The fqw[y]ar faith, "forfuth y wot no more;
My lord ws bad, I not the cauſſ quharfore."   3144
<small>The black knight returns to the field.</small>
The blak knycht, horfit, to the feld can few
Als frefch as he was in the morow new;
<small>The six comrades follow him.</small>
The fex falowis folowit hyme ilkone,
And al in front on to the feld ar goñ;   3148
<small>[Fol. 39 a.]</small>
Rycht frefchly one thar ennemys thai foght,
And many o fair poynt of armys vroght.
<small>Malangin's host is discomfited by king Ydras; and retreats to join the second line, commanded by the Conquest-king;</small>
[T]han hapnyt to king malangins oft
By ydras king difcumfit was, & loft,   3152
And fled, and to the conqueſt-king ar goñe,
Thar boith the batellis affemblit In to one;
King malengynis in to his hart was wo,
For of hyme-felf no better knycht mycht go;   3156
<small>so that 40,000 are now opposed to 15,000 of Arthur's.</small>
Thar xl thoufand war thai for xv.
Than mycht the feld rycht perellus be fen
Of armyt knychtis gaping one the ground;
Sum deith, and fum with mony a grewous wond;   3160
For arthuris knychtis, that manly war and gud,
Suppos that vthir was o multitude,
Refauit tham well at the fperis end;
But one fuch wyſſ thai may not lang defend.   3164

THE BLACK KNIGHT'S PROWESS. 93

The blak knycht faw the danger of the feld, The black knight,
And al his doingis knowith quho beheld, knowing who is beholding him,
And ek remembrith in to his entent
Of the mefag that fche haith to hyme fent: 3168
Than curag, ftrenth encrefing with manhed,
Ful lyk o knycht one to the feld he raid,
Thinking to do his ladice love to have, thinks to have
Or than his deth befor hir to refave. 3172 his lady's love, or die before her.
Thar he begynyth in his ferſ curag
Of armys, as o lyoune in his rag;
Than merwell was his doing to behold;
Thar was no knycht fo ftrong, nor yhit fo bold, 3176
That in the feld befor his fuerd he met,
Nor he fo hard his ftrok apone hyme fet,
That ded or wondit to the erth he focht;
For thar was not bot wonderis that he wrocht. 3180 He works nothing but wonders;
And magre of his fois euerilkone,
In to the feld oft tymys hyme alon and often passes alone through the field.
Throuch and throuch he paffith to & fro;
For in the ward[1] it was the maner tho 3184
That non o knycht fhuld be the brydill tak
Hyme to oreft, nore cum behynd his bak,
Nor mo than on at onys one o knycht
Shuld ftrik, for that tyme worfchip ftud fo rycht. 3188
Ʒhit was the feld rycht perellus and ftrong
Till arthuris folk, fet thai contenyt longe;
Bot in fich wyſ this blak knycht can conten, [Fol. 39 b.]
That thai, the wich that hath his manhed fen, 3192 He fights in such wise as to encourage all who see his deeds.
Sich hardyment haith takyne In his ded,
Them thocht thai had no maner cauſ of dred,
Als long as he mycht owthir ryd or go,
At euery ned he them recomfort fo. 3196
Sir kay haith with his falowis al the day Sir Kay and his fellows follow him all day
Folowit hyme al that he can or may,

---

[1] Another spelling of *warld*, i.e. world, which occurs in the fuller form in l. 3212.

And wondir well thai have in armys p*r*ewit,
And w*it*h thar manhed oft thar folk relewit ;   3200
Bot well thai faucht in diue*r*ſ placis fere,

But at last they are nearly all overpowered by numbers.
W*it*h multitud ya*r* folk confuſit were,
That long in ſich wyſ my*ch*t thai no*ch*t conteñ.

Sir Kay sends Gawane's squire with a message to Sir Harwy that he ought not to suffer the best knight that ever bore arms to be surprised,
S*i*r kay, that hath ſ*i*r gawans qſquyar*is* ſen,   3204
He clepit hyme, and haith hyme prayt ſo,
That to ſ*i*r harwy the rewell wil he go,
And ſay to hyme, "ws think hyme ewil awyſit ;
For her throuch hyme he ſufferit be ſuppriſit   3208
The beſt kny*ch*t that eue*r* armys bur ;
And if it ſo befell of adwentur,
In his defalt, that he be ded or lamyt,
This warld ſal have hyme vtraly defamyt.   3212

nor six knights of the Round Table to be discomfited.
And her ar of the round table alſo
A faloufchip, that ſall in well and wo
Abid w*it*h hyme, and furt*h* for to endur
Of lyf or deth, this day, thar adwentur ;   3216
And if ſo fal difcumfyt at thai bee,
The king may ſay that wond*er* ewill haith he
Contenit hyme, and kepit his honore,
Thus for to tyne of chevalry the flour ! "   3220

The squire takes the message.
The ſqw[y]ar hard, and furt*h* his way Raid,
In termys ſchort he al his meſag ſaid.
S*i*r harwy faith, "y wytneſ god, that I
Neue*r* in my days comytit tratory,   3224
And if I now begyne In to myne eld,
In ewill tyme fyrſt com I to this feld ;

Sir Harwy says that Sir Kay shall have no cause to reprove him.
Bot, if god will, I ſal me ſon difcharg.
Say to ſ*i*r kay, I ſal not ber the charg,   3228
He ſal no mat*er* have me to rapref,
I ſal amend this mys if that I lef."
The ſqwyar went and tellit to ſ*i*r kay ;

Sir Harwy comes to support them ;
And ſ*i*r harwy, in al the haſt he may,   3232
Aſſemblyt hath his oft*is*, & onoñ

[Fol. 40 *a*.] In gr*et* deſyre on the feld is gon

Before his folk, and haldith fur*th* his way;
Don goith his fper, and ewyne before f*ir* kay 3236
So hard o kny*ch*t he ftrykith in his ten
That horſ and he lay boith apone the gren.
S*ir* gawan faw the count*er* that he maad,
And leuch for al the farues that he had: 3240
That day f*ir* harwy prewyt in the feld   *and proves him-*
Of armys more than longith to his eld,   *self a better war-*
   rior than might
   have been ex-
For he was more than fyfty yher of ag,   *pected of one so*
   old.
Set he was ferſ and ʒong in his curag; 3244
And fro that he aſſemblyt his bataill
Doune goith the folk of galot*is* al haill;   *Galiot's folk are*
   beaten.
For to wi*th*ſtond thai war of no poware,
And yhit of folk x thoufand mo thei vare. 3248

Kyng valydone, that fauch on fuch o wyſ   *King Valydone*
   comes to support
   them.
His falowis danger*it* w*ith* thar ennemys,
W*ith* al his folk, being freſ and new,
Goith to the feld onon, them to reſſkew; 3252
Thar was the feld ry*ch*t p*er*ellus aʒañe,
Of arthuris folk ful many on var ſlan.

Bot angus, quhich that lykith not to bid,   *Angus comes to*
   aid Arthur's men.
And faw the p*er*ell one the tother ſid, 3256
His ſted he ſtrok, and w*ith* his oſt is gon
Whar was moſt ned, and thar the feld has ton.

Kyng clamedyus makith non abaid,   *Clamedyus comes*
   to aid Galiot's
Bot w*ith* his oſt one to the ſid he raid. 3260 *men.*

And ywons king, that haith his cu*m*myn ſen,   *Ywons encoun-*
   ters Clamedyus.
Encount*er*it hyme in myddis of the greñ.
The aucht batell*is* aſſemblyt one this wiſ;
On ather half the clamore and the cryiſ 3264 *Great clamour*
   and lamentable
Was lametable and petws for til her,   *cries on either*
   side.
Of kny*ch*t*is* wich in diue*r*ſ placis ſere
Wondit war, and fallyng to and fro,
ʒhit galyot*is* folk war xx thoufand mo. 3268

The blak kny*ch*t than on to hyme-felf he faid: *The black knight*
   bids himself re-
"Remembir the, how yhow haith ben araid,   *member love's*
   power over him;

    Ay fen ye hour that yow was makid knycht,
    With love, aȝane quhois powar & whois mycht   3272
    Yow haith no ftrenth, yow may It not endur,
    Nor ȝhit non vthir erthly creatur ;

and that only his lady's mercy or his life's end can amend him.
    And bot two thingis ar the to amend,
    Thi ladice mercy, or thi lyvys end.   3276
    And well yhow wot that on to hir prefens,

[Fol. 40 b.]
    Til hir eftat, nor til hir excellens,
    Thi febilneſſ neuermore is able
    For to attan, fche is fo honorable.   3280
    And fen no way yow may fo hie extend,

He counsels himself to strive for her thanks,
    My verray confell is, that yow pretend
    This day, (fen yow becummyne art hir knycht
    Of hir comand, and fechtit in hir fycht),   3284
    And well yow fchaw, fen yow may do no mor,
    That of refone fche fal the thank tharfore ;

and to be ashamed of every point of cowardice.
    Of euery poynt of cowardy yow fcham,
    And in til armys purcheſſ the fum nam."   3288
    With that of love in to o new defir

Swift as a crossbow-bolt he seeks the field.
    His fpere he ftraucht, and fwift as any wyre
    With al his forſſ the nereft feld he foght ;
    His ful ftrenth in armys thar he vroght,   3292
    In to the feld rufching to and fro,
    Doune goith the man, doune goith the horſſ alfo ;
    Sum throw the fcheld is perfit to the hart,
    Sum throw the hed, he may It not aftart.   3296

His sword carves the head from some, and cuts the arms of others in twain.
    His bludy fuerd he dreuch, that carwit fo
    Fro fum the hed, and fum the arm in two ;
    Sum in the feld fellit is in fwoñ,
    Throw fum his fuerd goith to the fadill doune.   3300
    His fois waren abafit of his dedis,
    His mortell ftrok fo gretly for to dred Is ;

When his foes see him, they leave the place for dread of death.
    Whar thai hyme faw, within a lytall fpace,
    For dreid of ded, thai levyng hyme the place,   3304
    That many o ftrok ful oft he haith forlorñ ;
    The fpedy horſſ away the knycht hath borñ.

In to his wyrking neuermore he feft,
Nor non abaid he makith, nor areft. 3308
His falowis, fo in his knychthed affuryd, *His knightly deeds assure his fellows.*
Thai ar recomfort, thar manhed is recoueryt,
And one thar fois ful ferfly thai foght,
Thar goith the lyf of many o knycht to nocht. 3312
So was the batell wonderful to tell,
Of knychtis to fe the multitud that fell,
That pety was til ony knycht to feñ *It was pitiful to see the knights gaping upon the green.*
The knychtis lying gaping on the gren. 3316
The blak knycht ay continewit fo faft,
Whill¹ many one, difcumfit at the laft,
Are fled, and planly of the feld thei pas: [Fol. 41 a.]
And galyot haith wondyr, for he was 3320 *Galiot asks his men why they flee.*
Of mor powar, and afkit at them qwhy
As cowartis thai fled fa fchamfully?
Than faith o knycht, for wondit in the brayne, *A knight replies, that whoever likes may go and see marvels.*
"Who lykith, he may Retwrn azayne 3324
Frome qwhens we come, merwalis for to fee,
That in his tyme neuer fich fauch hee."
"Marwell," quod he, "that dar I boldly fay *Galiot asks, what marvels; and the knight tells him there is a knight who vanquishes all;*
Thay may be callit, and quhat thai ar, I pray?" 3328
"Schir, in the feld forfuth thar is o knycht,
That only throw his body and his mycht
Wencuffith all, that thar may non fuften
His ftrokis, thai ar fo fureows and ken. 3332
He farith as o lyone or o beyre, *who fares as a lion or a bear;*
Wod in his rag, for fich is his affere.
Nor he the knycht in to the armys Red, *to whom the red knight bears no comparison.*
Wich at the first affemble in this fted 3336
Wencuffith all, and had the holl renown,
He may to this be no comparyfoune,
Fore neuer he fefith fen the day vas goñ,
Bot euermore continewit in to one." 3340

¹ MS. "Whilk."

Galiot says he will go and see.	Quod galiot, " in nome of god and we Al, be tyme, the futhfaftneſſ fal see."
Galiot is armed, rallies the flyers, and encourages his men.	[T]han he in armys that he had is gon, And to the feld with hyme aȝane hath ton 3344 Al the flearis, and foundyne [in]¹ fich aray His folk, that ner difcumfyt al war thay ; Bot quhen thai faw cummyne our the plan Thar lord, thai tuk fich hardement aȝañ, 3348
They shout their war-cries.	That thar effenȝeis lowd thai gon to cry. He chargit tham to go, that ware hyme by, Straucht to the feld, with al thar holl forſſ ; And thai, the wich that fparit not the horſſ, 3352 All redy war to fillyng his command, And frefchly went, withowten more demand : Throw qwich thar folk recoueryt haith thar place,
All think a new host is coming.	For al the feld prefwmyt that thar was 3356 O new oft, one fuch o wyſſ thai foght ;
Arthur's folk determine rather to die than fly.	Whar arthuris folk had paffith al to nocht, Ne war that thai the better war ilkoñe, And at thai can them vtraly difpoñe 3360
[Fol. 41 b.]	Rathar to dee than flee, in thar entent, And of the blak knycht haith fich hardyment ; For at al perell, al harmys, and myfchef, In tyme of ned he can tham al ralef. 3364 [T]har was the batell dangerus & ftrong, Gret was the pres, bath perellus & throng ;
The black knight is borne to the ground.	The blak knycht is born on to the ground, His horſſ hyme falyth, that fellith dethis wound. 3368
The six comrades go to the earth.	The vi falowis, that falowit hyme al day, Sich was the preſſ, that to the erth go thay ; And thar in myd among his ennemys He was about enclofit one fich wyſſ 3372
None know where he is.	That quhare he was non of [his] falowis knew, Nor mycht nocht cum to help hyme, nore refkew.

¹ The sense, but not the metre, requires " in."

And thus among his ennemys allon
His nakid fuerd out of his hond haith ton; 3376 *He defends himself with his sword.*
And thar he prewit his wertew & his ftrenth;
For thar was none within the fuerdis lenth
That came, bot he goith to confufioune.
Thar was no helme, thar was no habirioune, 3380 *No helm nor habergeon may resist his sword*
That may refift his fuerd, he fmytith so;
One euery fyd he helpith to and fro,
That al about the compas thai mycht ken;
The ded horß lyith virflyng with the men. 3384
Thai hyme affalʒeing both with fcheld & fpere,
And he aʒane; as at the ftok the bere   *He fares like a bear at the stake, that snubs the hardy hounds.*
Snybbith the hardy houndis that ar ken,
So farith he; for neuer mycht be fen   3388
His fuerd to reft, that in the gret rout
He rowmyth all the compas hyme about.

[A]nd galiot, beholding his manhed,
Within his-felf wonderith of his ded,   3392 *Galiot wonders at his deeds;*
How that the body only of o knycht
Haith fich o ftrenth, haith fich affere & mycht;
Than faid he thus, "I wald not that throw me,
Or for my cauß, that fuch o knycht fuld dee, 3396 *and says that such a knight shall not die on his account.*
To conquer all this world that is fo larg."
His horß than can he with his fpuris charg,
A gret trunfioune In to his hond hath ton,
And in the thikeft of the preß is goñ, 3400
And al his folk chargit he to feß.   *He charges all his folk to cease;*
At his command thai levyng al the preß;
And quhen he had departit all the rout,   [Fol. 42 a.]
He faid, "fir knycht, havith now no dout." 3404
Wich anfwerit, "I have no cauß to dred."
"ʒis," quod he, "fa euer god me fped,   *and assures the black knight that he will himself warrant him from all harm.*
Bot apone fut quhill ʒe ar fechtand here,
And yhow defendith apone fich manere, 3408
So hardely, and ek fo lyk o knycht,
I fal my-felf with al my holl mycht

	Be yhour defens, and varand fra al harmys;	
	Bot had yhe left of worſchip In til armys,	3412
	What I have don I wold apone no wyſſ;	
	Bot ſen yhe ar of knychthed ſo to prys,	
	ȝhe ſal[1] no maner cauſſ have for to dred:	
He offers him as many horses as he needs; and proposes that they shall never again part.	And ſet yhour horſſ be ſalit at this ned,	3416
	Diſpleſſ yhow not, for-quhy ȝe ſal not want	
	Als many as yhow lykith for to hawnt;	
	And I my-ſelf, I ſal yhowr ſqwyar bee,	
	And, if god will, neuer more ſal wee	3420
He 'lights from his horse, and gives him to Lancelot, who thanks him.	Depart;" with that, anon he can to lycht	
	Doune frome his horſſ, and gaf hyme to yᵉ knycht.	
	The lord he thonkit, and the horſſ hath ton,	
	And als ſo freſch one to the feld is gon,	3424
	As at no ſtrokis he that day had ben.	
	His falowis glad, one horſſ that hath hym ſen,	
	To galiot one vthir horſſ thai broght;	
	And he goith one, and frome the feld he focht,	3428
Galiot returns to his host, and chooses a band of 10,000 men.	And to the plan quhar that his oftis were;	
	And brandymagus chargit he to ſtere	
	Efter hyme, within a lytill ſpace,	
	And x thouſand he takyne with hym haſſ.	3432
	Towart the feld onon he can to Rid,	
	And chargit them befor ye oſt to byd.	
The trumpets, clarions, horns, and bugles are sounded.	Wp goith the trumpetis, and the claryownis,	
	Hornys, bugillis blawing furth thar ſownis,	3436
	That al the cuntre reſownit hath about;	
Arthur's folk despair.	Than arthuris folk var in diſpar & dout,	
	That hard the noys, and ſaw the multitud	
	Of freſch folk; thai cam as thai war wod.	3440
The sable knight, still fearless,	[B]ot he that was withowten any dred,	
	In ſabill cled, and ſaw the gret ned,	
	Aſſemblyt al his falowis, and arayd;	
harangues his men, saying,	And thus to them in manly termes ſaid:	3444

MS. "ſalt."

"What that ȝe ar I knaw not yhour eſtat,   [Fol. 42 *b*.]
Bot of manhed and worſchip, well I wat,
Out throuch this warld yhe aw to be commendit,
This day ȝe have ſo knychtly yhow defendit.   3448
And now yhe ſee how that, aȝanis the nycht,
Yhour ennemys pretendit with thar myght
Of multitud, and with thar new oſt,
And with thar buglis and thar wyndis boſt   3452
Freſchly cummyng In to ſich aray,
To iſyne yhow one owtrag¹ or affray.
And now almoſt cummyne Is the nycht,
Quharfor yhour ſtrenth, yhour curag, & yhovr mycht
Yhe occupye in to ſo manly wyſs,
That the worſchip of knychthed & empryſs
That yhe have wonyng, and ye gret renown
Be not yloſt, be not ylaid doune.   3460
For one hour the ſufferyng of diſtreſs,
Gret harm It war yhe tyne the hie encreſs
Of vorſchip, feruit al this day before.
And to yhow al my conſell is, tharfore,   3464
With manly curag, but radour, yhe pretend
To met tham ſcharply at the ſperis end,
So that thei feil the cold ſperis poynt
Out-throw thar ſcheldis, in thar hartis poynt.   3468
So fal thai fynd we ar no-thing affrayt;
Whar-throuch we fall the well leſs be aſſayt.
If that we met them ſcharply in the berd,
The formeſt fal mak al the laif afferd."   3472
And with o woyſs thai cry al, "ſir knycht,
Apone yhour manhed, and yhour gret mycht,
We fal abid, for no man ſhall eſchef
Frome yhow this day, his manhed for to pref."   3476
And to his oſt the lord ſir yvane ſaid,
"Yhe comfort yow, yhe be no-thing affrayd,

        ¹ MS. "owtray." See Glossary.

THE POEM ABRUPTLY ENDS.

Ws ned no more to dreding of fuppriß;

the strength of their enemies.   We fe the ftrenth of al our ennemys."   3480

Thus he faid, for he wend thai var no mo,

Sir Gawane, however, knew better.   Bot fir gawan knew well It vas not fo;

For al the oft*is* my*ch*t he fe al day,

And the gret hoft he faw quhar y*a*t it lay.   3484

Gallot also exhorts his men.   [A]nd galiot he can his folk exort,

Befeching them to be of good comfort,

And fich econter

[*The rest is wanting.*]

NOTES.

[It may be observed, once for all, that the expression *in to* repeatedly occurs where we should simply use *in*; and *one to* is in like manner put for *unto*. The ending *-ith* (for *-ed*) is frequent in the past tense, and *-it* (also for *-ed*) in the past participle, though this distinction is not always observed. A still more noticeable ending is *-ing* (for *-en*) in the infinitive. Observe further that the letters *v*, *u*, and *w* are perfectly convertible, and used quite indiscriminately; so that *wpone* means *upon*; *vthir* means *uthir*, i. e, *other*: *our* is put for *over*; *vounde* signifies *wound*, etc.]

Page 1, line 1. *The soft morow.* This nominative case has no verb. A similar construction occurs in the first lines of Books II. and III. 4. *Uprisith—his hot courss*, Upriseth in his hot course; *chare*, chariot. 6. *sent*, sendeth; so also *stant*, standeth, l. 326. 8. *valkyne*, waken. 10. *gyrss*, grass. 11. *assay*, assault. 13. *wox*, voice. 17. *frome I can*, from the time that I did. 18. *It dewit me*, it availed me. Jamieson gives "*Dow*, 1. to be able; A.S. *dugan* (*valere*), to be able. 2. to avail; Teut. *doogen*."

P. 2, l. 23. *hewy ȝerys*, heavy years. 24. "Until that Phœbus had thrice gone through his full circuits" (lit. spheres). See the peculiar use of "pas" in other places. 26. "So, by such a manner, was my lot fated;" see l. 41. 28. *carving can*, did cut. 30. *be the morow*, by the morn. 36. *neulyngis*, newly, anew. 43. *walkith*, walked. 50. *I-clede*, y-clad, clad. Ch. has *clede*. 54. "No one within thought he could be seen by any wight outside."

P. 3, l. 56. *clos it*, enclose it; the MS. has *closit*. 57. *alphest*. This reading of the MS. is an error for *alcest*. See Chaucer, Prologue to Legend of good women, l. 511:

"The grete goodnesse of the quene Alceste,
That turned was into a dayesye,"

Alceste being the contracted form of Alcestis. 59. *Wnclosing gane*, did unclose. 60. "The bright sun had illumined the spray, and had updrawn (upwarped) into the lusty air the night's soft (sober) and moist showers; and had made the morning soft, pleasant, and fair." With this difficult passage we should compare l. 2477. 66. *Quhill*, until. 67. *till ony vicht*, to any wight. 69. *Bot gladness til the thochtful, euer mo*, etc., " But, as for gladness to the melancholy man, evermore the more he seeth of it, the more wo he hath." 73. *represent*, represented (accented on the second syllable). 74. *Al day gan be sor*, etc., "All the day, my spirit began to dwell in torment, through sorrow of thought;" *be sor*, by sorrow (A.S. *sorh*). 77. *Ore slep, or how I wot*, "Or sleep, ere I knew how." 83. *A-licht*, alighted. 84. *levis in to were*, livest in doubt.

P. 4, l. 91. *be morow*, by morrow; at early morn. 99. *set*, although. 103. *weil accordinge*, very fitting. 105. *long ore he be sonde*, (It is) long ere he be sound. 108. *seith, for to consel*, saith, that as for concealing or shewing, etc. 109. *althir-best*, lit. best of all; see Chaucer's use of *alderfirst, alderlast*.

P. 5, l. 127. *lat be thi nyss dispare*, let be thy nice (foolish) despair. 128. *erith*, earth. 134. *schall hyme hating*, shall hate him. The termination *-ing* is here the sign of the infinitive mood after the verb *shall*. 140. *Set*, although. 146. *tak one hand and mak*, undertake and compose; *trety*, treatise; *vnkouth*, unknown, new. 151. *belevis*, believe will please thy lady. 160. *yis*, this.

P. 6, l. 161. *troucht*, truth. 163. *discharge*, release. 170. *spir*, sphere. 171. "At command of a wise (god from) whose vision," etc. We sometimes find in old English the adjective "a wise" used absolutely for "a wise man." See "Le Morte Arthur," ed. F. J. Furnivall, l. 3318. 175. *tynt*, lost. 177. *be this worldis fame*. Here again, as in many other passages, "be" expresses with relation to, as regards. 185. *yaim*, them. 191. *demande*, demur.

P. 7, l. 198. *Quhill*, until. 200. *conten*, treat; lit. contain. 202. Lancelot is here called the son of Ban, king of Albanak; so again in l. 1447. 204. *redis*, read. 214. "I will not waste my efforts thereupon." 219. *unwyst*, unwist, unknown. 225. *nome*, name. 226. *Iwondit to the stak*, very deeply wounded; but there is no doubt about the origin of the phrase. See Glossary. 228. *astart*, get rid of it, escape it.

P. 8, l. 240. *dedenyt to aras*, deigned to pluck out. 244. *hurtare*, hurter. 245. *Iwond*, wounded. 248. *ful wicht*, full nimble. 251. *of quhome*, by whom. 253. *send*, sent. 257. *pasing vassolag*, surpassing prowess. 260. "Passed down into the fell caves." 264. *tane*, taken. 266. *cwre*, care.

P. 9, l. 267. *gart be maid*, caused to be made. 271. *awoue*, vow. 275. *in to that gret Revare*, in that great river. 284. *o gret confusione of pupil and knychtis, al enarmyt*, a great medley of people and knights, all fully armed. Stevenson actually reads *unarmyt!* 294. *I wil report*; both here and in l. 320 we should almost expect to find "*I nil report;*" i.e. I will not tell. It must mean, "I will

tell you why I omit to mention these things." Compare lines 266, 320. 297. *thing*, think.
P. 10, l. 305. *veris*, wars. 306. *be the wais*, by the ways. 307. *Tuex*, betwixt; *accorde*, agreement. 314. *mot*, must. 316. *stek*, concluded. 319. *most conpilour*, very great composer. 320. "As to whose name I will only say, that it is unfit," etc. 326. *stant*, standeth. 328. *yroung*, rung. 330. *beith*, shall be; observe the *future* sense of *beith* in this place. 331. *suet*, sweet. 332. "His soul in bliss preserved be on that account." 334. *and this endit*. Whether *endit* here refers to *inditing* or *ending* is perhaps doubtful.

NOTES TO BOOK I.

P. 11, l. 336. If by *aryeit* is here meant the *sign*, not the *constellation* of Aries, the day referred to is April 1 or 2, according to Chaucer's "Astrolabie." 338. *bewis*, boughs. 340. *makyne gone*, did make. 341. *in ther chere*, after their fashion. (For *chere*, see Glossary.) 345. *auerding to*, belonging to. 351. *Anoit*, annoyed. 352. *For why*, wherefore; so also *for-thi*, therefore. 354. *can*, began. 355. *sende*, sent. 358. *heryng*, hear (infin. mood). In the next line it occurs as a present participle. 362. *to pas hyme*, to go, depart. 364. *meit*, to dream of; *aperans*, an appearance, apparition.
P. 12, l. 365. *hore*, hair. 375. *vombe*, womb; hence bowels. 377. *stert*, started. 384. *gert*, caused. 390. *traist*, trust. 397. *demande*, demur, delay. 398. *at*, that.
P. 13, l. 407. *whill*, until. 408. *the*, they. 410. *to viting*, to know. 412. *shauyth al hall*, sheweth all whole. 414. *chesith*, chooseth. 422. *shire*, sir. 424. *fore to awysing*, in order to take counsel. 432. All this about *astronomy* (i. e. astrology) should be compared with Gower; Conf. Amantis, lib. vii; ed. Pauli, vol. 3, pp. 133, 134. Arachell, Nembrote, Moises, Hermes are there mentioned as astrologers. 433. The MS. has "set" (*not* with a long *s*). Mr Stevenson has "fet," which would seem right.
P. 14, l. 435. *nembrot*, Nimrod; see *Genesis and Exodus* (E. E. T. S.), l. 659. 436. *herymes*, miswritten for *herymes*, i. e. Hermes. 439. "The which they found were wondrously evil set." 440. *his sweuen met*, dreamed his dream. 443. *waryng in to were*, were in doubt. 444. *danger*, power to punish; compare Shakspere's use of the word. 457. *but delay*, without delay. 459. *stondith heuy cherith*, stood heavy-cheered, was sad in his demeanour. 465. *fundyng*, found. 466. *depend to*, depend upon.
P. 15, l. 475. *tone*, taken. 478. *assey*, test. 481. *record*, to tell out, speak. 487. *preseruith It allan*, is preserved alone. 499. *affy in-tyll*, rely upon. 500. *failye*, fail. 504. *there clergy*, their science.
P. 16, l. 519. "Through the watery lion, who is also faithful,

and through the leech and eke the water also, and through the counsel of the flower." It is very possible this passage is partly corrupt; l. 520 should certainly be (as may be seen from lines 2010, 2056), " And throuch the leich withouten medysyne."

The meanings of lion, leech, and flower are fully explained, however, in lines 2013-2120. 524. *weyne,* vain. 527. *passid nat his thoght,* left not his thoughts. 531. *rachis,* braches, dogs. 533. *grewhundis,* grayhounds. 536. This purely conjectural line is merely inserted to carry on the sense. It is imitated from line 3293. In the next line we should read "grewhundis," rather than "grewhund." 538. *Befor ther hedis,* before their heads.

P. 17, l. 545. "All armed, as was then the fashion." 546. *salust,* saluted. 548. *kend,* known. 549. *lewyth,* liveth. 552. The rime requires "land," as in l. 638. 553. *yald hyme our,* yield him over. 554. *if tribut,* give tribute. 566. *recist,* resist; *mone bee,* must be. 568. *be,* by. 569. *day moneth day,* ere this day month ; comp. l. 1162.

P. 18, l. 577. *fairhed,* fair-hood, beauty. 587. *magre myne entent,* in spite of my intention. 591. *nome,* took. 593. *Inquere at,* inquire of. 596. *wes,* was. 599. *rase,* rose. 605. *accordith,* agree thereto. 606. *recordith,* belongith. 607. *visare,* wiser.

P. 19, l. 621. *This spek I lest,* this I list to speak. 622. *varnit,* warned. 626. "Though the season of the year was contrary." 627. *atte,* at the. 629. *the ilk,* that (Scotch *thilk*). 632. *Melyhalt,* the name both of a hill, and of the town built upon it. 636. *affray,* terror. 642. *wnconquest,* unconquered. 643. *cwre,* care.

P. 20, l. 649. *nemmyt,* named. 652. *were,* war. 654. *or than to morn,* earlier than to-morrow. 660. *our few,* over few. 677. *northest,* north-east.

P. 21, l. 686. *fechteris,* fighters. 688. *holde,* held. 691. *presone,* prison. 697. *peite,* pity. 699. The metre of Lancelot's lament is that of Chaucer's "Cuckoo and Nightingale," and was very possibly copied from it. *Qwhat haue y gilt,* what crime have I committed. 702. *ago,* gone. 703. *nat,* naught; *me glaid,* gladden me. 706. *til haue,* to have. 709. *Sen thelke tyme,* since that time.

P. 22, l. 718. *of remed,* for a remedy. 719. *sesith,* ceaseth. 723. *with this lady,* by this lady. 728. *laisere,* leisure. 731. *diuerss wais sere,* divers several ways. 733. *bur,* bore. 735. *cher,* car. 740. *dout,* to fear. 745. *but were,* without doubt. This expression often occurs.

P. 23, l. 751. *few menye,* small company; an oddly sounding expression to modern ears. 753. *cold,* called. 754. *hot,* hight, was named. 755. *but in his cumpany,* unless he had with him. 757. *He saith ;* the speaker is the captain of the hundred knights, called in l. 806 *Maleginis.* 768. *als fell,* just as many. 777. *hard,* heard. 781. *clepit,* called.

NOTES. 107

P. 24, l. 793, *as he wel couth*, as he well knew how. 796. *sen*, seen. 800. *sen*, since. 806. *was hot*, was hight, was named. 809. *In myde the borde and festinit in the stell*, In the midst they encounter, and fastened in the steel. See l. 850. 812. *Rout*, company. 815. *ferde*, fourth. 817. *sauch thar latter batell steir*, saw their last division stir.

P. 25, l. 820. *gane his mortall fell*. A word seems here omitted; if after *mortall* we insert *strokis*, the sense will be, "His enemies began his mortall strokes to feel." 825. *worth*, worthy. It would improve the metre to read *worthy* (l. 875). 828. *In to were*, in war, in the strife. 829. *hyme bure*, bore himself. 839. *to-for*, heretofore. 841. *Atour*, i. e. *at over*, across. 842. *assall*, assault. The rime shews we should read *assaill*, as in l. 855. 849. *socht atour*, made their way across. The use of *seke* in Early English is curious.

P. 26, l. 861. *setith his payn vpone*, devotes his endeavours to. 868. *al to-kerwith*, wholly cutteth in pieces. 880. *dirk*, dark. 883. *tan and slan*, taken and slain.

P. 27, l. 895. It frequently occurs in the MS. that a space is left at the beginning of a line, and the first letter of the line is omitted. It is evident that the intention was that the first letter should be illuminated, and that this, after all, was not done. Here, for instance, the T is omitted, as indicated by the square brackets. So also in l. 1083, etc. 897. *pasing home*, go home. 899. *was vent*, had gone. 905. *dulay*, delay. So also *duclar* for *declare*. 907. *comyne*, came. 908. *ill paid*, displeased. 909. *homly*, humbly. Stevenson reads *hourly*, but this is wrong; see l. 914. 911. *carful*, full of care, unhappy. 912. *withouten were*, without doubt. 914. *lawly*, lowly. 918. *wight*, with (unusual, and perhaps wrong).

P. 28, l. 924. *leife*, live. 929. *eft*, after. 933. *thar longith*, there belongeth. 943. *I was for til excuss*, I had some excuse. 944. "Because I did behove (to do it), out of very need." 946. *lefe it but*, leave it without. 953. *ma*, make. 954. *ga*, go. 955. *of new*, anew. 958. *But if that deth or other lat certan*, "Except it be owing to death or other sure hindrance."

P. 29, l. 960. *be hold*, be held. MS. *behold*. Stevenson suggested the alteration, which is certainly correct. 961. *withthy*, on the condition that. 965. *promyt*, promise; *als fast as*, as soon as. 973. *ferd*, fourth. 982. "Where we shall decide the end of this war."

P. 30, l. 997. *cag*, cage, prison. 999. *amen*, pleasant. 1000. *vodis*, woods. 1004. *lust*, pleasure (Ch.). But the line is obscure; unless we read "*diuersitee*." 1009. "His spirit started (owing to the) love (which) anon hath caught him," etc. 1012. *at*, that. 1014. "(As to) whom they know not at all." 1019. *sen at*, since that. 1022. *the dewod*, devoid thee. 1024. *and*, if. 1026. *be ony mayne*, by any mean.

P. 31, l. 1027. *y red*, I advise. 1035. *To warnnyng*, to warn.

1040. *our the furdis*, over the fords. 1044. *oyer*. So in MS.; the *y* representing the old *th* (þ); other. 1046. *hufyng*, halting. 1050. *worschip*, honour. "It were more expedient to maintain your honour." 1058. *wonk*, winked. 1062. *vare*, aware.

P. 32, l. 1064. The meaning of "ferst-conquest" is "first-conquered" (*conquest* being Old Fr. for conquered). It is explained in l. 1547 as having been a title given to the king whom Galiot first subdued. 1067. *ferss*, fierce. 1070. *suppos*, although. 1073. *he*; viz. the shrew. 1077. The MS. has "fched." 1080. *ymen*, I mean. 1095. *tais*, takes.

P. 33, l. 1109. *Galyo.*, put for *Galiotes*, the genitive case-ending being often omitted, after a proper name especially. 1110. *prewit*, proved, tried. 1129. *traist*, trust. 1131. *that euery thing hath cure*, that (of) everything hath care.

P. 34, l. 1135. "Aye from the time that the sun began to light the world's face, until he was gone." 1137. *o forss*, perforce. 1141. *taiis*, takes. 1142. *hecht*, promised. 1151. *failȝeis*, fail. 1154. *fet*, fetched. 1156. *stant*, standeth. 1162. *resput*, respite. 1166. *very knychtis passing*, weary knights go.

P. 35, l. 1170. *till spere*, to inquire. 1177. *ne wor his worschip*, had it not been for his valour. 1187. *qwheyar*, whether. 1191—4. "And fond," etc. These four lines are now for the first time printed. They were omitted by Stevenson, evidently by accident. 1196. *Per dee*. Fr. *par Dieu:* an oath common in old ballads, generally in the form *pardy*. 1197. *vsyt*, used. 1198. "I advise that we go unto his arms" (armour). 1203. *haill*, whole.

P. 36, l. 1207. *abwsyt*, abused, i.e. made an ill use of. 1208. *vsyt*, used. 1209. *suppos the best that lewis*, even though (it were) the best that lives. 1217. *on slep*, asleep. The prefix *a-* in English is due to the Saxon *on*. 1221. *al to-hurt*, etc. See note in Glossary on the word *To-kerwith*. 1225. *sauch*, saw; *rewit*, rued, pitied. 1233. *one syd a lyt*, a little on one side. 1236. *our mekill*, over much.

P. 37, l. 1240. *yarof*, thereof. 1241. *ruput*, repute, think. 1242. *ablare*, abler, readier. 1253. Insert a comma after *thret*, and destroy that after *lowe*. The meaning perhaps is, "But what if he be appealed to and threatened, and (meanwhile) his heart be elsewhere set to love." Observe that *and* is often the third or fourth word in the sentence it should begin. See l. 2833. 1258. *ȝhe tyne yowr low*, you lose your love. 1260. *conclusit*, ended. 1265. *mokil*, much. 1268. *of new*, anew, again. 1273. *pan*, pain.

NOTES TO BOOK II.

P. 38, l. 1279. *thocht*, anxiety. 1284. *apperans*, i.e. vision, as in l. 364. 1295. *aqwynt*, acquainted; Burns uses *acquent*. 1297. *com*, coming.

NOTES. 109

P. 39, l. 1316. "So far out of the way you go in your course." Compare l. 1797. 1317. "Thy ship, that goeth upon the stormy surge, nigh of thy revels (i. e. because of thy revels) in the gulf it falls, where it is almost drowned in the peril." 1321. "In the wretched dance of wickedness." See the curious uses of the word "daunce" in Chaucer. 1323. *the son*, thee soon. 1330. *powert*, poverty; *as the-selwyne wat*, as thyself knows. 1334. *in to spousag*, in wedlock.

P. 40, l. 1343. The word *diuerss* is required to complete the line; cf. l. 731. 1352. *suppriss*, oppression. 1354. *wedwis*, widows. 1367. *that ilke*, that same. 1369. *sufferith*, makest to suffer.

P. 41, l. 1379. Eccles. iv. 9, 10. 1387. *yow mone*, thou must. 1392. *her-efter leif*, hereafter live. 1401. A comma is scarcely needed after "*sapiens*." It means "The fear of the Lord is the beginning of wisdom." Prov. ix. 10.

P. 42, l. 1409. *to ryng wnder his pess*, to reign under His peace, by His permission. Roquefort gives *pais*, licence, permission. 1420. *arour*, error. 1427. *leful*, lawful.

P. 43, l. 1447. Ban, king of Albanak, was Lancelot's father. See l. 202, 1450. 1474. The MS. has "affit."

P. 44, l. 1491. *tak the bak apone themself*, turn their backs. 1500. *yewyne*, given. 1504. *till*, to ; redundant. 1506. *stand aw*, stand in awe. So also in l. 2684. The same expression occurs in *The Bruce*, iii. 62, ed. Pinkerton, p. 42, ed. Jamieson ; and also in *Havelok*, l. 277, where the word *in*, supplied from conjecture, should be struck out.

P. 45, l. 1537. *throw his peple*, by his people. 1541. *Thus falith not*, etc., "Except wise conduct falleth to a king." 1546. It may be right to retain the spelling of the MS.—"kinghe;" for, though strange and unusual, it occurs again in l. 2527.

P. 46, l. 1556. *wende*, weened. 1560. *in to his contrare*, against him. 1568. *trewis*, truce. 1575. *his powar*, his chief army. 1576. *by the yhere*, by the ear, privately. 1579. *cold*, called ; as in l. 753.

P. 47, l. 1597. *home fair*, go home. 1608. *And;* redundant in modern English. For many of the precepts given by Amytans the author must have been indebted to Gower, or, at any rate, to the author of the *Secreta Secretorum*. See Gower ; Conf. Amantis ; ed. Pauli, lib. vii ; vol. 3, pp. 152—159. And cf. Tyrwhitt's note to the Canterbury Tales, l. 16915 ; and Warton's Hist. Eng. Poetry.

P. 48, l. 1628. *lest*, least ; *low*, law. It requires care to distinguish the two meanings of *low*, viz. *love* and *law*. 1633. *Iug*, judge.

P. 49, l. 1660. *sar*, sorely. 1666. A line omitted. The inserted line is purely conjectural.

P. 50, l. 1704. *pupelle*, people. 1708. *Inwyus*, envious. 1716. *longith*, belongeth. 1717. *the lykith*, it likes thee, thou art pleased.

P. 51, l. 1724. *betak til hyme*, confer upon him. 1730. *essy*,

NOTES.

easy. 1736. *for the nonis,* for the occasion. See White's Ormulum. 1739. *vn to the vorthi pur yow if,* unto the worthy poor thou give. 1742. *set nocht of gret substans,* though not of great value. 1754. *alowit,* approved of.

P. 52, l. 1761. *tynith,* loseth. 1763. *atonis,* at once. 1771. *resawe,* receive. 1773. *with two,* also.

P. 53, l. 1791. *well less, al-out,* much less, altogether. The punctuation hereabouts in Stevenson's edition is very wild. 1795. *wys,* vice; *the wrechitness,* thy miserliness. 1797. *pass the courss,* go thy way. 1808. *vrech,* wretch; but here used instead of *miser.* 1812. *viss,* vice. 1814. *ben y-knawith,* are known (to be) (?). 1815. *dant,* daunt. 1822. *the ton,* the one.

P. 54, l. 1832. *beis var,* beware. 1834. *colde,* cool. 1852. *onys,* once. 1855. *whar-throw,* through which, whereby.

P. 55, l. 1864, *awn,* own. The metre requires the more usual form *awin.* 1879. *dispolȝeith,* despoileth. 1881. *For-quhi,* wherefore. In this line the MS. has "scrikth."

P. 56, l. 1899. *most nedis,* must needs. *Ye = the;* i. e. The one, He. 1909. *Mot,* might. 1917. *in* should be *into,* as elsewhere.

P. 57, l. 1940. *havith,* hath. 1950. *hot,* hight, is called.

P. 58, l. 1966. *wnepwnist,* unpunished. 1990. *omend,* amend; *spill,* destroy.

P. 59, l. 2011. *ayre,* are. 2012. *duclar,* declare; so also *dulay* for delay. 2017. *the god werray,* the Very God.

P. 60, l. 2036. *For-quhi,* wherefore. 2040. *mad,* made. 2041. *clergy,* science. 2062. *be the mycht dewyne,* by the might divine.

P. 61, l. 2069. *far,* fare. 2079. *helyth frome the ground,* heals from the bottom; i.e. effectually. 2100. *not sessith,* who ceaseth not.

P. 62, l. 2107. *Ne war,* were it not for; *hartly,* hearty; it occurs again four lines below. 2135. *yneuch,* enough. He means he will ask but one question more.

P. 63, l. 2148. *To passing home,* to go home. 2162. *the* xxiiij *day.* The first *i* in the MS. is like a "v" smudged over; we should read "xxiiij," as in l. 2155. The contraction is to be read *four and twentieth,* not *twenty-fourth;* so also in l. 610.

P. 64, l. 2190. *hal dure,* hall door. 2192. *o iorne most for to comend,* a journey most to be commended. 2194. *lowith,* love.

P. 65, l. 2212. *the fewar eschef thay,* the less they achieve. 2229. "For no adventure will prove so great, that ye shall not achieve it." 2241. *whill,* until.

P. 66, l. 2247. *galot;* so in MS. 2265. *grant mercy,* great thanks; Fr. *grand merci.* 2267. *quhy,* because.

P. 67, l. 2279. *thithingis,* tidings; probably an error of the scribe for *tithingis.* Stevenson has *chichingis!* 2284. *al-out,* altogether. 2304. *oft syss,* oft-times. See Glossary (*Syss*). 2306. *dante,* dainty. 2310. *tithandis,* tidings; compare l. 2279.

P. 68, l. 2323. *aw,* owe. 2328. *fantessy,* fancy, notion. 2334.

for no why, for no reason. 2337. *mon I fair*, must I go. 2338. *our son It waire*, over soon it were. 2342. *For-quhy*, because.

P. 69, l. 2352. *nor* has the force of *but*. 2366. *be ony men*, by any means. 2368. *on of tho*, one of them. 2375. *chen of low*, chain of love. 2376. *and if ȝhe may deren*, an if you may declare.

P. 70, l. 2409. *hartly raquer*, heartily require. 2416. *gar ordan*, cause to be provided.

P. 71, l. 2428. *prewaly disspone*, privily dispose. 2436. *ellisquhat;* I suppose this means, "he was on fire *elsewhere.*" 2448. *hamlynes*, homeliness. 2452. *fest throw al the ȝher eliche*, feast through all the year alike.

P. 72, l. 2469. *commend*, commended. 2470. *he drywith*, he driveth, pursueth. The reading is not *drawith*, as in Stevenson.

NOTES TO BOOK III.

P. 73, l. 2471. This line is too long, and the sense imperfect; but there is no doubt about the reading of the MS. 2474. *Awodith*, expels. 2475. *doune valis*, falls down; for it is evident that *valis* is an error for *falis*, the mistake having arisen from confusion with the succeeding line. 2480. *cled*, clad. 2487. *bygonen*, begun. In the next line Stevenson has *sown;* but the true reading is *Rown*, run; as in l. 2820. 2492. *barnag*, baronage, nobility.

P. 74, l. 2522. *but dulay*, without delay; *the*, they. 2524. *thar com*, their coming. 2530. *in the dogre*, in its (due) degree.

P. 75, l. 2545. *Or that*, ere that. 2552. *he and hate*, high and hot. 2558. *the can*, they began.

P. 76, l. 2574. *hyme mak*, prepare himself; or perhaps simply, make (for the field), go. 2582. *helmys last; last* clearly means *laced;* see l. 2250. 2594. *ȝhit*, although. 2599. *dout*, fear. 2600. *is assemblit*, made an attack. The peculiar use of *assemble* must always be borne in mind. 2601. *erd*, earth.

P. 77, l. 2612. *found till gwyans*, go to Gwyans. 2614. *til esquyris thei sewyt*, after Esquyris they followed. 2619. *one to the melle socht*, made their way to the mêlée. 2627. *don bore*, borne down. 2630. Fifty thousand. It would appear that Galiot had 40,000, of whom 10,000 were held *in reserve;* so that in l. 2632 only 30,000 are mentioned. See l. 2569, 2647.

P. 78, l. 2646. *ten*, sorrow, vexation. 2656. *resauf*, receive. 2663. *at thar come*, at their coming; *led*, put down. 2670. *biding one the bent*, abide on the grassy plain.

P. 79, l. 2679. "That, despite their efforts, they must needs retire." 2684. *stud aw*, stood in awe; see note to l. 1506. 2693, 4. These lines do not rime. But we should certainly read *felde, erde* having slipped in from confusion with l. 2691. The knight of Galloway goes *to the field*, i. e. joins battle.

P. 80, l. 2712. *On ayar half*, on either side. The MS. omits *to*. 2713. *of*, off. 2714. *noiss*, nose. 2731. *Bot nocht forthi*, But not on that account.

P. 81, l. 2754. *harmys*, loss. 2761. *aucht to ses*, ought to cease. 2765. *at*, that. 2768. *my lef*, my leave, permission. 2770. *in to cage*, in prison.

P. 82, l. 2802. *commandit*, commended.

P. 83, l. 2819. *one athir half*, on either side. 2820. *rown*, run. 2821. *howyns;* an ungrammatical form; perhaps *howyng* is meant. 2827. *one hycht*, on height; i. e. aloud. 2829. *sterith*, stirreth. 2833. "The lady of Melyhalt made (her way) to him, and immediately caused his couch to be placed before a window." Mr Stevenson reads,

"Of Melyhalt the lady to hyme maid
Incontinent his couche, and gart he [1] had," etc.

i. e. "The lady immediately made his bed for him," etc. 2841. *wencust*, vanquished. After this word we should perhaps insert "at," as in l. 3336.

P. 84, ll. 2877-2880. These lines were printed by me for the first time, four lines having been here again omitted by Mr Stevenson. 2880. *but weyne*, without doubt. 2884. *to led and stere* to lead and direct.

P. 85, l. 2893. *Endlong*, along. 2894. *weryne*, were. 2913. *let*, hinder.

P. 86, l. 2925. *dulay*, delay; as in several other places. 2938. *fek*, effect. 2944. *ȝude*, went. 2947. *fair*, welfare.

P. 87, l. 2964. *Whill*, until. 2970. *ho*, stop, pause. 2971. *veryng In affray*, were in terror. 2972. *rovm*, room. 2978. *socht*, made his way. 2984. *disponit*, intends; but we must insert "not," to complete the sense and the metre.

P. 88, l. 2998. *eschevit* (used passively), is achieved. 3003. *o knycht*, a single knight. 3005. *tais*, takes. 3006. *fays*, foes. 3013. *onys or the nycht*, once ere the night. 3015. *that ȝhe have gilt to mend*, to amend that in which ye have trespassed.

P. 89, l. 3052. *Do at I may*, Do that which I can.

P. 90, l. 3065. This line is printed by Mr Stevenson,

"Curag can [   ] encresing in [1] his hart";

but it is not clear that a word is wanting, for the metre is as complete as in many other lines; whilst, as regards the sense, "the knycht" is probably a nominative without a verb, and l. 3065 means, "Courage did increase in his heart." Or the reader may, if he pleases, insert "fele." Compare l. 3058. 3066. *lap*, leaped. 3079. Observe the omission of the word "neither" in this line. 3080. *persit*, pierced. 3086. *onan*, anon. A.S. *on-án*.

[1] But the MS. has "be;" also "melyhat" instead of "Melyhalt."
[2] MS. has "to."

NOTES. 113

P. 91, l. 3093. *In samyne will*, with like intent. 3100. *bet axampil*, better example. 3104. *bot*, unless ; *me fall*, befall me. 3108. *one vthir*, another. 3120. *send*, sent. 3121. *lewit one*, left one. 3122. *but mercy*, without mercy.
P. 92, l. 3134. *deliuer besynes*, clever readiness. 3136. *aray*, livery. 3140. *Ee*, eye. 3146. *the morow new*, the early morning. 3160. *deith*, dead. 3162. *Suppos*, although.
P. 93, l. 3178. *Nor ;* we now use *but*. 3184. *ward ;* see Glossary. *tho*, then.
P. 94, l. 3200. *relewit*, relieved. 3201. *diuerss placis sere ;* as *sere = diuerss*, one of these words is redundant. So in l. 3266. 3207. *ewil awysit*, ill advised. 3217. "And if it so happen, that they be discomfited."
P. 95, l. 3240. *leuch*, laughed ; *sarues*, service. 3246. *al haill*, all whole. 3248. *x thousand mo*, ten thousand, and more. 3259. *abaid*, delay. 3263. *aucht*, eight. 3265. *petws for til her*, piteous to hear.
P. 96, l. 3297. *dreuch*, drew. 3299. *fellit*, fallen. 3304. *levyng*, leave.
P. 97, l. 3307. *sest*, ceased. 3321. *askit at*, asked of. 3331. *Wencussith*, vanquisheth. 3340. *in to one*, continually ; which is sometimes the sense of A.S. *on-án*.
P. 98, l. 3353. *to fillyng*, to fulfil. 3357. *soght*, came on ; see Glossary. 3359. *Ne war*, etc., "Had it not been that they were, individually, the better men." 3364. *ralef*, relieve. 3368. *fellith*, feeleth.
P. 99, l. 3384. *virslyng*, wrestling, *i. e.* entangled with ; a strong expression ! 3385. *assalȝeing*, assail. 3390. *rowmyth*, roometh, emptieth. 3403. *departit*, parted. 3404. *dout*, fear.
P. 100, l. 3412. *left*, failed. 3423. *The lord*, i. e. Galiot, as I suppose ; Mr Stevenson has, "The Lord." 3430. *stere*, to stir, move, come.
P. 101, l. 3450. *pretendit*, endeavour. 3457. *occupye*, employ. 3461. *For one hour*, etc., "On account of suffering distress for one hour." 3470. *the well less*, much less ; see l. 1791. 3471. *berd*, beard. 3473. *o woyss*, one voice. 3475. *eschef frome yhow*, not, *win* from you ; but, *withdraw* himself from you. See Glossary.
P. 102, l. 3481. *wend thai var no mo*, thought they were no more. 3487. *And sich enconter*, and such encounter. These three words are written at the bottom of the page as a catchword. The rest of the MS. is wanting.

GLOSSARIAL INDEX.

[As many of the words occurring in "Lancelot" are well explained either in Jamieson's Scottish Dictionary or in Roquefort's "Glossaire de la langue Romane," I have frequently referred to these works by means of the letters J. and R. Other abbreviations, as O.N. for Old Norse; Goth. for Mœso-Gothic; Su.-G. for Suio-Gothic, etc., will be readily understood. Ch. has also been used as an abbreviation for Chaucer. The various French, Danish, German, and other words referred to in the Glossary are merely added by way of illustration, to indicate in what direction a word may be most easily traced up. To ensure accuracy as far as possible, I have verified every foreign word by the aid of dictionaries, referring for Gothic words to my own Glossary, edited for the Philological Society; for Suio-Gothic words, to Ihre's Glossarium; for Icelandic words, to Egilsson; and for Old French words, to Roquefort and Burguy. Whatever errors occur below may thus, I hope, be readily traced.]

Abaid,) delay, tarrying, 1882,
Abyde,) 2147, 3069, 3308.
A.S. *abídan*, J.

Abasit,) abashed, humbled, di-
Abasyt, } spirited, cast down,
Abaysit,) 378, 1452, 2664.
Abasit of, dispirited by, 3301.
R. *abaiser*.

Abasit of (used passively), were dispirited by, 2243.

Abraid, awoke, 1231; (Ch.) A.S. *on-bredan*.

Abwsyt (abused), made an ill use of, 1207.

Access, a fever; or better, a fit of the ague; Lat. *accessus febris*, (Wright's Glossary), 31.

Accorde, to agree with, 1526. Fr. *s'accorder*.

Accordith, is suitable for, becomes, 1679, 1951; agree therewith, 605; is useful for, is fit for, 1204.

According for, suitable for, 1512. R. *accordant*.

Adred, terrified, 378, 2664. A.S. *on-drǽdan*, to dread.

Affek, effect, 382. Cf. *Fek*.

Afferd, afraid, 3472. A.S. *afered*, *afǽran*.

Affere, warlike preparation, 985; aspect, bearing, 3043, 3334, 3394. See J., who makes it of Teutonic origin; but it may be no more than the O.Fr. *afeire, afaire* = state, condition; as explained by Burguy.

Afferith, belongs to, suits, 1550.

Afferis, is suitable, 1690, 1961. R. *aferer*.

Affrait, terrified, from the verb *Affray* (Ch.), 2462, 3469. R. *effraer*.

Affray, terror, fright, 636, 3454. Fr. *effroi*.

GLOSSARIAL INDEX. 115

Affy in till, trust to, rely upon, 499, 1394. R. *affier.*
Afyre, on fire, 30, 251 ; hence, used allegorically, in love, 2436.
Agrewit, ⎱ aggrieved, vexed,
Aggrewit, ⎰ 1308, 1538 ; angry, enraged, 2618. R. *agrever.*
Ago, gone, 159. A.S. *of-gán.*
Aire, are, 1732.
Algait, Algat, always, 1996, 1792. Gothic *gatwô*, a street, way.
Al magre thine, in spite of thee, 115. An expression compounded of A.S. *al*, wholly ; *maugre* (Fr. *mal grè*), ill-will, and *thine* (A.S. *thín*, the gen. case of *thú*, thou).
Al-out, altogether, 1676, 1791, etc.
Alowit, approved, 1754. Fr. *allouer.*
Als, (1) as ; (2) also.
Amen, ⎱ pleasant, 64, 999. Lat.
Ameyne, ⎰ *amœnus.*
Anarmyt, fully armed, 545, 620, 2219, 2771. See *Enarmyt.*
And, if, 1024, 1591 ; and if (= an if), if, 2376.
Anerly, only, 1476, 1696. A.S. *ǽn-líc.*
Anoit, ⎱ annoyed, vexed, 351,
Anoyt, ⎰ 2244.
Anoyt, annoyeth, 1407.
Anterous, (for Aunterous, the shortened form of Aventurous), adventurous, 2618. Fr. *aventure.*
Aparalit, apparelled, 338.
Aperans, an appearance, a vision, 364. So also Apperans, 1284.
Apone, upon, 765, etc.
Appetit, desire, 2722. Ch. has *appetite* as a verb, to desire.
Aqwynt, acquainted, 1295. Burns uses *acquent.*
Aras, to pluck out, 240. Fr. *arracher.*
Araid, disordered, afflicted, 3270.

See *Araye* in Halliwell. The examples there given shew that to *araye* sometimes actually signifies to *disorder.*
Arest, stop, delay, 678, 3072, 3308. Fr. *arrêt.*
Arly, early, 4, 384, 975. A.S. *árlíce.*
Artilʒery, implements of warfare, 2538. See R. *artillerie.* Compare 1 Samuel, xx. 40.
Assay, (1) assault, trial, 11, 35, 112, 712 ; attack, 537, 2662. As a verb, to assault, attack, assail, 570, 1044. Fr. *assaillir.* (2) to essay, attempt, 2936 ; to test, 478, 982. Fr. *essaier.*
Assaid, ⎱ assaulted, 1224, 2641.
Assayt, ⎰
Assall, assault, attack, 842. We should perhaps read "assaill," as in l. 855.
Assalʒeing, assail (3 pers. *plural*), 3385.
Assemblay, an assembling of knights for a combat, a tournament, 267.
Assemble, a hostile meeting, combat, battle, 978, 3336. See J.
Assemblyng, encountering, 2588.
Assemblyng on, attacking, 2956.
Assey, to test, 478. See Assay.
Astart, to start away from ; hence to escape from, avoid, 228, 3296. Ch. has *asterte.*
At, that, 1019, etc. Compare Dan. *at ;* O.N. *at.*
Atour, at over, i. e. across, 841, 849, 873 ; in excess, in addition, besides, 1775.
Ather, either, 2629, 2819, 3264. A.S. *ǽgther.*
Atte, at the, 627, 1055.
Aucht, eight, 3263. Compare Ger. *acht.*
Auentur, adventure, 601.
Auer, ever, 273, etc.

Auerding to, belonging to (?), 345. The sense seems to point to the A.S. *and-weardian*, to be present, Goth. *and-wairths*, present.

Aventur, Auentoure, adventure, 80, 222.

Aw, owe, deserve; the present tense of the verb of which *ought* is the past tense; 3447. A.S. *áh, áhte*.

Awalk, awake, 1049. Goth. *wakan*. The form *awalk* occurs in Dunbar,

"*Awalk*, luvaris, out of your slomering."
(The Thistle and the Rose.)

Awant, boast, 2136. As a verb, 1588; and as a reflective verb, 2196, 2386. Fr. *se vanter*. Ch. has *avante*.

Awin, own, 89. A.S. *ágen*.

Awodith, maketh to depart, 2474. See *Avoid* in Nares' Glossary, edited by Halliwell and Wright.

Awow, } vow, 234, 242, 246.
Awoue, } Ch. has *avowe*.

Awys, consideration, advisement, 558.

Awyſſ the, advise thee, consider, 1913.

Awyſſ, } to consider, 424, 429.
Awyſing, } Fr. *s'aviser*.

Awysment, advisement, consideration, 360, 680.

Ay, ever, continually, 1135, 1486. A.S. *á*.

Ayar (*written instead of* Athar), either, 2712.

Ayre, are, 2011.

Ayanis, 744, } against.
Aȝanis, 1164, 2283, } A.S. *ongean*.

Aȝane, Aȝeine, again, 3253, 380.

Bachleris, bachelors; a name given to novices in arms or arts, 1689. See *bacheler* in R.

Banaris, tanners, 770.
Bartes, 2897. } *See* Bertes.
Bartiis, 3041. }
Barnag, baronage, nobility, 2492. See *barniez* in R.

Batell, a battalion, division of an army, 784, 808, etc.

Be, by. A.S. *be*.

Behest, promise, 2766. A.S. *behæs*.

Behufis, behoves, 579. A.S. *behófan*, often used impersonally.

Behuſſ, } it behoves, it is necessary
Behwſſ, } sary (to do), 944, 2342; apparently contracted from *behufis*.

Beleif, *in phr.* ore belief = beyond belief, 112.

Bent, a grassy plain (properly a coarse grass; in German, *binse*), 2670. J.

Bertes, a parapet, a tower, 1007, 1118, 2815. R. *bretesche*, from Low Latin *brestachia*.

Betak til, to confer upon, 1724. A.S. *be-tǽcan*, in the sense, to assign.

Betakyne, betoken, 2014. A.S. *be-tǽcan*, in the sense, to shew.

Bewis, boughs, 338. A.S. *boh*.

Billis, letters, 142. Fr. *billet*.

Blindis, blindness (?), 1903.

Borde, to meet in a hostile manner, encounter, 809. We find in R. *border*, to joust, fight with lances. Compare Fr. *aborder*, and Spenser's use of *bord*. See *horde* in Burguy.

Bot, (1) but; (2) without. In general, *without* is expressed by *but*, and the conjunction by *bot*; but this distinction is occasionally violated.

Bown, ready, prepared, 1036. O.N. *búinn*, past part. of *búa*, to prepare. Su.-G. *boa*, to prepare. J.

Bretis, fortifications, forts, 874;

GLOSSARIAL INDEX. 117

"properly wooden towers or castles: *Bretachiœ*, castella lignea, quibus castra et oppida muniebantur, Gallis *Bretesque*. Du Cange." Jamieson. See *Bertes*.

Bukis, books, 434, 1862.

Burdis, boards, i. e. tables, 2198. A.S. *bórd*, which means—1. a plank; 2. a table, etc.

Bur, bore, 733, 778.

But, without; common in the phrase *but were*, without doubt.

But if, unless, except, 958.

Byhecht, } promised, 1485, 2791.
Byhicht, } A.S. *be-hǽtan*.

Byknow, notorious for, known to be guilty of, 1627. Compare "I *know* nothing *by* myself" (1 Cor. iv. 4). Compare also Dan. *bekiende*, to make known.

By, near at hand, 1535, 2916.

Cag, } cage, prison, 997, 2770.
Cage, }

Can, an auxiliary verb, used nearly as we now use *did*.

Careldis, plural of Careld, a merry-making, revel (?), 1318. "*Caraude*, réjouissance;" and "*Caroler*, danser, se divertir, mener une vie joyeuse." Roquefort.

Catifis, wretches, 2102. R. *caitif*, *captif*. Compare Ital. *cattivo*.

Chalmer, chamber, 2281, 2308, 2427, 2808. J.

Chare, } chariot, 4, 735. R. *cher*.
Cher, }

Charge, load, 693. Fr. *charge*; see *discharge* in the line following (694), meaning to shake off a load.

Chargit, gave attention to, 710, 2454. Fr. *se charger de*.

Chen, chain, 2375.

Cher, car, chariot, 735. See *Chare*.

Chere, cheer, demeanour, 83, 341, 695; sad demeanour, outward grief, 2718. Fr. *chère*; compare Ital. *ciera*, the face, look.
  "*Wepinge* was hyr mosté *chere*."
  (Le Morte Arthur, l. 726.)

Cheß, choose, 1611, 1636, 2368. A. S. *ceósan*; Ger. *kiesen*; Dutch *kiezen*.

Clariouns, clarions, 771, 789.

Clepe, to call, 90, 99. A.S. *clepan*.

Clepit, callest, 93; called, 781.

Clepith, is called, 1919.

Clergy, science, knowledge, 504, 511, 2041. R. *clergie*.

Closine, closed, concluded, 316.

Closith, enclosed, shut up, 427.

Cold, called, 753, 1579.

Commandit, commended, 2802.

Comprochit, approached, 2472, 2509.

Conpilour, compiler, poet, 319.

Conquest, conquered, 574; Fyrst-conquest, first conquered, 1545, etc.

Conseruyt, preserved, 332.

Conten (used as a reflective verb), to demean oneself valorously, to maintain one's ground, 823, 1107, 1130. See R. "*contenement*, contenance, conduite, maintien, posture."

Contenit hyme, behaved himself, 3219; Contenit them, 2634.

Contenyt, endured, 3190.

Contretioun, contrition, 1415, 1426.

Contynans, demeanour, 1693, 1747.

Counter, encounter, attack, charge, 3239.

Couth, could, 793. A.S. *cunnan*; past tense, *ic cúðe*.

Cowardy, cowardice, 1023, 3287.

Cownterit, encountered, 2609, 2621. J.

Crownel, coronal, corolla of a flower, 59. J.

Cummyne, ⎱ came, 807, 907.
Comyne, ⎰
Cumyne, 650, 1136, ⎫
Cumyng, 447, ⎬ come (past part.).
Cummyng, 2498, ⎭
Cunyng, knowledge, 1455.
Cusynace, 1270, ⎫
Cusynece, 2802, ⎬ kinswoman.
Cusynes, 2287, ⎪
Cwsynes, 1185, ⎭
Cwre, care, 98, 266, 643. Lat. *cura*. (N.B. Though *Cwre* = *cura*, yet *cura* should be distinguished from A.S. *cearu*.)

Danger, power to punish; "the power of a feudal lord over his vassals," (Wright), 444. Also, power to injure, 3006. See R. *dangier*.
Dans, (dance), in the phrase "wrechit dans," evil mode of life, 1321. See Chaucer's use of *daunce*; and compare—
"I sai ȝow lely how thai lye
Dongen doun alle in a *daunce*."
Lawrence Minot; quoted in Specimens of Early English, by R. Morris; p. 194.
Dede, 90, ⎱ death. Dan. *död*.
Ded, 3304, ⎰ A.S. *deað*. O.N. *dauði*.
Deden, deign, 949. J.
Dedenyt, deigned, 240.
Deid, died, 215.
Deith, dead (past part.), 3160.
Delitable, delightful, 1738. R. *delitable*.
Deliuer, nimble, clever, 3134.
Deliuerly, (cleverly), nimbly, lightly, 3089, 3131. R. *delivre*.
Demande, demur, 191, 397, 3052, 3354. See R. "*demander*, contremander, changer, revoquer l'ordre donné."
Depart, to part, 3421. R. *departir*.
Departit, parted, 3403.

Depaynt, painted, 46, 1703. Fr. *dépeint*. Ch. *depeint*.
Depend me, waste or consume (my powers), 214; possibly miswritten for *despend*. Cf. *Dispendit*. Depend to, to concern, appertain to, 466.
Deren, to speak out, tell, 2376. R. *derainier*.
Dereyne, a plea, 2313; "haith o dereyne ydoo," hath appealed to trial by combat. R. *derainier*.
Des, daïs, high table, 2762. R. *deis*; Lat. *discus*.
Deuit, availed, 18. See note.
Devith, ⎱ deafen, 92, 94. "Su.-
Dewith, ⎰ G. *deofwa*; Icel. *deyfa*," J. Compare Dan. *döve*. Burns has *deave*.
Dewod the, devoid thyself, 1022.
Deuoydit was = departed, 1031. Compare *Awodith*.
Dewyſ, to tell, narrate, 373.
Discharg, to put aside one's liability, 163, 1665.
Diseß, lack of ease, misery, 707.
Disiont (Disioint?), disjointed, out of joint; hence uncertain, hazardous, 2907. "Disjoint, A difficult situation." Halliwell.
Dispendit, spent, 1808. R. *despendre*.
Dispens, expenditure, 1746. Fr. *dépense*.
Dispolȝeith, despoileth, 1879
Dispone, to dispose, provide; or, as a reflective verb, to be disposed to do, to intend, 54, 446, 980, 1590, 2428, 2462.
Disponit, declines (?); but much more probably, intends; and we must read "disponit not," 2984.
Dout, fear, 2599, 3404, 3438; (as a verb), to fear, 740, 1827. Ch. *doute*. R. *doubtance*.
Drent, drowned, 1319. A.S. *drencan*.

Dreſ (as a reflective verb), to direct oneself, proceed, go, 1975, 2288, 2486. Lat. *dirigere*.
Drywith, drives; "he drywith to the end," i.e. concludes, 2470.
Duclar, declare, 3022.
Dulay, delay, 681, 788, 2925.

Effere, shew, pomp, 2360. Compare *Affere*.
Efter, after, 217. A.S. *efter*.
Eld, old age, 3225, 3242. A.S. *yldo*. Gothic *alds*.
Elyk, Eliche, alike, 182, 2452.
Eme, uncle, 2572. A.S. *eám*.
Empit, emptied, empty, 180. A.S. *œmtian*.
Empleſ, to please, 2455. J.
Empriſ, worth, honour, 129, 269, 3458; cf. Romans of Partenay, l. 2013. Anxiety, oppression, 393. R. *emprindre*.
Enarmyt, fully armed, 285, 751, 2499. J.
Endit, indited, 138; indite, 206; inditing, poem (?), 334. If the meaning were, "this ends," the form "endis" would be required; besides which, the rime shews that the *i* is long; cf. ll. 138, 206.
Endlong, along, 2893. A.S. *andlang*; Ger. *entlang*.
Entent, intention, will, meaning, thoughts, 448, 1451, 1499, 2938. R. *entente*. Used by Chaucer.
Entermet, to intermeddle with, to have do with, 2914. R. *entremetre*.
Enweronyt, environed, 53.
Erde, earth, 1072, 1540, 2601. Compare Ger. *erde*.
Erdly, earthly, 498.
Erith, earth, 128. A.S. *eorð*.
Eschef (1. eschew), to shun, withdraw himself, 3475. R. *eschever*;

(2. achieve), to accomplish, 2212, 2513. R. *eschavir*. Eschef deith, to die, 2732.
Escheuit, achieved, 258.
Eschevit, is achieved, 2998.
Eſ, 174, } ease.
Eeſ, 706, }
Essenʒeis (ensigns), warcries, 3349, J. See also R. *enseigne*.
Euerilkon, every one, 1039, etc.
Exasy, extasy, 76. (Possibly miswritten.)
Exortith, beseecheth, 3026.
Extend, attain, 3281.

Failʒeis, fail, (3 pers. plu. indicative), 1151.
Fairhed (fairhood), beauty, 577. In A.S. *fægernes*, but in Dan. *förhed*.
Fall, to happen, befall, 493, 2139. A.S. *feallan*; Dan. *falde*.
Fallyng, fallen, 1217, 1322.
Falowschip, used as we now use company, 1105, 2687, etc.
Falʒeing, failing, 1499.
Falʒet, Falʒheit, failed, 1460, 1469, 1498, 1503.
Farhed, beauty, 2440. See *Fairhed*.
Fayndit (feigned), dissembled, 2397.
Fays, foes, 3006. A.S. *fáh*.
Fechtand, fighting, 2691, 3127, 3407. Ger. *fechten*.
Fechteris, fighters, 686.
Feill, knowledge, skill, 2854. J. A.S. *félian*.
Fek (effect), sum, amount, result, drift, 2938. Fr. *effet*.
Fell, to feel, 820, 2131.
Fellith, feeleth, 3368.
Fell, many; als fell, as many, 768. A.S. *féala*; Gothic *filu*.
Fell, horrible, 260. A.S. *fell*, cruel, fierce.
Ferde, fourth, 815, 973, 2285. Compare Dan. *fierde*.

Ferleit, wondered, 3117. A.S. *fǽr-líc*, sudden, fearful. Burns has *ferlie*.
Fet, fetched, 433, 1154. A.S. *feccan*, past tense, *ic feahte*.
Fongith, catcheth, seizeth, 1922. A.S. *fangan;* Goth. *fahan*.
Forfare, to fare amiss, to perish, 1348. A.S. *for-faran*.
Forlorn, lost, 3305. A.S. *forloren;* cf. Goth. *fra-liusan*.
For-quhy ; see *For-why*.
For-thi, } (there-fore), on that account, 332, 2261, 2731. A.S. *forthý;* where *thý* (Gothic *thê*) is the instrumental case of *se*, that.
For-wrocht (for-wrought), overworked, wearied out, 888. A.S. *forwyrcan*.
For-why, 798, 925, 2209, } for For-quhy, 2171, 2342, 2290, } the reason that, because that.
Found, to advance, go, 2612. J. A.S. *fundian*, to try to find, go forward.
Franchis, generosity, 230. R. *franchise*.
Fremmytneß, strangeness, alienation, 1508. A.S. *fremdnes*.
Froit, enjoyment, 1644 ; fruit, 2088, 2109. R. *fruit*.
Frome, from the time that, 17, 1432. Goth. *frums*, a beginning.
Fruschit, broken, dashed in pieces, 1201. R. *frois*, broken ; from the verb *froier*.
Fundyne, 497, (found (past Fundyng, 465,) part.).
Fyne, faithful, true, 519. See R. "*fine*, fidéle ;" and "*fine*, foi."
Fyne, end, 1388, 2081. Fr. *fin*.

Ganith, is suitable for, 991. Icel. *gegna*. J. Compare Dan. *gavne*.
Ganyth, it ; it profits ; *used impersonally*, 121. R. *gaagner*.

Gare, to cause, 910, 2416. Dan. *giöre ;* Icel. *göra*.
Gart, caused; 267, 2777.
Gentilleß, 917, 1847. See *Gentrice*.
Gentrice, 130 2757, } courtesy, Gentriß, 2790. } nobleness. R. *gentilesse*.
Gere, gear, equipment, armour, 2777. A.S. *gearwa*.
Gert, 384. See *Gart*.
Giffis, give thou, (lit. give *ye*, the plural being used in addressing the king), 463. A.S. *gifan*.
Gifyne, given, 1752.
Gilt, offended, done wrong, 699, 3015. A.S. *gyltan*.
Grewhundis, greyhounds, 533, 537. "O.N. *grey, grey-hundr*, a bitch." Wedgwood.
Gowerne the, conduct thyself, 1598.
Grawis, groves, 2481. Ch. *greves*.
Gyrß, grass, 10. A.S. *gærs*.
Gyß, guise, fashion, custom, 545. Ch. *gise*.

Haade, had, 2150.
Habariowne, habergeon, 2889. From *haubergeon*, the French form of Ger. *halsberge*. See *Hawbrek*.
Habirioune, habergeon, 3380.
Heill, whole, 3246. A.S. *hæl*.
Haknay, an ambling horse for a lady, 1730. R. *hacquenée*.
Half ; *in the phrase* on arthuris half, i. e. on Arthur's *side*, 883. Compare use of Germ. *halb*.
Halk, a hawk, 1736, 2482. A.S. *hafoc*.
Hall, }
Hoil, } various spellings of Haill, Holl, } whole.
Hail, }
Hals, neck, 1054. A.S. *hals*. Goth. *hals*.

Hant, to exercise, practise, 2191. Fr. *hanter*, lit. to frequent.
Hardement, 801, 2669,) hardi-
Hardyment, 900, 3362,) hood, boldness. R. *hardement*.
Harrold, herald, 1047.
Hate, hot, 2552.
Havith, hath, 1940; have, 3404.
Hawbrek, 1070, 1200,) hauberk,
Hawbryk, 3112,) neck-defence; Ger. *hals-berge*, armour for the neck.
Hawnt, to use, 3418. See *Hant*.
Hawntis, exercise, 2772.
He, high, 1969, 2552. A.S. *háh*.
Hecht, hight, is called, 2140; was called, 2290.
Hecht, to promise, 3101; promised (*past part.*), 1142. A.S. *hátan*.
Hedis, heads, 538, 869.
Hewy, 442,) heavy. A.S. *hefig*.
Heuy, 459,)
Hie, 550,) high. See *He*.
Hye, 297,)
Hienes, highness, 126.
Ho, pause, stop, cessation, 2970. According to J. radically the same with the verb *Houe*, or *How* (see *Houit*). The Dutch, however, use *hou*, hold! from *houden*, to hold.
Holl, whole, 106, 745.
Hore, hair, 365.
"Holȝe were his yȝen and vnder campe hores."
(Early English Alliterative Poems; *ed.* Morris. See Poem B. l. 1695.) The meaning of the line quoted is, "Hollow were his eyes, and under bent hairs."
Hot, hight, was called, 754, 806; is called, 1950. A.S. *hátan* (neuter).
Houit, delayed, tarried, halted, 996. "W. *hofian, hofio*, to fluctuate, hover, suspend," Morris.
Hovith, stays, halts, 2829.
Howit, halted, 2814, 2842.
Howyns, halts, tarries, 2821. Probably miswritten for "howyng."
Hufyng, halting, delaying, 1046.
Hundyre, a hundred, 756, 1554.

I, in, 332. Dan. *i*; Icel. *í*.
Iclosit, y-closed; i. e. enclosed, shut in, 53.
If, to give, 554. In lines 1718-1910 the word occurs repeatedly in several forms; as *iffis, iffith*, giveth; *iffis*, give ye (put for give thou); *ifyne*, given, etc.
Ifyne, to give, 3454.
Iftis, gifts, 1741. In the line preceding we have *giftis*.
Ilk; the ilk (= thilk) that, 629, 1601. Literally, the ilk = the same. A.S. *ylc*. See 1367.
Ilk, each, 2211, etc. A.S. *ælc*.
Illumynare, luminary, 3.
Incontinent,) immediately, 253,
Incontynent,) 1215, 2647, 2834. Still used in French.
In-to-contynent (= Incontinent), 3020.
In to, used for "in;" *passim*.
Iornaye, journey, 680.
Irk, to become slothful, grow weary, tire, 2709. A.S. *eargian*.
Iuperty, combat, 2547. Fr. *jeu parti*, a thing left undecided; hence the meanings, 1. strife, conflict; 2. jeopardy, as in Ch. See J.; and Tyrwhitt's note to C.T. 16211.
Iwond, 245,) wounded. We
Iwondit, 226,) find in A.S. both *wúnd* and *wúnded*.
I-wyſſ, certainly, of a surety, 1709, 1925, 1938. A.S. *gewis*; Ger. *gewiss*. Often *wrongly* in-

terpreted to mean, *I know.* See *Wit.*

Kend, known, 548, 906.

Laif, the remainder (lit. what is *left*), 1802, 3472. A.S. *láf.* Burns has "the *lave.*"

Lametable, lamentable, 3265. The omission of the *n* occurs again in l. 2718, where we have *lemytable.*

Larges, liberality, 608, 1681, 1750. Fr. *largesse.*

Larg, prodigal, profuse, 2434.

Lat, impediment, 958. A.S. *lǽtan,* means (1) to suffer, (2) to hinder.

Lat, to let, permit (used as an auxiliary verb), 803.

Latith, preventeth, 1927.

Lawrare, a laurel, 82. Ch. *laurer.*

Learis, liars, 493.

Led, put down, beat down, depressed, overpowered, 2663. It is the past tense of A.S. *lecgan,* to lay, to cause to submit, to kill.

Lef, to live, 564, 3230.

Leful, lawful, 1427.

Legis, lieges, subjects, 1957. R. *lige;* Lat. *ligatus.*

Leich, leech, physician, 106. A.S. *lǽce;* Dan. *læge.* See 520, 2056.

Leif, to live, 952, 1392. A.S. *lybban;* Goth. *liban.*

Leir, to learn, 1993. Comp. D. *leeren.*

Lest, to list, to please, 555, 621. A.S. *lystan.*

Lest, to last out against, sustain, 811. A.S. *lǽstan.*

Lest, least, 1628.

Let, hindrance, 2495.

Leuch, laughed, 3240. A.S. *hlihan,* past tense *ic hloh.*

Lewis, liveth, 1209.

Lewith, left, deserted, 1854.

Liging, 376. The sense requires *lay,* i. e. the 3rd p. s. pt. t. indic., but properly the word is the present participle, *lying.*

Longith, belongeth, 738, 1921, 2429, 2778. Compare Dan. *lange,* to reach.

Longith, belonged, 3242.

Longyne, belonging, 433.

Lorn, lost, 2092; destroyed, 2740. See *For-lorn.*

Loſſ, praise, 1777. Lat. *laus.* Ch. has *losed,* praised.

Low,   } (1) law, 1602, 1628, 1636,
Lowe, } etc. (2) love, 29, 1620. It is sometimes hard to say which is meant. Compare Dan. *lov,* law; A.S. *luf,* love.

Luges, tents, 874, 881, 2500, 2680. Fr. *loge, logis;* Ger. *laube,* a bower, from *laub,* foliage; Gothic *laúf,* a leaf.

Lugyne, a lodging, tent, 891.

Lyt, a little, 1233. At lyte, in little, used as an expletive, 143.

Ma; short form of Make, 953.

Maad, made, 697.

Magre of, in spite of, 500, 960, 2679, 2702, 2711. Sometimes "magre" is found without "of." Fr. *mal gré.*

Matalent, } displeasure, anger,
Matelent, } 2169, 2660. In both cases Mr Stevenson wrongly has *maltalent.* R. *maltalent, mautalent.*

Mayne, 1026. See *Men.*

Medyre, mediator (?), 1624. I am not at all sure of this word, but we find in R. many strange forms of "mediator," such as *méener, méeisneres,* etc. In the Supplement to the "Dictionnaire de l'Academie" we find *mediaire,* qui occupe le milieu, from Low Lat. *mediarius.* N.B.

GLOSSARIAL INDEX. 123

In the MS. the "d" is indistinct. See *mediare* in Ducange.
Meit, to dream, 363. A.S. *mœtan*.
Mekill, much, 876, 1236. Mokil, 1265.
Melle, contest, battle, 2619. Fr. *melée*, J.
Memoratyve, mindful, bearing in remembrance, 1430. Fr. *mémoratif*.
Men, mean, way; "be ony men" = by any means, 2366; so, too, "be ony mayne," 1026. Fr. *moyen*.
Men, to tell, declare, 510. A.S. *mœnan*.
Menye, a company, multitude (without special reference to number); whence "a few menye," a small company, 751. Apparently from A.S. *menigu;* Ger. *menge;* but it may have nothing to do with the modern word *many*, and is more probably from the O.F. *maisnée*, a household.
Met, dreamt, 440. See *Meit*.
Meyne, 41. See *Men*.
Misgyit, misguided, 1663. R. *guier*.
Mo, more, 3187, etc. A.S. *má*.
Mon, man, 96.
Moneth, month, 569. A.S. *mónað;* Goth. *menoth*.
Morow, morning, 1, 30, 64, 341. Goth. *maúrgins*.
Mot, must, 195. A.S. *ic mót*.
Mys, a fault, 1888, 1937, 3230. A.S. *mis*. Do o myſ, to commit a fault, 1926.
Mysour, measure, 1830.
Myster, need, 1877, 2322. Ch. *mistere;* R. *mester;* Lat. *ministerium*. Cf. Ital. *mestiere*.

Nat, naught, 703. Shortened from A.S. *ná wuht*, i.e. *no whit*.

Nece, nephew, 2200, 2245, 2720. R. *niez*.
Nedlyngis, of necessity, 2337, J. A.S. *neádinga*.
Nemmyt, considered, estimated, 649, 2852. A.S. *nemnan*, to name, call.
Ner, near, 441.
Neulyngis, newly, again, 36, J. A.S. *niwe-líce* (?).
Newis, for Nevis, nieves, fists, 1222. Icel. *hnefi*. Dan. *nœve*. Burns has *nieve;* Shakspeare *neif*.
Noght, not, 1182.
Noiſ, nose, 2714. R. *néis*.
Nome, name, 226, 320, 1546, 3341. Fr. *nomme*.
Nome, took, 591, 1048. A.S. *niman*, past tense, *ic nám*.
Northest, north-east, 677.
Not (shortened from Ne wot), know not, 522, 3144. A.S. *nát*, from *nitan* = *ne witan*.
Not, naught, 720. See *Nat*.
Noyith, annoyeth, 904. Fr. *nuire*. Lat. *nocere*.
Noyt, annoyed, offended, 471.
Nys, } (nice), foolish, 127, 1946.
Nyce, } Fr. *niais*.

O, a, an, *passim;* one, a single, 2998, 3003, 3393, etc.
Obeisand, obedient, 641.
Obeſ, obey, 2134.
Oblist, obliged, 969.
Occupye, to use, employ, 3457; to dwell, 75. Lat. *occupare*.
Of, with, 66.
Oft-syſ, oft-times, 2304, 2594, 2789, 2885, 2929. See *Syſ*.
On, and, 519. Possibly a mistake.
One, on, often used for In; One to = unto.
Onan, } anon, 158, 1466, 2602,
Onone, } etc. The form "onan,"
Onon, } l. 3086, suggests the

GLOSSARIAL INDEX.

derivation of *anon;* viz. from A.S. *on-án,* in one; hence, forthwith, immediately.

Onys, once, at some time or other, 3013; at onys, at once, 3187.

Opin, 1286, ⎫
Opine, 13, ⎬ open.

Or, ere, before, 77, 1887, 2545. A.S. *ǽr.*

Ordand, to set in array, 784; to prepare, procure, 1713. R. *ordener;* Lat. *ordinare.*

Ordan, to provide, 2416, 2777.

Ordynat, ordained, 490. See l. 507.

Orest (=Arest), to arrest, stop, 3186.

Orient, east, 5.

Oucht, it; it is the duty of (= Lat. *debet*), 2995. Strictly, we should here have had "it owes" (*debet*), not "it ought" (*debuit*). See *Aw.*

Ourfret, over-adorned, decked out, 71, 2480. A.S. *frœtwian,* to trim, adorn.

Out-throng (= Lat. *expressit*), expressed, uttered, 65. A.S. *út,* out, and *þringan,* to press.

Owtrag, outrage, 3454. R. *outrage;* Ital. *oltraggio,* from Lat. *ultra.* The MS. has *outray,* probably owing to confusion with *affray* in the same line. We find "owtrag" in l. 2578.

Oyß, to use, 1701, J.

Paid, pleased; ill paid, displeased, 908. Low Lat. *pagare,* to pay, satisfy.

Palȝonis, pavilions, tents, 734; *plural of*

Palȝoune, a pavilion, a tent, 1305. R. gives *pavillon,* a tent; cf. Low Lat. *papilio,* a tent.

Pan, pain, 1273.

Pas hyme, to pace, go, 362.

Paß, to go, 1213.

Pasing, pacing, departing, 371; surpassing, 303, 346, 689, etc.

Pens, to think of, 1431. Fr. *penser.*

Planly, at once, 3319. J. gives "Playn, out of hand, like Fr. *de plain.*" In the same line "of" = off.

Plant, plaint, complaint, 137. Fr. *plainte.*

Plesance, Plesans, pleasure, 941, 1939.

Plessith, pleases, 68.

Possede, to possess, 578. Fr. *posseder.*

Poware, a power, a strong band of men, 2647. We now say *force.*

Powert, poverty, 1330, 1744.

Pref, to prove, 2229, 3476.

Prekand, pricking, spurring, 3089. See the very first l. of Spenser's *Faerie Queene.*

Prekyne, 2890, showy (?), gaudy (?). J. gives "Preek, to be spruce; to crest; as 'A bit *preekin* bodie,' one attached to dress; *to prick,* to dress oneself." Compare D. *prijcken.*

Pretend, to attempt, aspire to, 3282, 3465. Fr. *prétendre.* So, too, in lines 559, 583.

Pretendit, endeavour, attempt, 3442.

Process, narration, 316. Wright gives "Proces, a story or relation, a process." The writer is referring to his prologue or introduction.

Promyt, to promise, 965.

Proponit, proposed, 361, 445.

Pupil, people, 285.

Puple, people, 1367, 1498, 1520.

Pur, 1648, ⎫
Pure, 1697, ⎬ poor.
Pwre, 1655, ⎭

Quh-. Words beginning thus begin in modern English with Wh. Thus, Quhen = when, etc.
Quhilk (whilk), which, 184. A.S. *hwylc* = Lat. *qualis* rather than *qui*.
Quhill, while, *used as a noun*, 1229, 1293. A.S. *hwíl*, a period of time.
Quhill, until, 24, 198. See *Whill*.
Quhy; the quhy = the why, the reason, 123, 1497.
Qwhelis, wheels, 736. A.S. *hweol*.
Qwheyar, whether, 1187.
Quhois, } whose, 171, 1297.
Qwhois, }

Rachis, hounds, 531. Su-G. *racka*, a bitch, which from the v. *racka*, to race, course. Perhaps connected with *brach*.
Radur, fear, 1489, J. From Su-G. *rædd*, fearful; Dan. *ræd*.
Raddour, 2133, } fear.
Radour, 1835, 3465, }
Raid, rode, 3070, 3260, etc.
Ralef, relieve, 3364.
Ramed, remedy, 117. See *Remed*.
Randoune, in, 2542. The corresponding line (l. 739) suggests that *in Randoune = al about*, i.e. in a circuit. But if we translate it by "in haste," or "in great force," we keep nearer to the true etymology. In Ogilvie's Imperial Dictionary, *s.v.* Random, we find the Nor. Fr. *randonnée* explained to mean the "sweeping circuit made by a wounded and frightened animal;" but the true meaning of *randonnée* is certainly *force, impetuosity;* see R., Cotgrave, etc. In Danish, *rand* is a surrounding edge or margin; while in Dutch we find *rondom* round about.

Raquer, require, 2409.
Raſ, race, swift course, 3088. A.S. *rǽs*. Compare Eng. *mill-race*, and D. *ras*.
Recidens, delay, 2359. R. *residier*, to defer.
Recist, resist, 566, 660, 2578.
Recounterit, met (in a hostile manner), encountered, 2958. Fr. *rencontrer*.
Record, witness, testimony; hence value, 388. R. *record*.
Recorde, to speak of, mention; hard recorde, heard say, 121, 595.
Recorde, speak out, 454, 481. See R. *recorder*.
Recordith, is suitable, belongs, 606.
Recourse, to return, 1798. Lat. *recurrere*.
Red, to advise, 1027, 1198. A.S. *rǽdan*; Goth. *rêdan*.
Relewit (relieved), lifted up again, rescued, 2617. Fr. *relever*. J.
Remede, 89, } remedy.
Remed, 718, }
Remuf, remove, 655.
Report, to narrate, 266; to explain, 294; to state, 320.
Reprefe, reproof, defeat, 764.
Reput, he reputed, i.e. thought, considered, 743.
Resauit, received, 2796.
Resawit, received, kept, 2106. We should have expected to find "reseruit."
Resonite, resounded, 66.
Resydens, delay 670. See *Recidens*.
Revare, 275, }
Rewar, 2893, } river.
Rewere, 2812, }
Reweyll, proud, haughty, 2853. R. *revelé*, fier, hautain, orgueilleux. Compare Lat. *rebellare*.
Richwysneſ, righteousness, 1406. A.S. *rihtwísnes*.

GLOSSARIAL INDEX.

Rigne, 94, 1527, ⎫ a kingdom. Fr.
Ring, 1468, ⎬ *régne.* Ch.
Ringe, 1325, ⎭ *reyne.*
Rignis, kingdoms, 1858.
Rignis, Rignith, reigneth, 1825, 782.
Ringne, a kingdom, 1952.
Rout, a company, a band, 812, 2956, 3403. Rowt, 2600.
Rowmyth, roometh, i.e. makes void, empties, 3390. A.S. *rúmian.*
Rown, run; *past part.* 2488, 2820.
Rwn, run, 2545.
Rygnis, kingdoms, 1904.
Ryne, to run, 113. See 2952.
Ryng, to reign, 1409, 2130.

Sa, so, 3322, 3406. Dan. *saa.*
Saade, said, 698.
Salust, saluted, 546, 919, 1553, 2749. Ch. *salewe.*
Salosing, salutation, 1309.
Sar, sorely, 1660.
Sauch, saw, 817, 1219, 1225. A.S. *ic seáh*, from *seón.*
Schawin, shewn, 2387.
Schent, disgraced, ruined, 1880. A.S. *scendan;* Dan. *skiænde.*
Schrewit, accursed, 1945.
Scilla, the name of a bird, also called Ciris, 2483.
——— " plumis in avem mutata vocatur Ciris, et a tonso est hoc nomen adepta capillo."—(Ovid, Met. viii. 150.)
Screwis, shrews, ill-natured persons, 1053. More often used of males than females in old authors.
Sedulis, letters, 142. R. *cedule.*
Sege, a seat, 2258. Fr. *siége.*
Semble, a warlike assembly, hostile gathering, 988, 2206.
Semblit, assembled, 845. G. *sammeln;* from Goth. *sama,samana.*
Semblyng, encountering, 2951. See *Assemble.*

Sen, since, 709, 800, etc. Sen at, since that. In Piers Plowman we find *syn.*
Septure, sceptre, 666.
Sere, several, various, 594, 731, 746. "Su-G. *sær,* adv. denoting separation." J. Cf. Lat. *se-.*
Sess, to cease, 14, etc. Fr. *cesser.*
Set, although.
Sew, to follow up, seek, 2326. R. *suir;* Fr. *suivre.*
Sew, to follow up, go, proceed, 3145. Sewyt, 2614.
Shauyth, shewith, 412.
Sice, such, 2115. Scotch, *sic.*
Snybbyth, snubs, checks, 3387. Comp. D. *sneb,* a beak; *snebbig,* snappish.
Sobing, sobbing, moaning, 2658.
Socht, ⎱ sought to go; and hence,
Soght, ⎰ made his (or their) way, proceeded, went, 2619, 3179, 3357, 3428. Sought one, advanced upon, attacked, 3149, 3311. Sought to, made his way to, 3130. A.S. *sécan,* past tense *ic sóhte,* to seek, approach, go towards.
Sor, sorrow, anxiety, 74. A.S. *sorh;* Goth. *saúrga.*
Sort, lot, fate, 26. Fr. *sort.*
Sound, to be consonant with, 149. See Gloss. to Tyrwhitt's Chaucer. Lat. *sonare.*
Soundith, 1811. " So the puple soundith," so the opinion of the people tends.
" As fer as *souneth* into honestee."
(Chaucer : *Monkes Prologue.*)
Soundith, tend, 1943; tends, 149.
Sown, sound, 1035. Fr. *son.*
Sownis, sounds, 772, 3436.
Spent, fastened, clasped, 2809. A.S. *spannan,* to clasp, join. Comp. Dan. *spænde,* to stretch, span, buckle together.

Spere, } sphere, 6, 170 ; speris,
Spir, } spheres, circuits, 24.
Spere, to inquire, 1170. A.S. *spirian*, to track. Cf. G. *spur*.
Sperithis, spear's, 810.
Spill, to destroy, ruin, 1990. A.S. *spillan*.
Spreit, spirit, 81, 364.
Stak, 226. J. gives "to the steeks, *completely;*" and this is the sense here. See Jamieson: s.v. "Steik." Halliwell gives *stake*, to block up; also *steck*, a stopping place (cf. Shakespeare's *sticking-place*, Macb. i. vii. l. 60). In the N. of France it is said of one killed or severely wounded, *il a eu son estoque*, he has had his belly-ful; from *estoquer*, to cram, satiate, "stodge." Compare Ital. *stucco*, cloyed. It has also been suggested that *to the stak* may mean to the *stock*, i.e. up to the hilt, very deeply.
Start, started up, leapt, 994, 1094.
Stede, stead, place, 218, 1124. A.S. *stede*.
Steir, to stir, 817. A.S. *stirian*.
Stekith, shuts, 1651. Ger. *stecken*. Burns has *steek*.
Stek, shut, concluded, 316.
Stell, steel, 809. Stell commonly means a stall, or fixed place; but the form *stell* for *steel* occurs; e.g. "Brounstelle was heuy and also kene." *Arthur*, l. 97.
Sterapis, 3056, } stirrups. A.S.
Steropis, 3132, } *sti-rap* or *stige-ráp*, from *stigan*, to mount, and *ráp*, rope.
Stere, ruler, arbiter, 1020; control, guidance, 1974.

Stere, to rule, control, 1344, 2884, A.S. *stýran*.
Stere, to stir, move, go, 3430. See *Steir*.
Sterith, stirreth, 2829.
Sterf, to die, 1028. A.S. *steorfan*.
Sterit, governed, 612. A.S. *stýran*.
Stert, started, 377.
Stok, the stake to which a baited bear is chained, 3386.
Stour, conflict, 1108, 2607, 3124. R. *estour*.
Straucht, stretched out, 3090. A.S. *streccan*, past part. *gestreht*.
Strekith, stretcheth, i.e. exciteth to his full stride, 3082.
Subiet, 1799,
Subeitis, 1828, } subject; subjects.
Subiettis, 1878,
Sudandly, Sodandly, suddenly, 1009, 1876.
Suet, sweet, 331.
Suppris, (surprise), overwhelming power, 691, 860, 2651; oppression, 1352. Fr. *surprendre*, to catch unawares.
Supprisit, overwhelmed, 1237, 1282; overpowered, 2705, 3208. Supprisit ded, suddenly killed, 3125.
Surryȝenis, surgeons, 2726.
Suth, sooth, true, 110. A.S. *sóð*.
Suthfastnes, truth, 1183. A.S. *sóðfæstnes*.
Sutly, soothly, truly, 963.
Swelf, a gulf such as is in the centre of a whirlpool, a vortex, 1318, J. A.S. *swelgan*, to swallow up.
Sweuen, a dream, 440. A.S. *swefn*.
Swth, sooth, true, 2753. See *Suth*.
Syne, 2026, } sin.
Synne, 2029, }
Syne, afterwards, next. J. 45, 794, etc.
Syþ, times, 3054. A.S. *sið*.

Tais, 1095, 3005,) takes. Abbre-
Taiis, 1141.) viated, as
"ma" is from "make." See *Ma*.
Tane, taken, 264.
Ten, grief, vexation, 2646, 3237.
A.S. *teonan*, to vex.
Tennandis, tennants, vassals holding fiefs, 1729. R. *tenancier*.
Than, then, 3111.
The, (1) they, (2) thee, (3) thy.
Thelke, that, 709. See l. 629, where *the ilk* occurs; and see *Ilk*.
Thir, these, those, 2734, 2745, 2911, 3110, etc.
Thithingis, tidings, 2279. A.S. *tidan*, to happen.
Tho, then, 545, 2221; them, 2368.
Thoore, there, 628. Thore, 1102.
Thrid, third, 370, 2347, 2401. A.S. *þridda*.
Throng, closely pressed, crowded, 3366. A.S. *þringan*.
Til, to; til have, to have, 706.
Tint, lost, 1384. See *Tyne*.
Tithandis, tidings, 2310.
Tithingis, tidings, 902, 2336.
To, too, besides, 3045.
Togidder, together, 254.
To-kerwith, carves or cuts to pieces; al to-kerwith, cuts all to pieces, 868. A.S. *to-ceorfian*. The prefix *to-* is intensive, and forms a part of the verb. See Judges ix. 53: "All to-brake his skull;" i.e. utterly brake; sometimes misprinted "all to break" (!).
Ton, taken, 1054, 1071.
Ton, one; the ton, the one, 1822. The tone = A.S. *þæt áne*.
To-schent, disfigured, 1221. The intensive form of the A.S. verb *scendan*, to shame, destroy. In the same line we have *to-hurt*, and in the next line *to-rent*, words modelled on the same form. We find, e.g., in Spenser, the forms *all to-rent, all to-brus'd*. (See the note on the prefix *To-* in the Glossary to William of Palerne.)
Tothir, the other, 2536. The tothir = A.S. *þæt oþere*, where *þæt* is the neuter gender of the definite article. Burns has *the tither*.
Toyer (= tother), the other; *y* being written for the A.S. þ (*th*), 2571, 2584.
Traist, to trust, to be confident, 390, 1129, 1149, J. Trast, 1659.
Traisting of (trusting), reliance upon, or expectation of, 25, J.
Translat, 508,) to transfer, re
Transulat, 2204,) move.
Tratory, treachery, 3224. See R. *traitor*.
Trety, treatise, 145. Fr. *traité*.
Trewis, truce, 1568, 2488, 2545.
Tronsione, 239,) a trun-
Trunscyoune, 2962, } cheon, a
Trownsciown, 2890,) stump of
a spear. Fr. *tronçon*; from Lat. *truncus*. In the last passage it means a sceptre, *bâton*.
"One hytte hym vpon the oldé wouride Wyth A tronchon of an ore;" (oar.) (Le Morte Arthur, l. 3071.)
Troucht, truth, 161.
Tueching, 403,) touching.
Tweching, 386,)
Tyne, to lose, 1258, 1387. Icel. *týna*.
Tynith, loseth, 1761.
Tynt, lost, 175, 1384, 1521.

Unwist, unknown, 1140.

Valis, falls; we should read "falis," 2475.
Valkyne, to waken, 8. See *Awalk*
Vall, billow, wave, 1317. Ger. *welle*, a wave; *quelle*, a spring;

GLOSSARIAL INDEX.

Icel. *vella*, to *well* up, boil. Cf. also A.S. *wæl*; Du. *wiel*; Lancashire *weele*, an eddy, whirlpool. So, too, in Burns:—
"Whyles owre a linn the burnie plays,
As thro' the glen it wimpl't;
Whyles round a rocky scaur it stays,
Whyles in a *wiel* it dimpl't."

Varand, to warrant, protect, 3411. R. *warandir*.
Varnit, warned, 622.
Vassolag, a deed of prowess. Pasing vassolag, surpassing valour, 257. R. has *vasselage*, courage, valour, valourous deeds, as indicative of the fulfilment of the duties of a *vassal*. We now speak of rendering *good service*.
Vassolage, valour, 2724.
Veir, were, 818.
Veris, wars, 305. See *Were*.
Veryng, were, 2971. A.S. *wǽron*.
Vicht, a wight, a person, 10, 55, 67. A.S. *wiht*.
Virslyng, wrestling, struggling, 3384. J. gives the forms *warsell*, *wersill*.
Visare, wiser, 607.
Viting, to know, 410. A.S. *witan*.
Vncouth, lit. *unknown*; hence little known, rare, valuable, 1734. A.S. *uncúð*.
Vodis, woods, 1000.
Vombe, womb, bowels, 375. Goth. *wamba*.
Vondit, wounded, 700.
Vpwarpith, warped up, i.e. drawn up, 63. See Note to this line. It occurs in Gawain Douglas's prologue to his translation of the 12th Book of the Æneid. Du. *opwerpen*, from Goth. *wairpan*, to cast.
Vsyt, used, 1197, 1208.
Vyre, a cross-bow bolt, 1092. R. *vire*: cf. Lat. *vertere*.

Wald, would, 419, 470, etc.
Walkin, to waken, wake, 1239. See *Awalk*.
Wapnis, weapons, 241. A.S. *wǽpen*, or *wǽpn*.
Ward, world, 3184. Grose's Provincial Dictionary gives *Ward* = world; and the omission of the *l* is not uncommon; see *Genesis and Exodus* (E.E.T.S.), ll. 32, 1315.
Wassolage, valour, 2708. See *Vassolag*.
Wat, know, 512.
Wawasouris, vavasours, 1729. A *Vavasour* was a sub-vassal, holding a small fief dependent on a larger fief; a sort of esquire. R. *vavaseur*.
Weil, very. Weil long, a very long time, 79. Comp. Ger. *viel*, J.
Wencussith, vanquisheth, 3331; vanquished, 3337.
Wencust, vanquished, 2841.
Wend, (1) to go, 2191; (2) weened, thought, 3481.
Wentail, ventaile, a part of the helmet which opened to admit air, 1056. R. *ventaile*; from Lat. *ventus*.
Were, (1) war. Fr. *guerre*. R. *werre*, 308, etc. (2) doubt, 84, etc. "But were," without doubt. A.S. *wǽr*, cautious, *wary*. (3) worse, 1930. Burns has *waur*.
Wering, weary, 58. A.S. *wérig*.
Werray, very, true, 1262, 2017.
Werroure, warrior, 248.
Weriour, warrior, 663.
Wers, worse, 515.
Weryng, were, 2493.
Wex, to be grieved, be vexed, 156.
Weyn, vain, 382, 524.
Weyne, *in phr*. but weyne, without doubt, 2880. A.S. *wénan*, to ween, to suppose.

GLOSSARIAL INDEX.

Whill, until, 1136, J. Formed from A.S. *hwil*, a period of time.
Wice, advice, counsel, 1909. Shortened from Awys.
Wichsaif, vouchsafe, 355, 1391.
Wichsauf, *id.* 2364.
Wicht, wight, person, 131.
Wicht, strong, nimble, 248. "Su-G. *wig*," J. Sw. *vig*.
Wight, with, 918. Possibly miswritten.
Wist, knew, 225, 1047. See *Wit*.
Wit, to know, 268. A.S. *witan*; pres. *ic wát*, past tense, *ic wiste*.
Wit, knowledge, 2504.
With, by, 723.
Withschaif, vouchsafe, 1458.
With-thy, on this condition, 961. See *For-thy*.
Wnkouth, little known, 146. See *Vncouth*.
Wnwemmyt, undefiled, 2097. A.S. *wam, wem*, a spot.
Wnwyst, unknown, secretly, 219, 269.
Wod (wood), mad, 3334, 3440. A.S. *wód*. Goth. *wóds*.
Woid, mad, 2695. Perhaps we should read *woud*.
Wonde, wand, rod, or sceptre of justice, 1601, 1891. J.
Wonk, winked, 1058.
Wonne, to dwell, 2046. A.S. *wunian*.
Worschip, honour, 1158, 1164. A.S. *weorð-scipe*.
Wot, know, 192, etc. See *Wit*.
Wox, voice, 13. Lat. *vox*.
Woyß, voice, 3473.
Wrechitnes, misery, 2102; miserliness, niggardliness, 1795, 1859.
Wy, reason; "to euery wy," for every reason, on all accounts, 2356. Compare *Quhy*.
Wycht, strong, nimble, 2592. See *Wicht*.

Wynyth, getteth, acquireth, 1832.
Wyre, a cross-bow bolt, 3290. See *Vyre*.
Wys, vice, 1795. Wysis, 1540.

Y, written for "th." Thus we find "oyer" for "other," etc. The error arose with scribes who did not understand either the true form or force of the old symbol þ.
Yaf, gave, 387.
Yald, yield, 553; yielded, 558. A.S. *gildan*.
Yclepit, called, 414.
Yef, give, 563.
Yeif, give, 923.
Yer, year, 610. Used instead of the plural "yeris," as in l. 3243.
Yewyne, given, 1500.
Ygrave, buried, 1800. Comp. Ger. *begraben*.
Yhere, ear, 1576.
Yher, year, 2064. Used instead of "yheris," 3243.
Yhis, yes, 1397.
Yis, yes, 514; this, 160.
Ylys, isles, 2858, 2882.
Ymong, among, 821.
Yneuch, enough, 2135. A.S. *genog*.
Yolde, yielded (to be), 951, 1088.
Ystatut, appointed, 2529. Fr. *statuer*.
Ywyß, certainly, 1798, 1942. See *Iwyß*.
Ʒeme, to take of, regard, have respect to, 665. A.S. *géman*.
Ʒere, year, 342.
Ʒerys, years, 23, 1432.
Ʒewith, giveth, 1772.
Ʒha, yes, 2843. Ger. *ja*.
Ʒhe, ye, 921. Observe that, as in this line, *ye* (A.S. *ge*) is the *nominative*, and *you* (A.S. *eów*) the *objective* case.
Ʒhed, went, 1486. Ch. has *yede*.

A.S. *ic eóde*, past tense of *gán*, to go. Goth. *ik iddja*, past tense of *gaggan*, to go.
Ӡher, year, 2064, 2274.
Ӡhing, young, 2868.
Ӡhis, yes, 1397.
Ӡhouth-hed, youth-hood, youth, 2772.
Ӡhud, went, 2696. See Ӡ*hed*.
Ӡis, yes, 3406.
Ӡolde, yielded, 291, 380, 951. A.S. *ic geald*, past tense of *gyldan*, to pay, to yield.
Ӡude, went, 2944. See Ӡ*hed*.

INDEX OF NAMES, ETC.

Albanak, 202, 1447.
Alexander, 1837.
Alphest, 57.
Amytans, 1304, 2446.
Angus, 2858.
April, 1.
Arachell, 434.
Ari s, 336.
Arthur (*passim*).
Ban, 202, 1447.
Bible, the, 1483.
Brandellis, 3086.
Brandymagus, 2884, 3430.
Camelot, 275, 280, 357, 407.
Cardole, 2153.
Carlisle, 347.
Christ, 2046.
Clamedeus, 2881, 3259.
Dagenet, 278.
Daniel, 1365.
Danʒelome, 435.
Esquyris, 2591, 2609, etc.
First-conquest king, 1064, etc.; 2568, etc.
Gahers, 3087.
Galiot (*passim*).
Galys Gwyans, 2605, 2613, etc.
Galygantynis, 599.
Galloway, 2690.
Gawane (*passim*).
Gwynans or Gwyans. See *Galys*.
Gyonde or Gyande, 302, 551, 637.
Harwy, 2853, 3206, etc.
Herynes (*i.e.* Hermes), 436.
Hundred knights, king of, 1545, 1554.

Jhesu, 2046, 2096.
Kay, 254, 355, 3081, etc.
Lady of the Lake, 220, 223.
Lancelot (*passim*); appears as the *red* knight, 991, etc.; as the *black* knight, 2430, etc.
Logris, 2301.
Maleginis, 806. See *Malenginys*.
Malenginys, 2873, 3151, 3155. See also *Hundred knights, king of*.
May, 12.
Melyhalt, 283, 895.
Melyhalt, lady of (*passim*).
Moses, 436.
Nembrot (*i.e.* Nimrod), 435.
Nohalt, 255.
Phœbus, 24, 2472, 2486.
Priapus, 51.
Round Table, 795, 3213.
Saturn, 2474.
Scilla, 2483.
Solomon, 1378.
Sygramors, 3083.
Titan, 335.
Valydone, 3249. See *Walydeyne*.
Vanore, 575. See *Wanore*.
Virgin (Mary), 2049, 2087, etc.
Venus, 309.
Wales, 599, 2153.
Walydeyne, 2879.
Wanore, 230.
Wryne, 2867.
Ydrus, 2851, 3152.
Ywan, 2606, 2618, etc.
Ywons, 2861.